BLUESMAN

Other great graphic novels from NBM:
750 cc Down Lincoln Highway
"Like a Gallic Jim Jarmusch road movie (though shorter), this slim motorcycle diary has its moments."
-Publishers Weekly

750cc DOWN LINCOLN HIGHWAY
BERNARD
CHAMBAZ
BARROUX
nbm

THE INITIATES
A Comic Artist And a Wine Artisan Exchange Jobs
"This intensely thought-provoking graphic novel makes us pause to consider our relationships with other people and asks us to think about who we are, what we do, and how we perceive and relate to the world around us."
-Publishers Weekly starred review

Étienne Davodeau
THE INITIATES
A Comic Artist and a Wine Artisan Exchange Jobs

See previews, get exclusives and order from:
NBMPUB.COM
We have hundreds of graphic novels available.
Subscribe to our monthly newsletter
Follow us on Facebook & Instagram (nbmgraphicnovels), Twitter (@nbmpub).

NBM
160 Broadway, Suite 700, East Wing,
New York, NY 10038
Catalog upon request

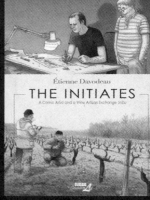

BLUESMAN

A twelve-bar graphic novel
by Rob Vollmar and Pablo G. Callejo

nbm GRAPHIC
NOVELS
Nantier · Beall · Minoustchine
NEW YORK

ISBN 978-1-68112-300-4
Library of Congress Control Number: 2022938027
© 2006, 2022 Rob Vollmar & Pablo G. Callejo
First printing August 2022
Printed in US
first paperback printing August 2022

Also available as an e-book 978-1-68112-301-1

1

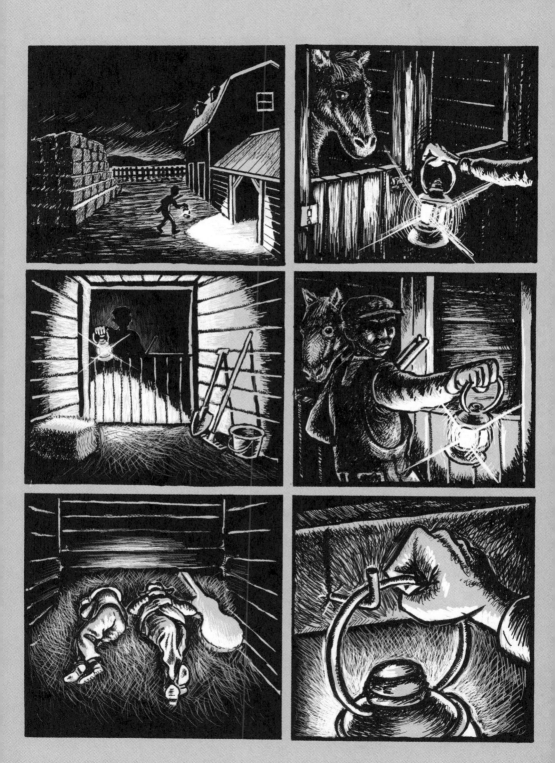

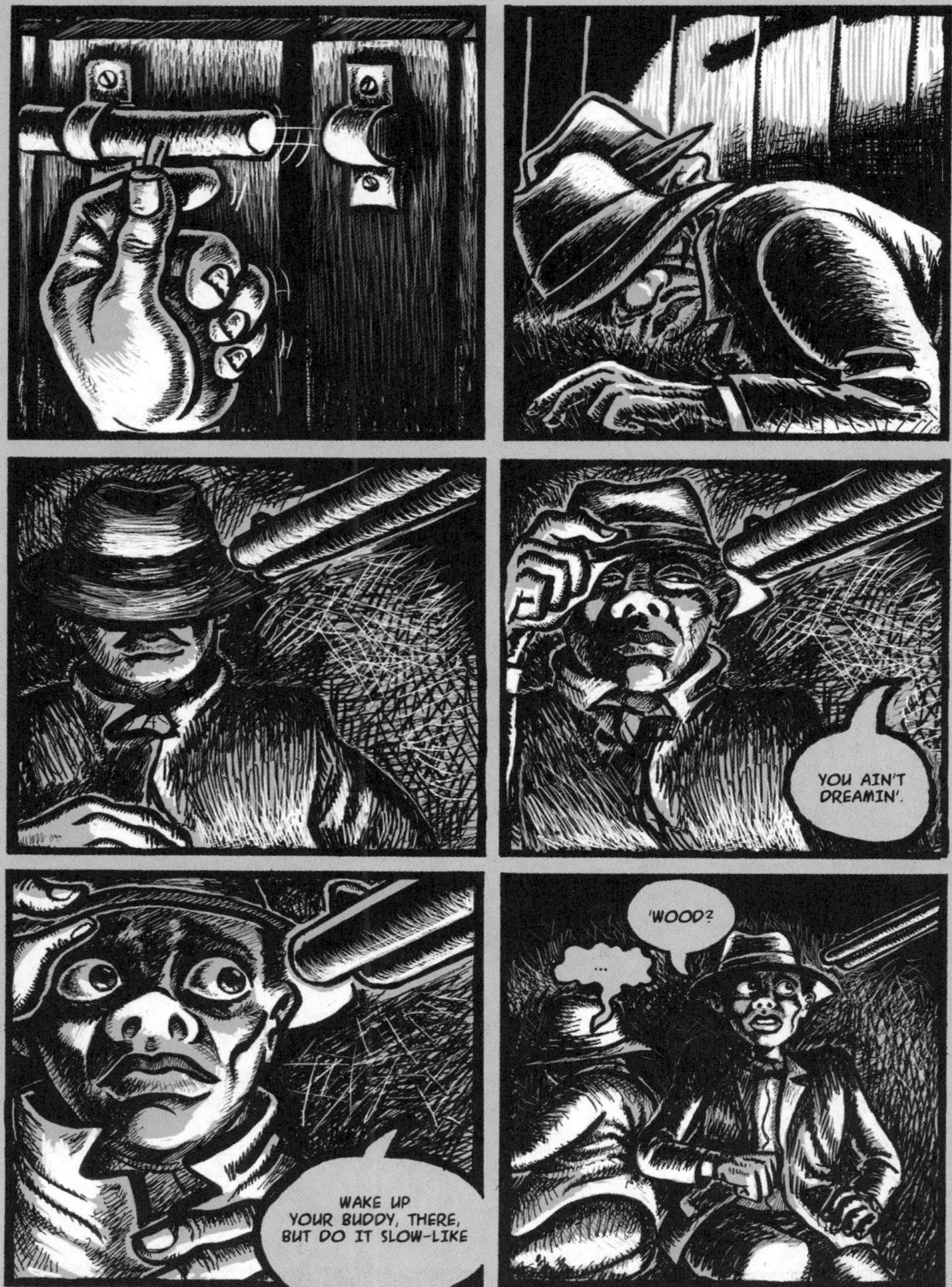
YOU AIN'T DREAMIN'.
WAKE UP YOUR BUDDY, THERE, BUT DO IT SLOW-LIKE
'WOOD?
...

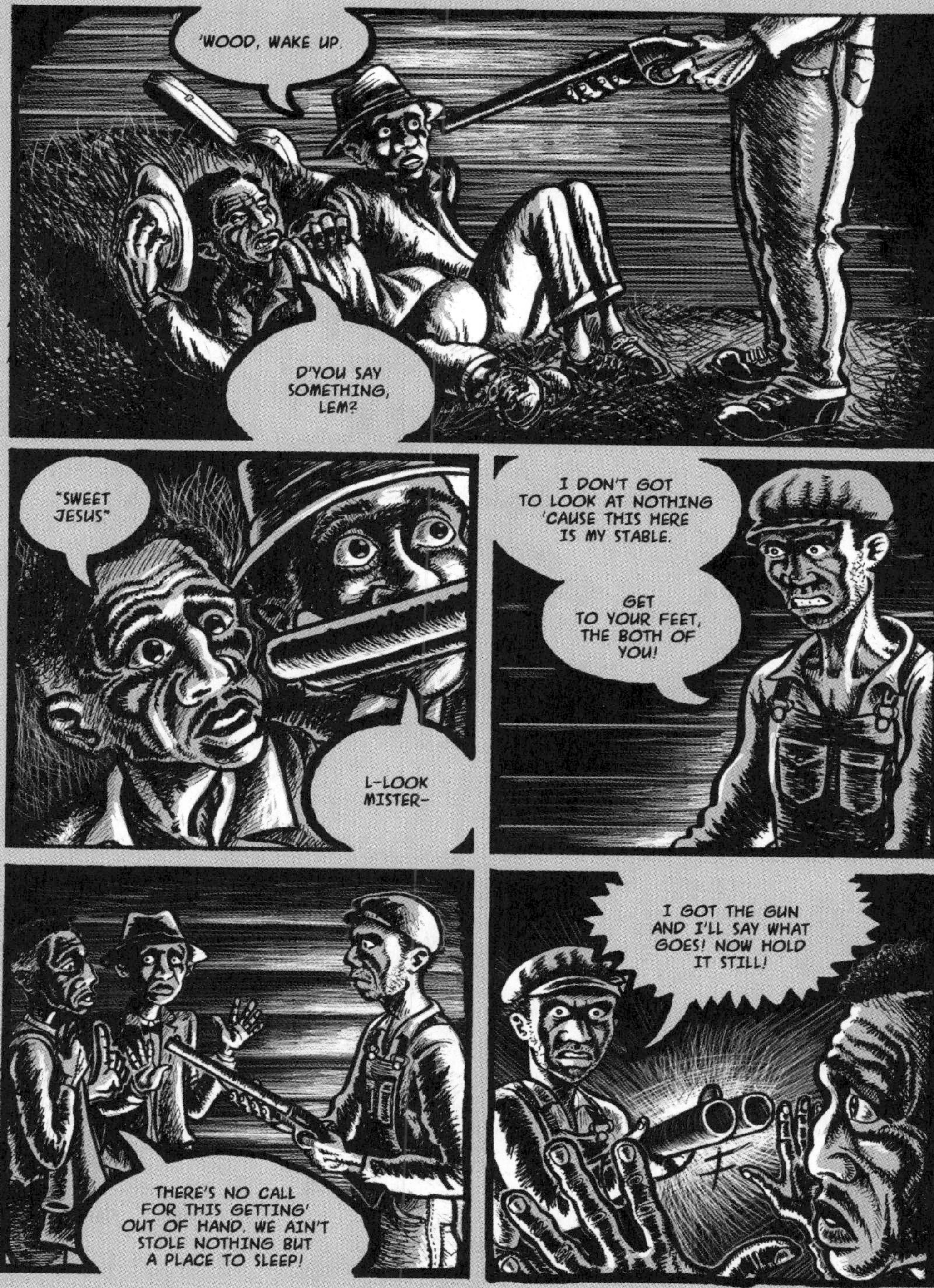
'WOOD, WAKE UP.
D'YOU SAY SOMETHING, LEM?
"SWEET JESUS"
L-LOOK MISTER-
I DON'T GOT TO LOOK AT NOTHING 'CAUSE THIS HERE IS MY STABLE.
GET TO YOUR FEET, THE BOTH OF YOU!
THERE'S NO CALL FOR THIS GETTING' OUT OF HAND. WE AIN'T STOLE NOTHING BUT A PLACE TO SLEEP!
I GOT THE GUN AND I'LL SAY WHAT GOES! NOW HOLD IT STILL!

WE DON'T WANT NO TROUBLE, MISTER.
LET ME GET MY GUITAR AND WE'LL BE OFF YOUR LAND BEFORE THE SUN IS UP.
YOU PLAY THAT?
YES, SIR. I DO. AND OL' IRONWOOD THERE, HE'S A RIGHT FINE PIANO PLAYER.
WE'RE TOURING THE COUNTRYSIDE, SPREADING GOD'S WORD THROUGH SONG.
OUR TRAVELS DIDN'T GET US TO THE NEXT TOWN BEFORE OUR LEGS GAVE OUT LAST NIGHT.
YOU'RE LUCKY I DIDN'T BLOW A HOLE IN THE BOTH OF YOU WHILE YOU WERE SLEEPING, RATTLING MY NERVES LIKE THAT FIRST THING IN THE MORNIN'.
SO YOU'RE PREACHERS, ARE YOU?
WELL, I 'SPOSE IT WOULD UPSET THE WIFE IF I SHOT UP A COUPLE PULPIT POUNDERS.
IN FACT...

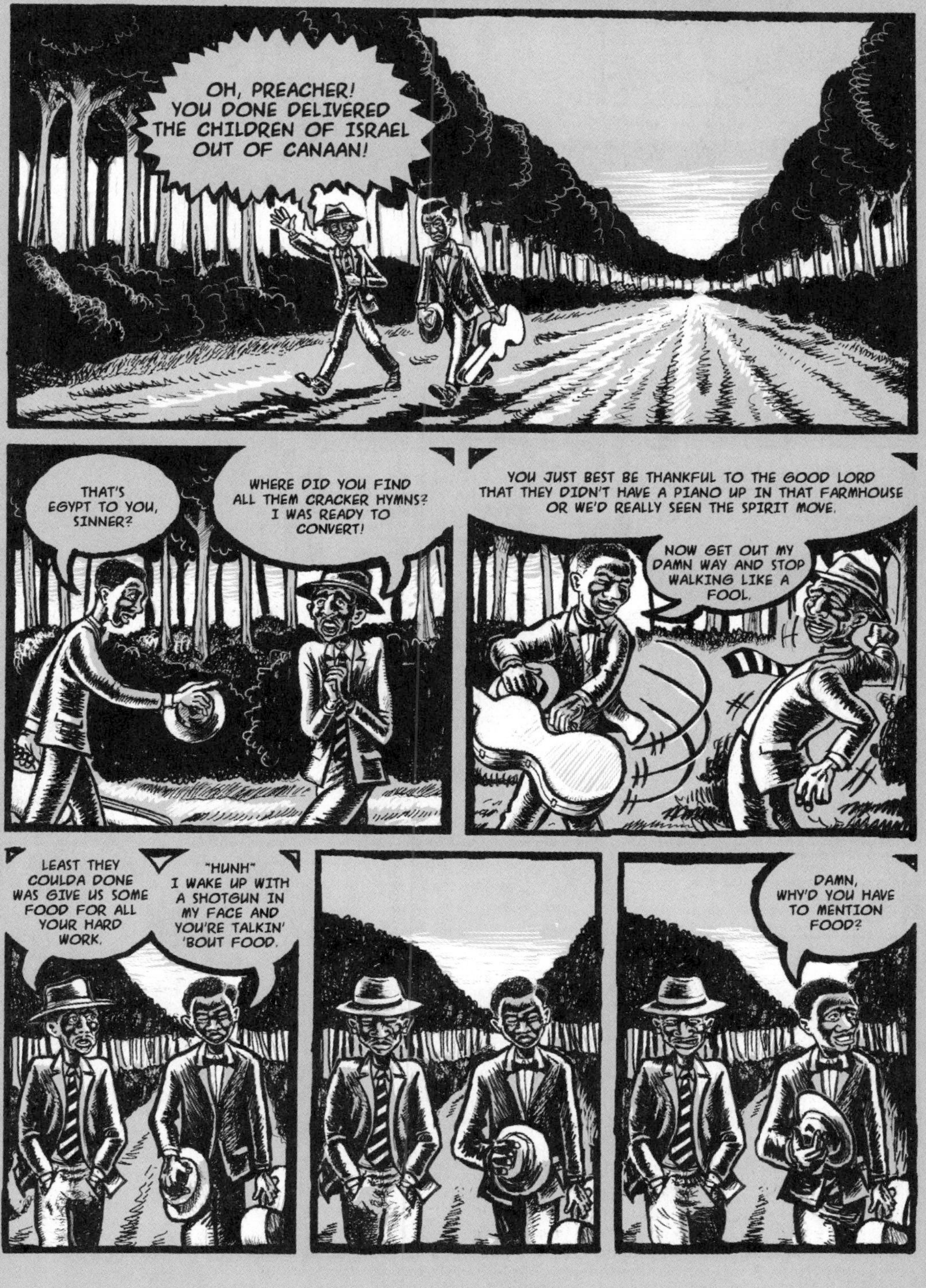
OH, PREACHER! YOU DONE DELIVERED THE CHILDREN OF ISRAEL OUT OF CANAAN!
THAT'S EGYPT TO YOU, SINNER?
WHERE DID YOU FIND ALL THEM CRACKER HYMNS? I WAS READY TO CONVERT!
YOU JUST BEST BE THANKFUL TO THE GOOD LORD THAT THEY DIDN'T HAVE A PIANO UP IN THAT FARMHOUSE OR WE'D REALLY SEEN THE SPIRIT MOVE.
NOW GET OUT MY DAMN WAY AND STOP WALKING LIKE A FOOL.
LEAST THEY COULDA DONE WAS GIVE US SOME FOOD FOR ALL YOUR HARD WORK.
"HUNH" I WAKE UP WITH A SHOTGUN IN MY FACE AND YOU'RE TALKIN' 'BOUT FOOD.
DAMN, WHY'D YOU HAVE TO MENTION FOOD?

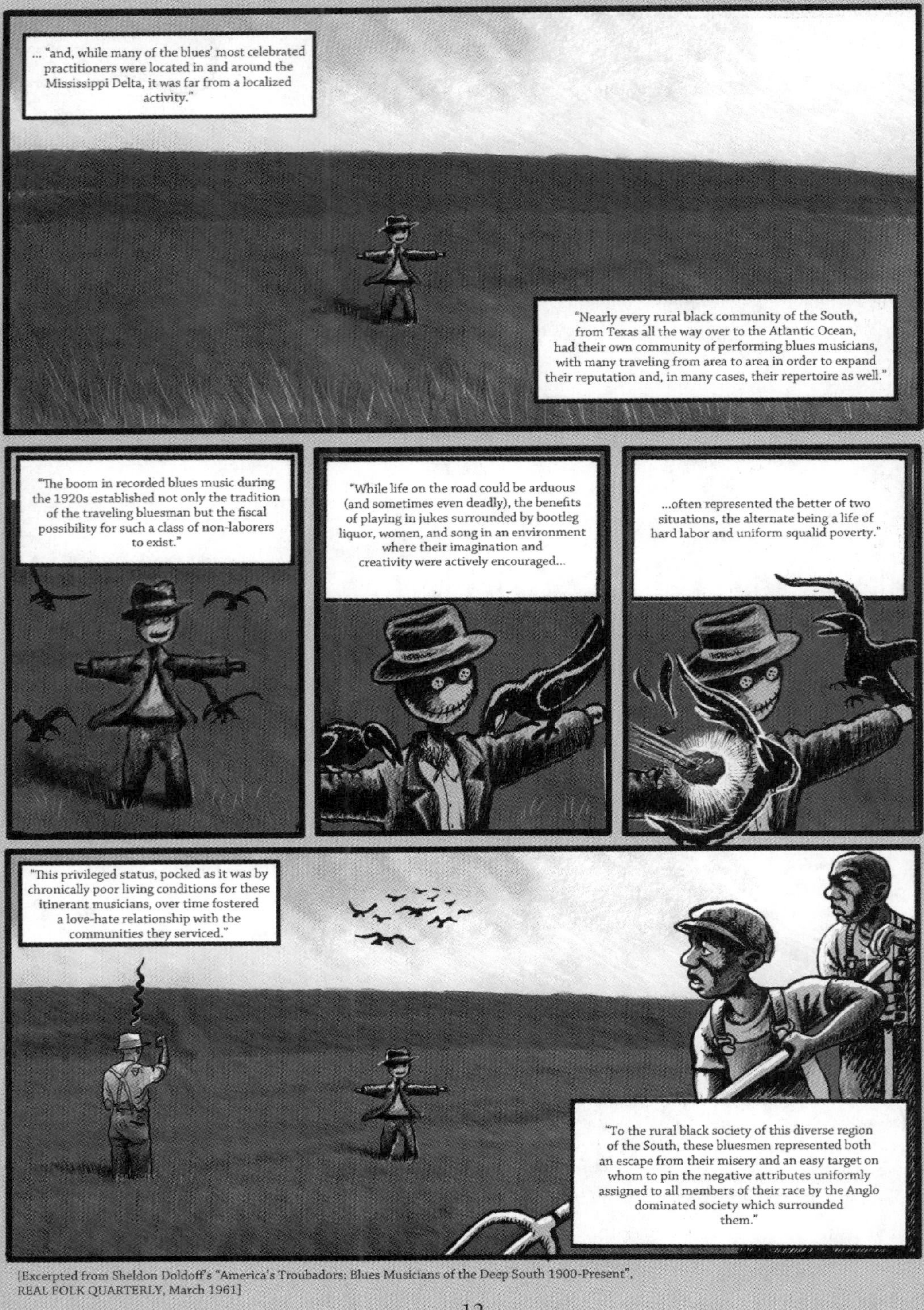
... "and, while many of the blues' most celebrated practitioners were located in and around the Mississippi Delta, it was far from a localized activity."
"Nearly every rural black community of the South, from Texas all the way over to the Atlantic Ocean, had their own community of performing blues musicians, with many traveling from area to area in order to expand their reputation and, in many cases, their repertoire as well."
"The boom in recorded blues music during the 1920s established not only the tradition of the traveling bluesman but the fiscal possibility for such a class of non-laborers to exist."
"While life on the road could be arduous (and sometimes even deadly), the benefits of playing in jukes surrounded by bootleg liquor, women, and song in an environment where their imagination and creativity were actively encouraged...
...often represented the better of two situations, the alternate being a life of hard labor and uniform squalid poverty."
"This privileged status, pocked as it was by chronically poor living conditions for these itinerant musicians, over time fostered a love-hate relationship with the communities they serviced."
"To the rural black society of this diverse region of the South, these bluesmen represented both an escape from their misery and an easy target on whom to pin the negative attributes uniformly assigned to all members of their race by the Anglo dominated society which surrounded them."

[Excerpted from Sheldon Doldoff's "America's Troubadors: Blues Musicians of the Deep South 1900-Present", REAL FOLK QUARTERLY, March 1961]

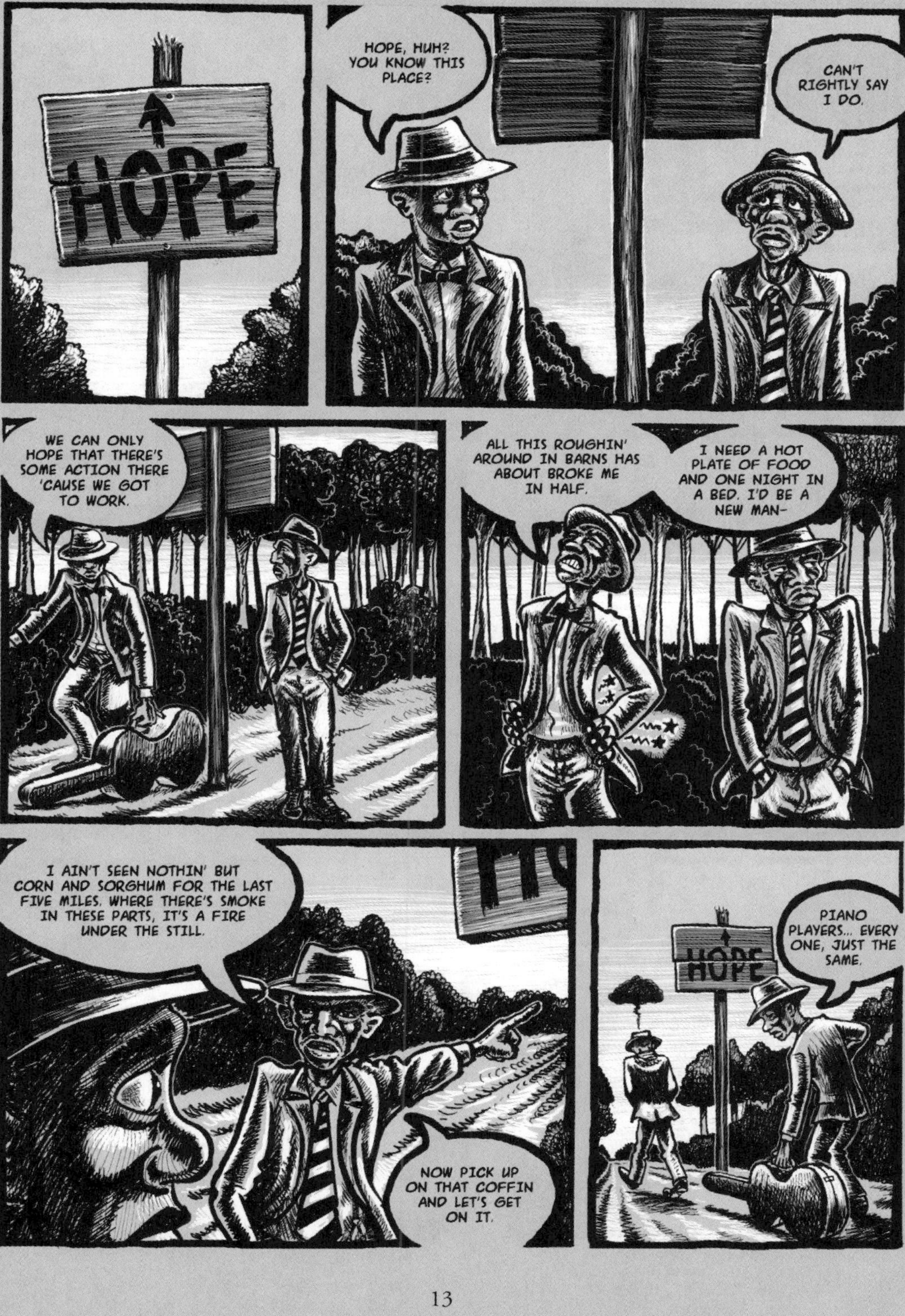
HOPE
HOPE, HUH? YOU KNOW THIS PLACE?
CAN'T RIGHTLY SAY I DO.
WE CAN ONLY HOPE THAT THERE'S SOME ACTION THERE 'CAUSE WE GOT TO WORK.
ALL THIS ROUGHIN' AROUND IN BARNS HAS ABOUT BROKE ME IN HALF.
I NEED A HOT PLATE OF FOOD AND ONE NIGHT IN A BED. I'D BE A NEW MAN–
I AIN'T SEEN NOTHIN' BUT CORN AND SORGHUM FOR THE LAST FIVE MILES. WHERE THERE'S SMOKE IN THESE PARTS, IT'S A FIRE UNDER THE STILL.
NOW PICK UP ON THAT COFFIN AND LET'S GET ON IT.
HOPE
PIANO PLAYERS... EVERY ONE, JUST THE SAME.

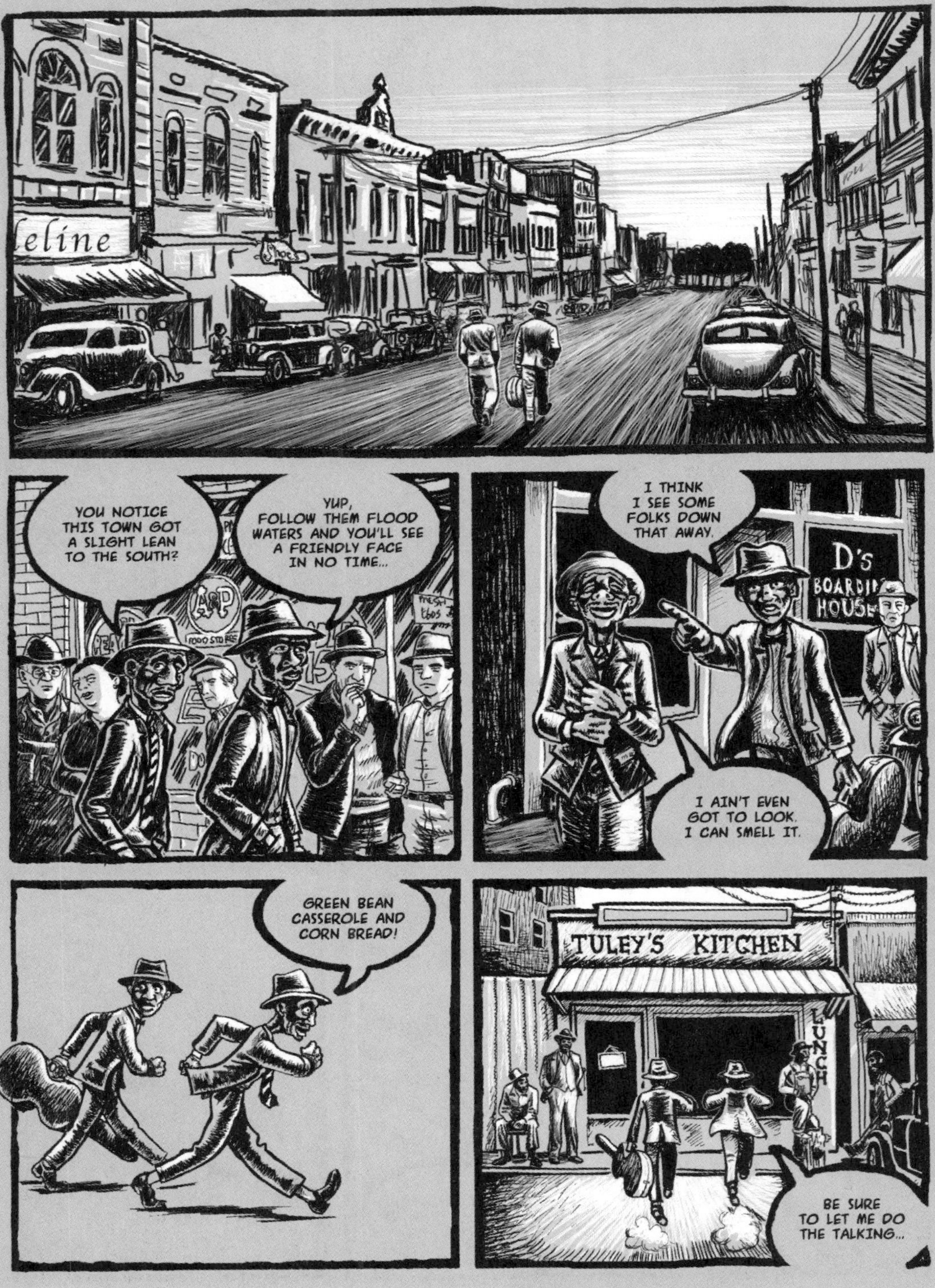

YOU NOTICE THIS TOWN GOT A SLIGHT LEAN TO THE SOUTH?
YUP, FOLLOW THEM FLOOD WATERS AND YOU'LL SEE A FRIENDLY FACE IN NO TIME...
I THINK I SEE SOME FOLKS DOWN THAT AWAY.
D's
I AIN'T EVEN GOT TO LOOK. I CAN SMELL IT.
GREEN BEAN CASSEROLE AND CORN BREAD!
TULEY'S KITCHEN
LUNCH
BE SURE TO LET ME DO THE TALKING...

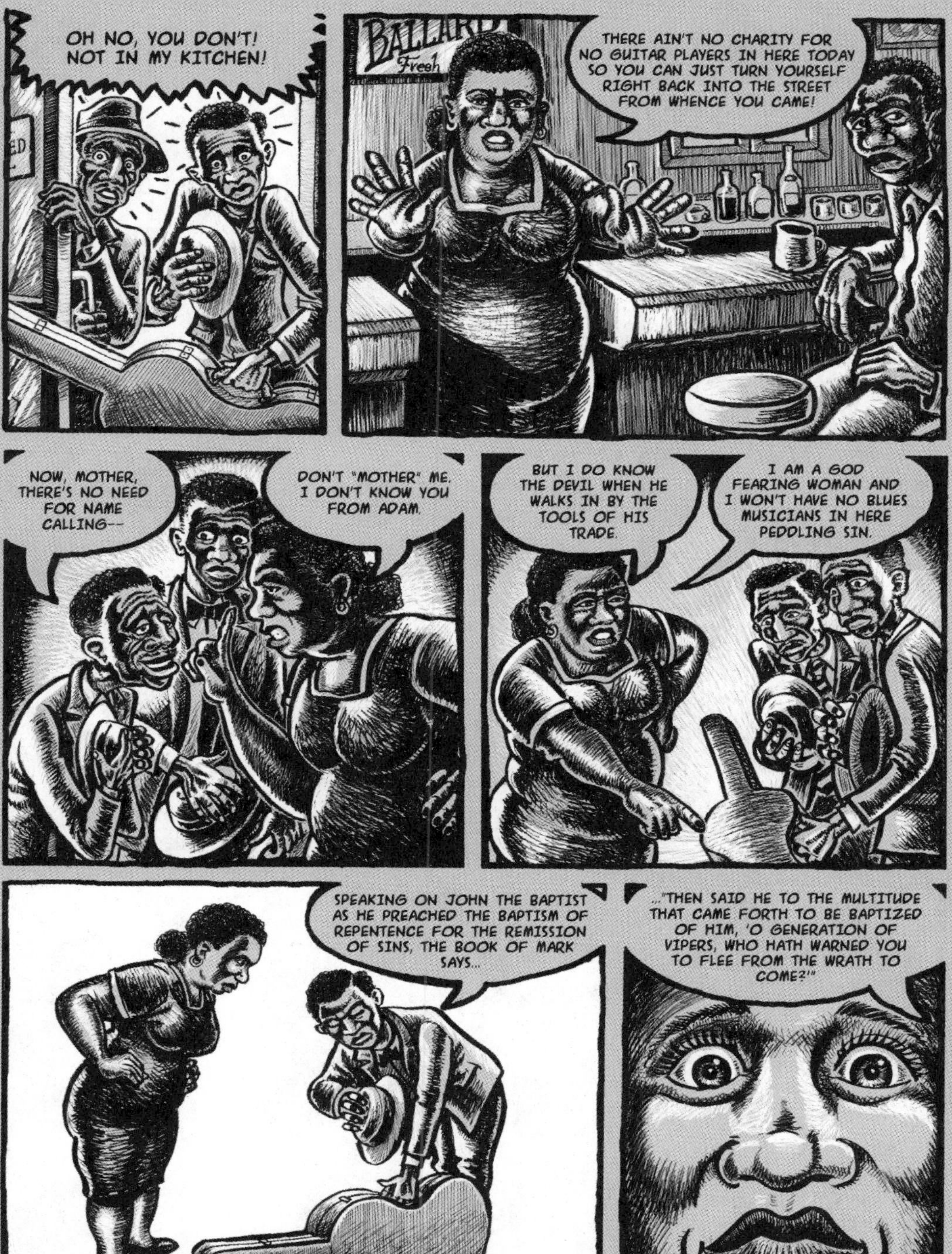
OH NO, YOU DON'T! NOT IN MY KITCHEN!
BALLARD Fresh
THERE AIN'T NO CHARITY FOR NO GUITAR PLAYERS IN HERE TODAY SO YOU CAN JUST TURN YOURSELF RIGHT BACK INTO THE STREET FROM WHENCE YOU CAME!
NOW, MOTHER, THERE'S NO NEED FOR NAME CALLING--
DON'T "MOTHER" ME. I DON'T KNOW YOU FROM ADAM.
BUT I DO KNOW THE DEVIL WHEN HE WALKS IN BY THE TOOLS OF HIS TRADE.
I AM A GOD FEARING WOMAN AND I WON'T HAVE NO BLUES MUSICIANS IN HERE PEDDLING SIN.
SPEAKING ON JOHN THE BAPTIST AS HE PREACHED THE BAPTISM OF REPENTENCE FOR THE REMISSION OF SINS, THE BOOK OF MARK SAYS...
..."THEN SAID HE TO THE MULTITUDE THAT CAME FORTH TO BE BAPTIZED OF HIM, 'O GENERATION OF VIPERS, WHO HATH WARNED YOU TO FLEE FROM THE WRATH TO COME?'"

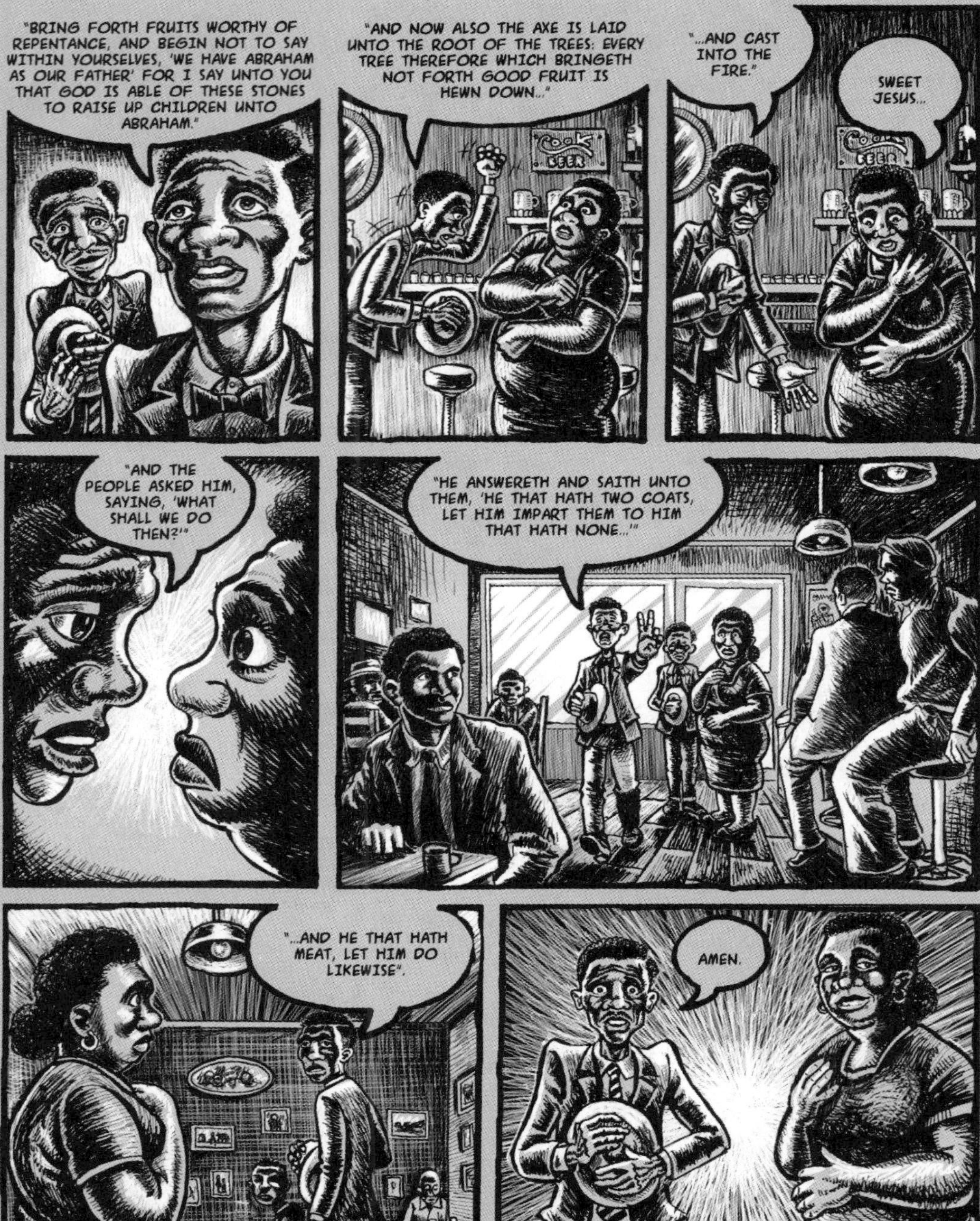
"BRING FORTH FRUITS WORTHY OF REPENTANCE, AND BEGIN NOT TO SAY WITHIN YOURSELVES, 'WE HAVE ABRAHAM AS OUR FATHER' FOR I SAY UNTO YOU THAT GOD IS ABLE OF THESE STONES TO RAISE UP CHILDREN UNTO ABRAHAM."
"AND NOW ALSO THE AXE IS LAID UNTO THE ROOT OF THE TREES: EVERY TREE THEREFORE WHICH BRINGETH NOT FORTH GOOD FRUIT IS HEWN DOWN..."
COOK BEER
"...AND CAST INTO THE FIRE."
SWEET JESUS...
"AND THE PEOPLE ASKED HIM, SAYING, 'WHAT SHALL WE DO THEN?'"
"HE ANSWERETH AND SAITH UNTO THEM, 'HE THAT HATH TWO COATS, LET HIM IMPART THEM TO HIM THAT HATH NONE...'"
"...AND HE THAT HATH MEAT, LET HIM DO LIKEWISE".
AMEN.

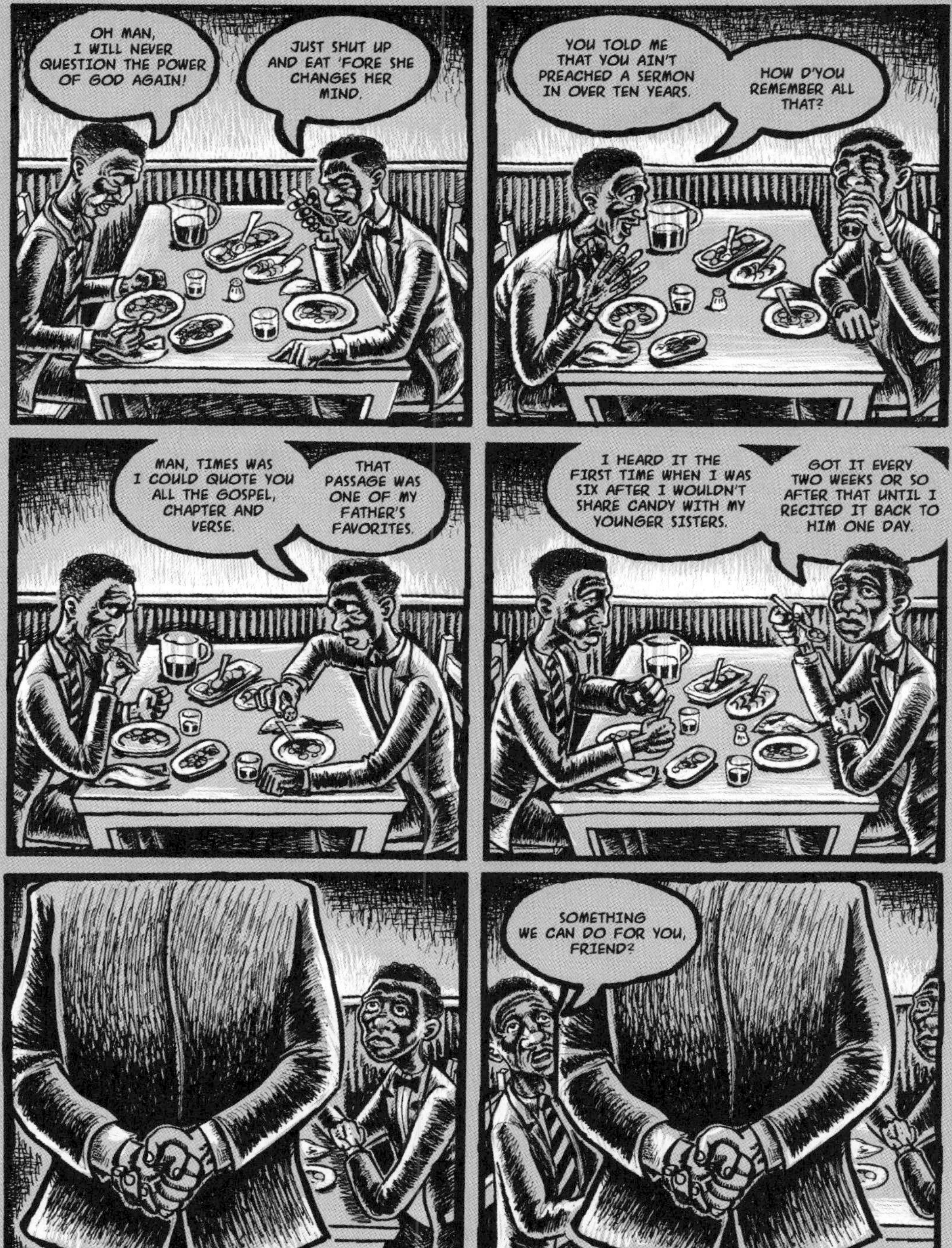
OH MAN, I WILL NEVER QUESTION THE POWER OF GOD AGAIN!
JUST SHUT UP AND EAT 'FORE SHE CHANGES HER MIND.
YOU TOLD ME THAT YOU AIN'T PREACHED A SERMON IN OVER TEN YEARS.
HOW D'YOU REMEMBER ALL THAT?
MAN, TIMES WAS I COULD QUOTE YOU ALL THE GOSPEL, CHAPTER AND VERSE.
THAT PASSAGE WAS ONE OF MY FATHER'S FAVORITES.
I HEARD IT THE FIRST TIME WHEN I WAS SIX AFTER I WOULDN'T SHARE CANDY WITH MY YOUNGER SISTERS.
GOT IT EVERY TWO WEEKS OR SO AFTER THAT UNTIL I RECITED IT BACK TO HIM ONE DAY.
SOMETHING WE CAN DO FOR YOU, FRIEND?

WHY, I JUST WANTED TO COME OVER AND THANK THE REVEREND HERE FOR HIS FINE SERMON EARLIER.

ALL IN THE SERVICE OF THE LORD.

OF COURSE, OF COURSE.

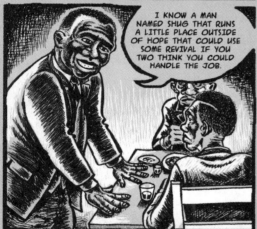

I KNOW A MAN NAMED SHUG THAT RUNS A LITTLE PLACE OUTSIDE OF HOPE THAT COULD USE SOME REVIVAL IF YOU TWO THINK YOU COULD HANDLE THE JOB.

IT SOUNDS LIKE WE'RE TALKIN' BUSINESS SO LET'S DROP THE SWEET TALK.

WHERE DO WE FIND THIS JUKE AND WHAT DOES IT PAY?

GIVE THIS DIME TO ANY BOY ON THE STREET AND HE'LL TAKE YOU THERE.

YOU'LL HAVE TO TALK TERMS WITH SHUG...

"...BUT WHEN YOU SEE THE ACTION FIRSTHAND, I THINK YALL'LL BE GLAD YOU CAME."

"TELL HIM, J.L. SENT YOU."

2

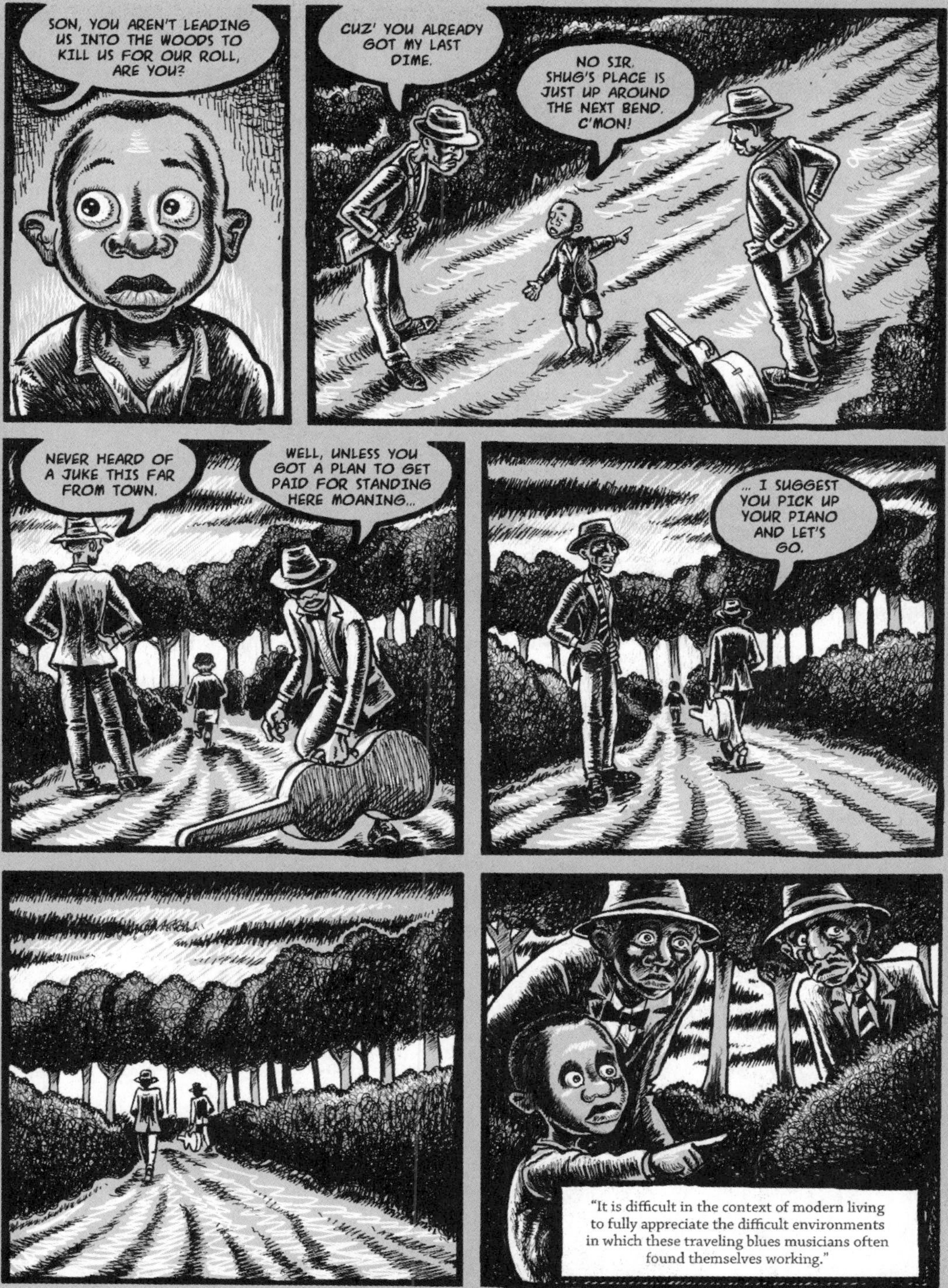
SON, YOU AREN'T LEADING US INTO THE WOODS TO KILL US FOR OUR ROLL, ARE YOU?
CUZ' YOU ALREADY GOT MY LAST DIME.
NO SIR. SHUG'S PLACE IS JUST UP AROUND THE NEXT BEND. C'MON!
NEVER HEARD OF A JUKE THIS FAR FROM TOWN.
WELL, UNLESS YOU GOT A PLAN TO GET PAID FOR STANDING HERE MOANING...
... I SUGGEST YOU PICK UP YOUR PIANO AND LET'S GO.
"It is difficult in the context of modern living to fully appreciate the difficult environments in which these traveling blues musicians often found themselves working."

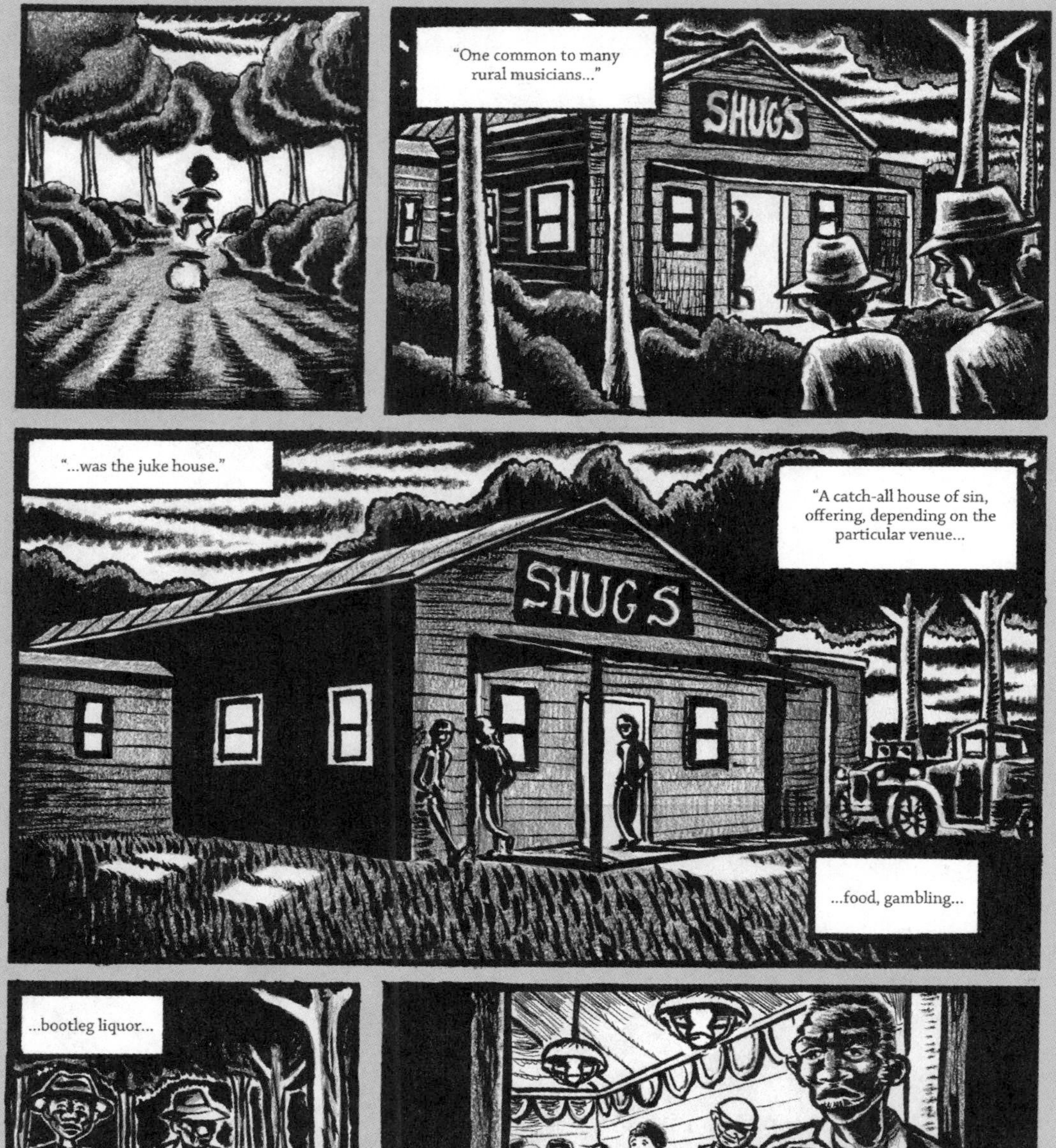
"One common to many rural musicians..."
SHUG'S
"...was the juke house."
"A catch-all house of sin, offering, depending on the particular venue...
SHUG'S
...food, gambling...
...bootleg liquor...
...prostitution, dancing, and, of course...

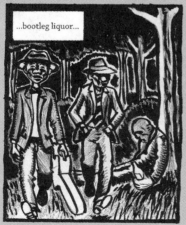

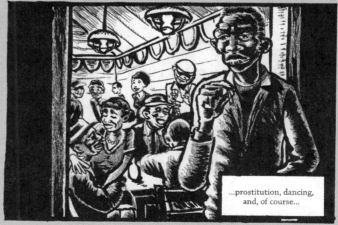

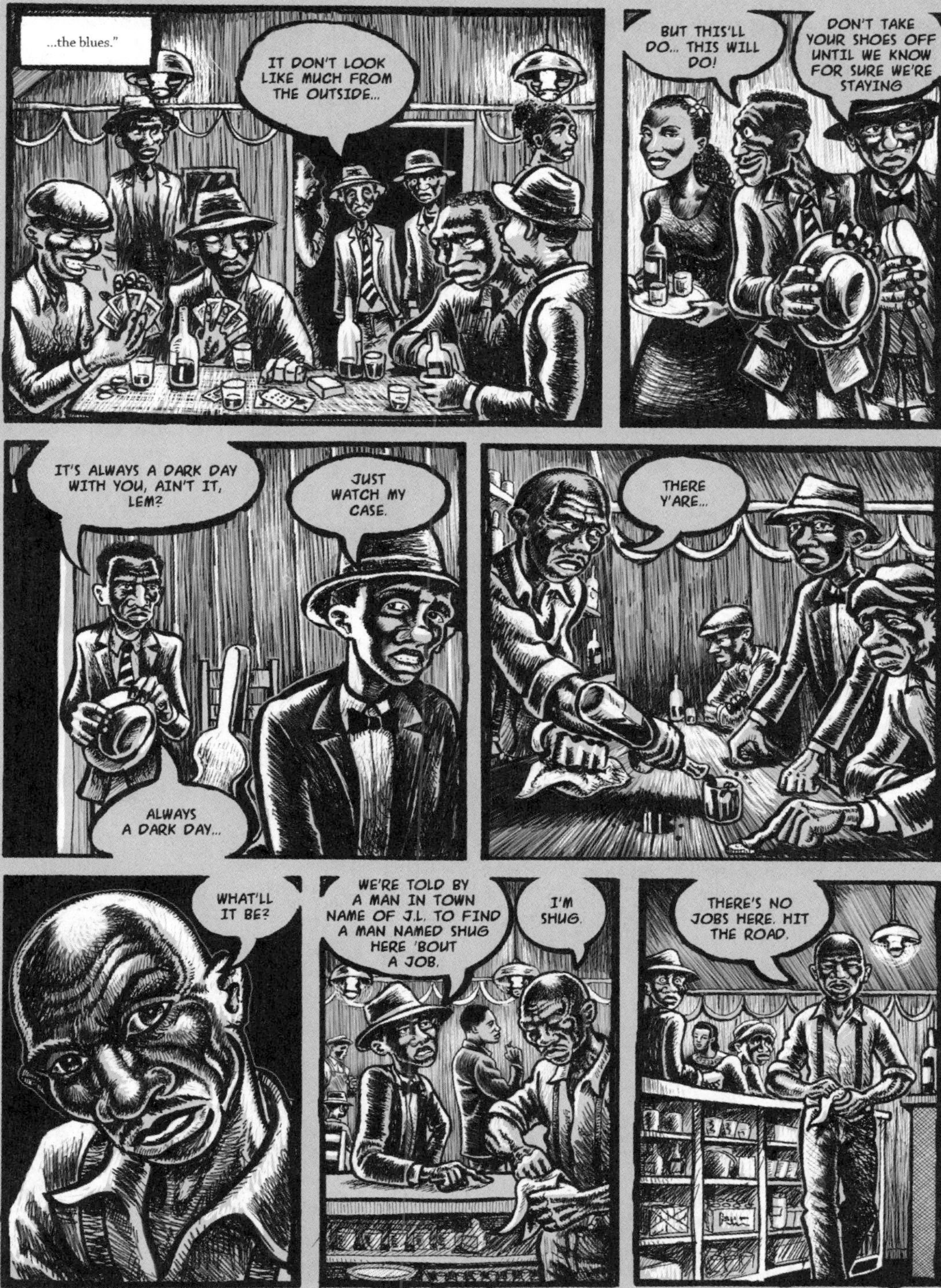
...the blues."
IT DON'T LOOK LIKE MUCH FROM THE OUTSIDE...
BUT THIS'LL DO... THIS WILL DO!
DON'T TAKE YOUR SHOES OFF UNTIL WE KNOW FOR SURE WE'RE STAYING
IT'S ALWAYS A DARK DAY WITH YOU, AIN'T IT, LEM?
JUST WATCH MY CASE.
ALWAYS A DARK DAY...
THERE Y'ARE...
WHAT'LL IT BE?
WE'RE TOLD BY A MAN IN TOWN NAME OF J.L. TO FIND A MAN NAMED SHUG HERE 'BOUT A JOB.
I'M SHUG.
THERE'S NO JOBS HERE. HIT THE ROAD.

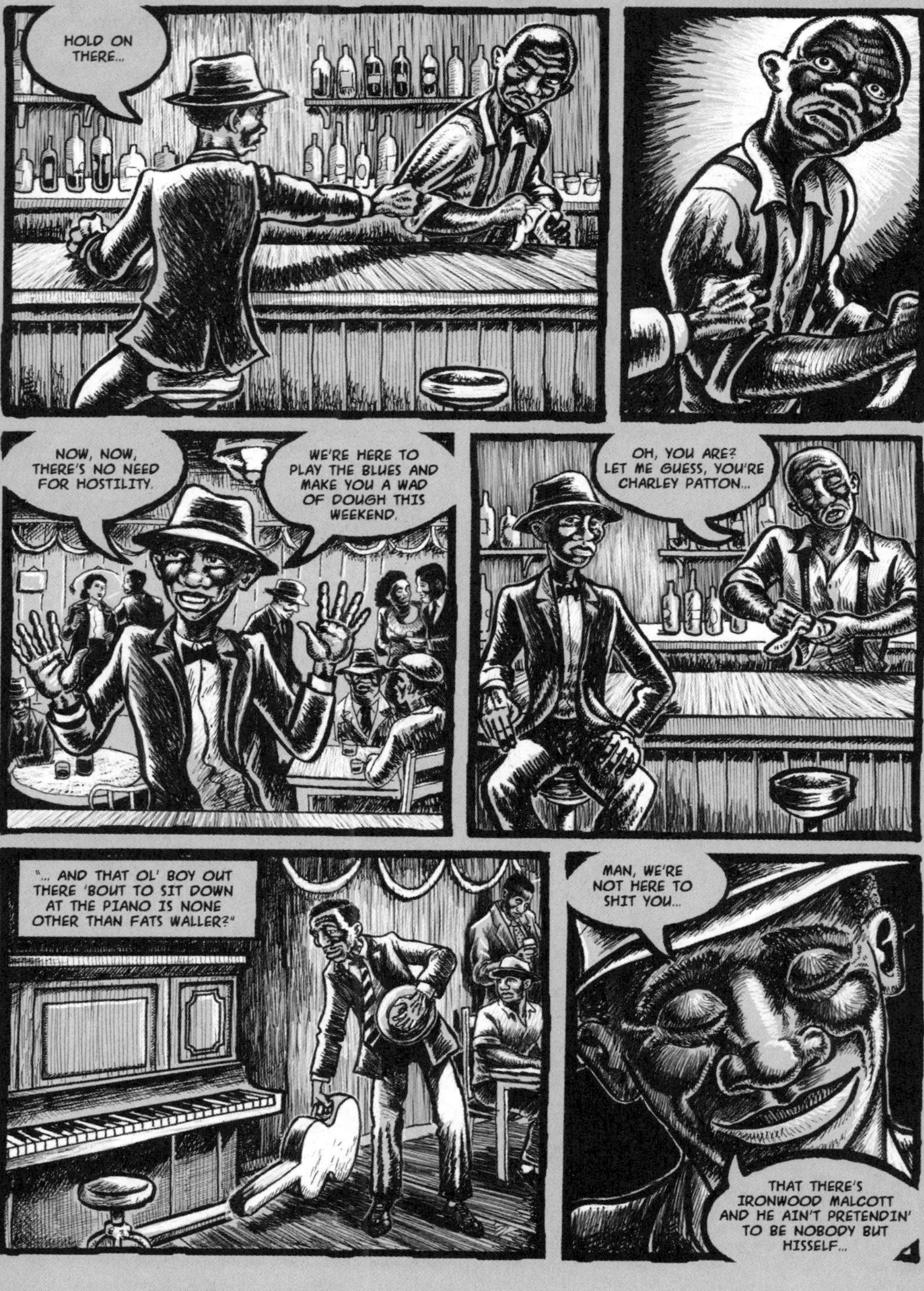
HOLD ON THERE...
NOW, NOW, THERE'S NO NEED FOR HOSTILITY.
WE'RE HERE TO PLAY THE BLUES AND MAKE YOU A WAD OF DOUGH THIS WEEKEND.
OH, YOU ARE? LET ME GUESS, YOU'RE CHARLEY PATTON...
"... AND THAT OL' BOY OUT THERE 'BOUT TO SIT DOWN AT THE PIANO IS NONE OTHER THAN FATS WALLER?"
MAN, WE'RE NOT HERE TO SHIT YOU...
THAT THERE'S IRONWOOD MALCOTT AND HE AIN'T PRETENDIN' TO BE NOBODY BUT HISSELF...

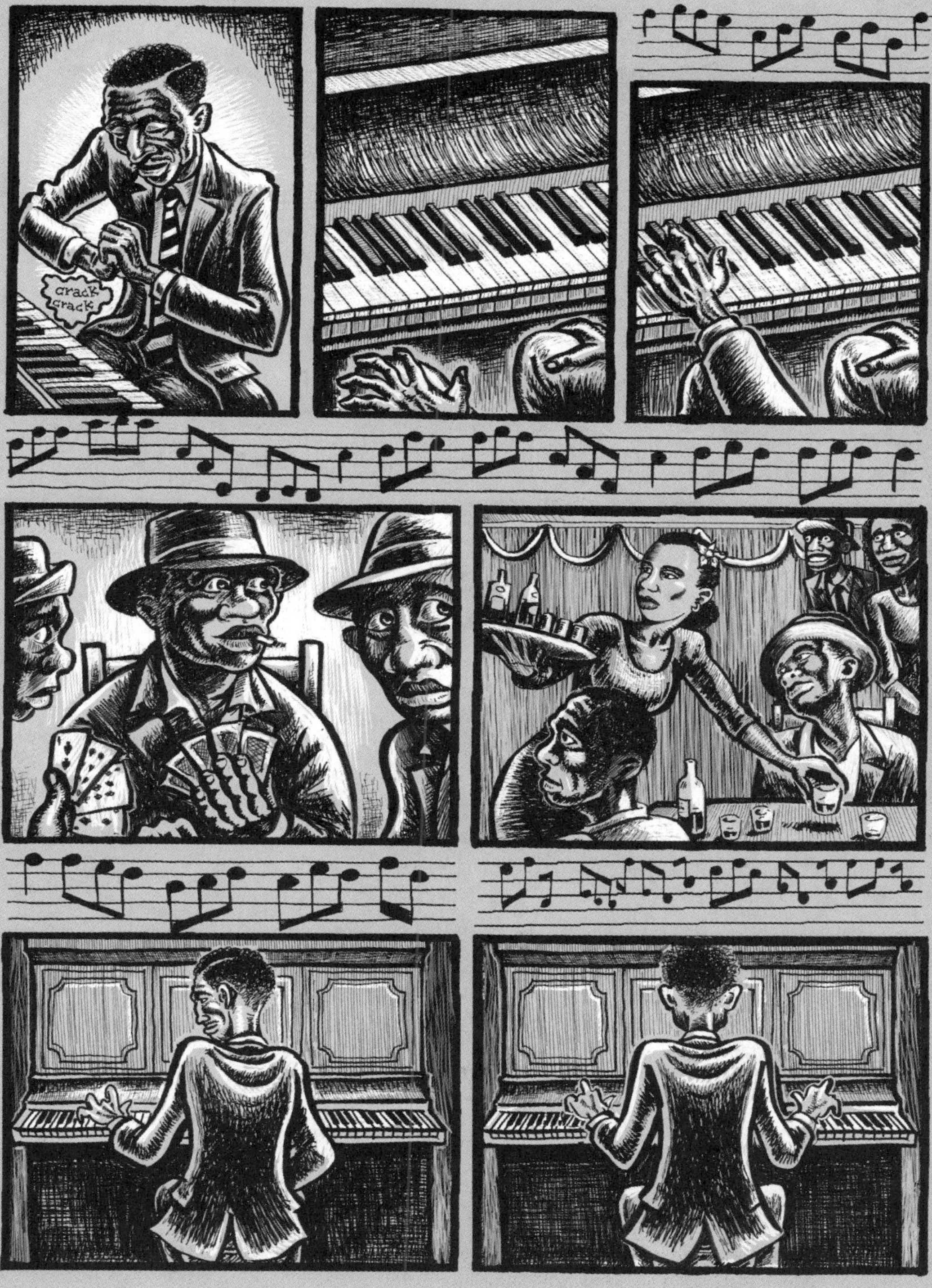
crack crack

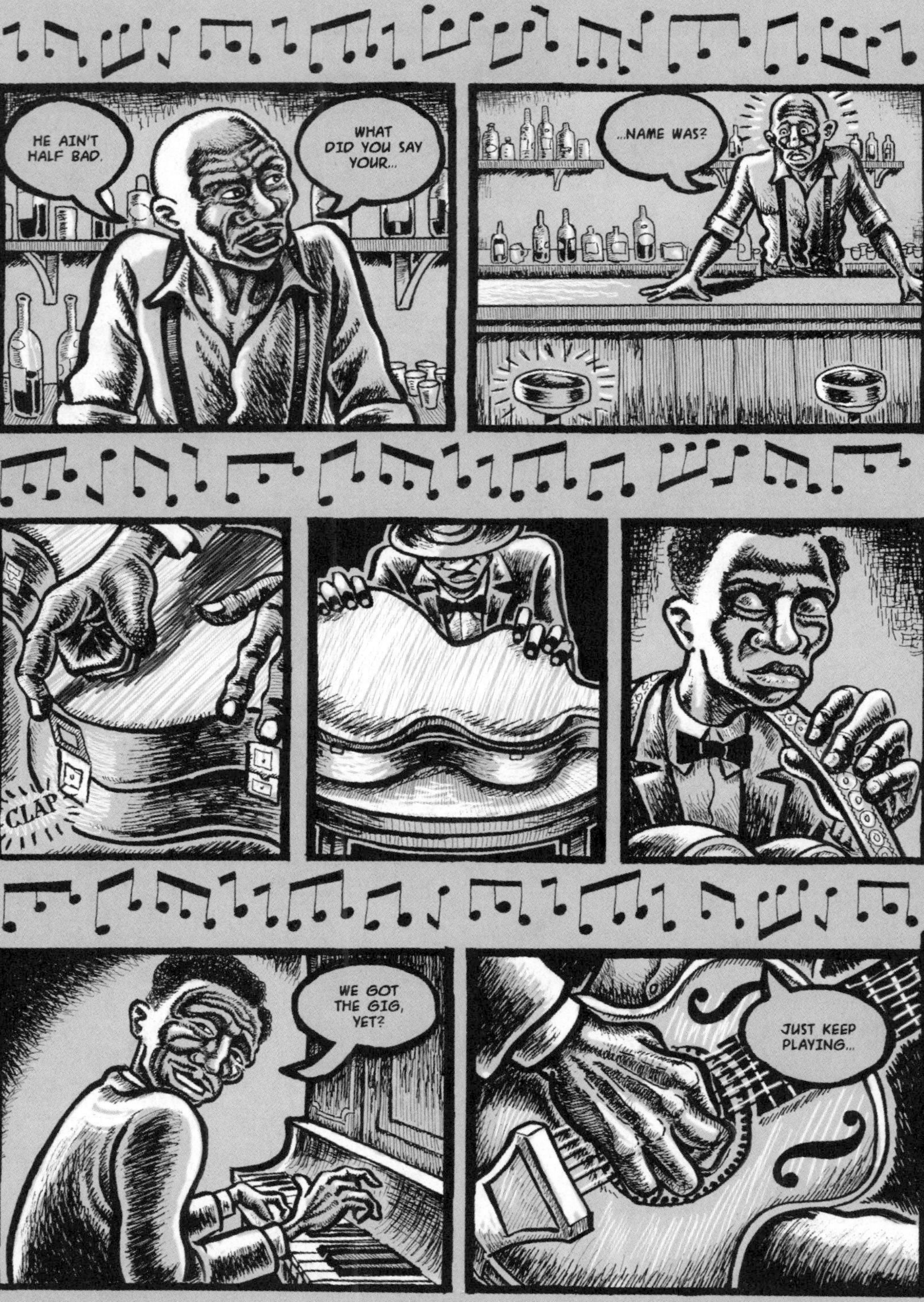

HE AIN'T HALF BAD.
WHAT DID YOU SAY YOUR...
...NAME WAS?
CLAP
WE GOT THE GIG, YET?
JUST KEEP PLAYING...

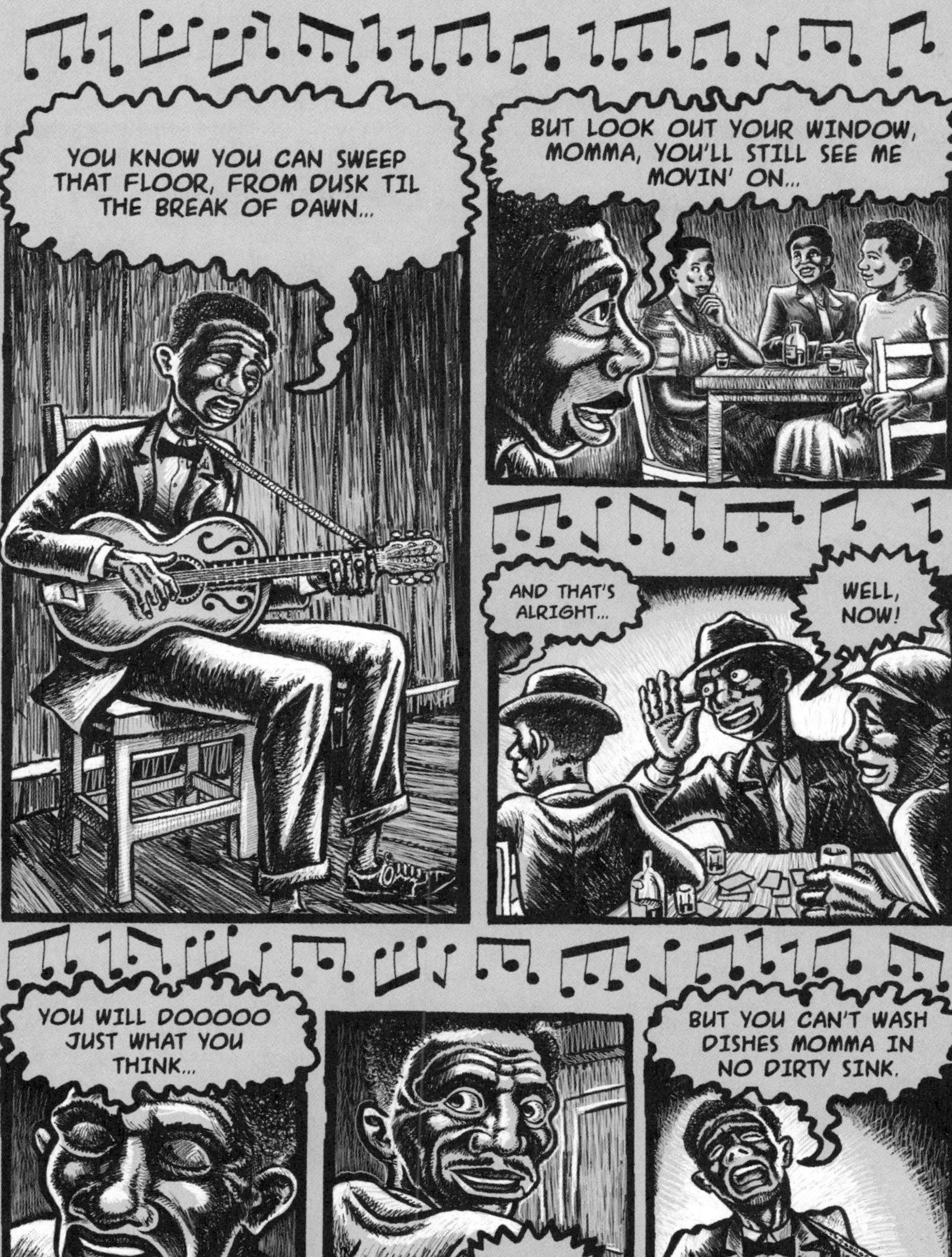
YOU KNOW YOU CAN SWEEP THAT FLOOR, FROM DUSK TIL THE BREAK OF DAWN...
BUT LOOK OUT YOUR WINDOW, MOMMA, YOU'LL STILL SEE ME MOVIN' ON...
AND THAT'S ALRIGHT...
WELL, NOW!
YOU WILL DOOOOO JUST WHAT YOU THINK...
THAT'S RIGHT, THAT'S RIGHT!
BUT YOU CAN'T WASH DISHES MOMMA IN NO DIRTY SINK.

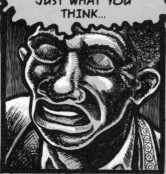

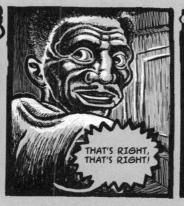

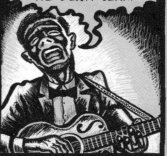

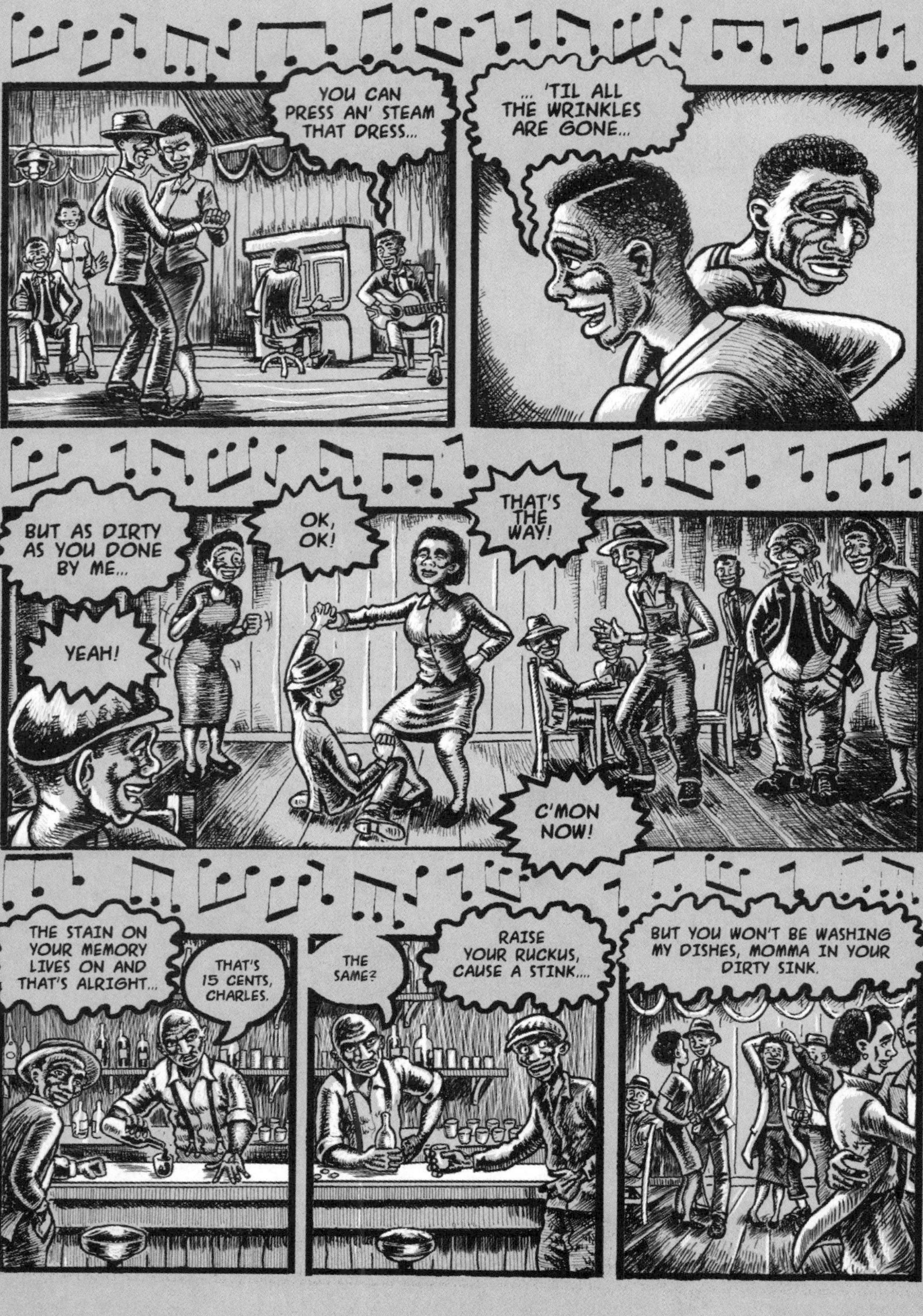
YOU CAN PRESS AN' STEAM THAT DRESS...
... 'TIL ALL THE WRINKLES ARE GONE...
BUT AS DIRTY AS YOU DONE BY ME...
OK, OK!
THAT'S THE WAY!
YEAH!
C'MON NOW!
THE STAIN ON YOUR MEMORY LIVES ON AND THAT'S ALRIGHT...
THAT'S 15 CENTS, CHARLES.
THE SAME?
RAISE YOUR RUCKUS, CAUSE A STINK....
BUT YOU WON'T BE WASHING MY DISHES, MOMMA IN YOUR DIRTY SINK.

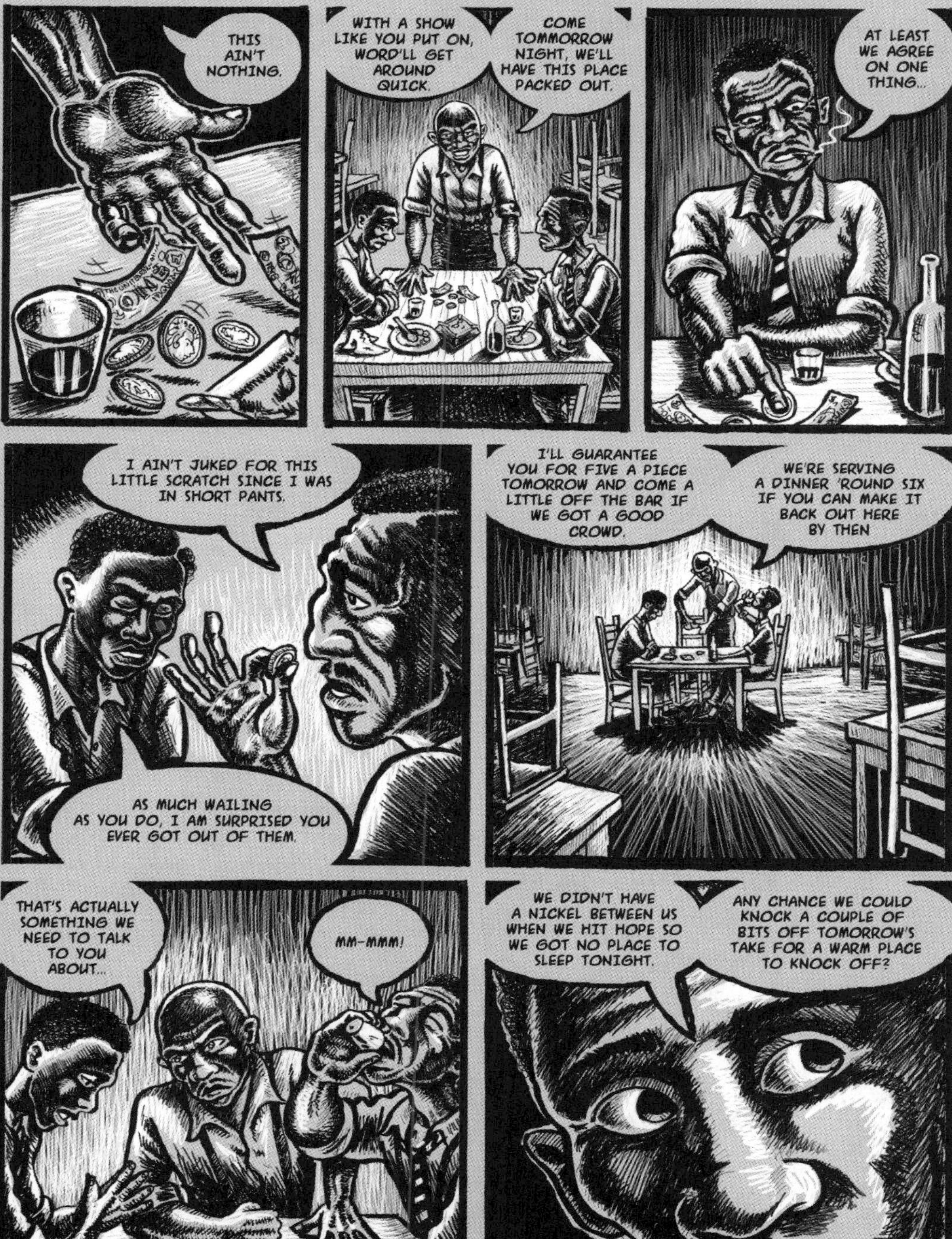
THIS AIN'T NOTHING.
WITH A SHOW LIKE YOU PUT ON, WORD'LL GET AROUND QUICK.
COME TOMORROW NIGHT, WE'LL HAVE THIS PLACE PACKED OUT.
AT LEAST WE AGREE ON ONE THING...
I AIN'T JUKED FOR THIS LITTLE SCRATCH SINCE I WAS IN SHORT PANTS.
AS MUCH WAILING AS YOU DO, I AM SURPRISED YOU EVER GOT OUT OF THEM.
I'LL GUARANTEE YOU FOR FIVE A PIECE TOMORROW AND COME A LITTLE OFF THE BAR IF WE GOT A GOOD CROWD.
WE'RE SERVING A DINNER 'ROUND SIX IF YOU CAN MAKE IT BACK OUT HERE BY THEN
THAT'S ACTUALLY SOMETHING WE NEED TO TALK TO YOU ABOUT...
MM-MMM!
WE DIDN'T HAVE A NICKEL BETWEEN US WHEN WE HIT HOPE SO WE GOT NO PLACE TO SLEEP TONIGHT.
ANY CHANCE WE COULD KNOCK A COUPLE OF BITS OFF TOMORROW'S TAKE FOR A WARM PLACE TO KNOCK OFF?

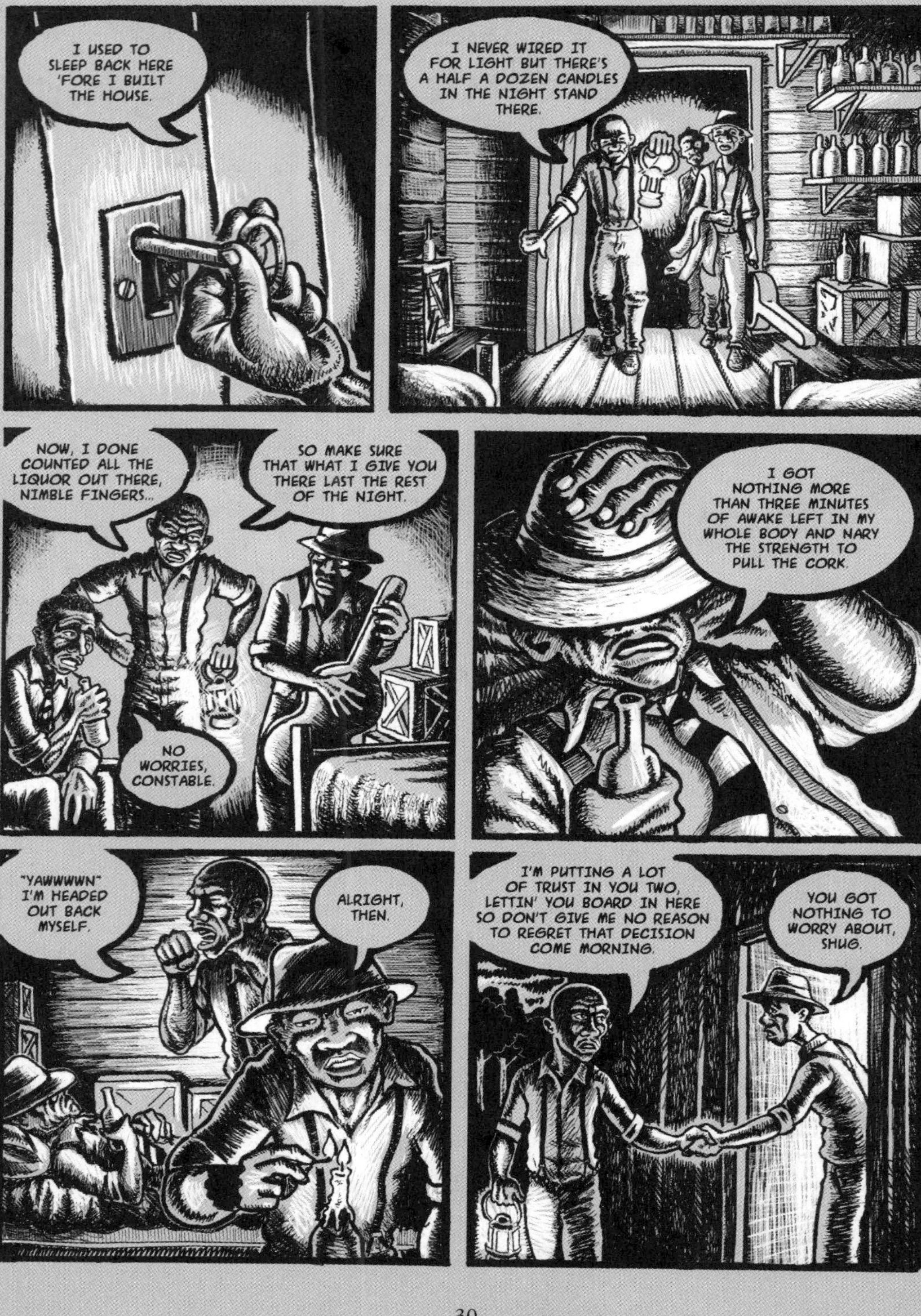
I USED TO SLEEP BACK HERE 'FORE I BUILT THE HOUSE.
I NEVER WIRED IT FOR LIGHT BUT THERE'S A HALF A DOZEN CANDLES IN THE NIGHT STAND THERE.
NOW, I DONE COUNTED ALL THE LIQUOR OUT THERE, NIMBLE FINGERS...
SO MAKE SURE THAT WHAT I GIVE YOU THERE LAST THE REST OF THE NIGHT.
NO WORRIES, CONSTABLE.
I GOT NOTHING MORE THAN THREE MINUTES OF AWAKE LEFT IN MY WHOLE BODY AND NARY THE STRENGTH TO PULL THE CORK.
"YAWWWWN" I'M HEADED OUT BACK MYSELF.
ALRIGHT, THEN.
I'M PUTTING A LOT OF TRUST IN YOU TWO, LETTIN' YOU BOARD IN HERE SO DON'T GIVE ME NO REASON TO REGRET THAT DECISION COME MORNING.
YOU GOT NOTHING TO WORRY ABOUT, SHUG.

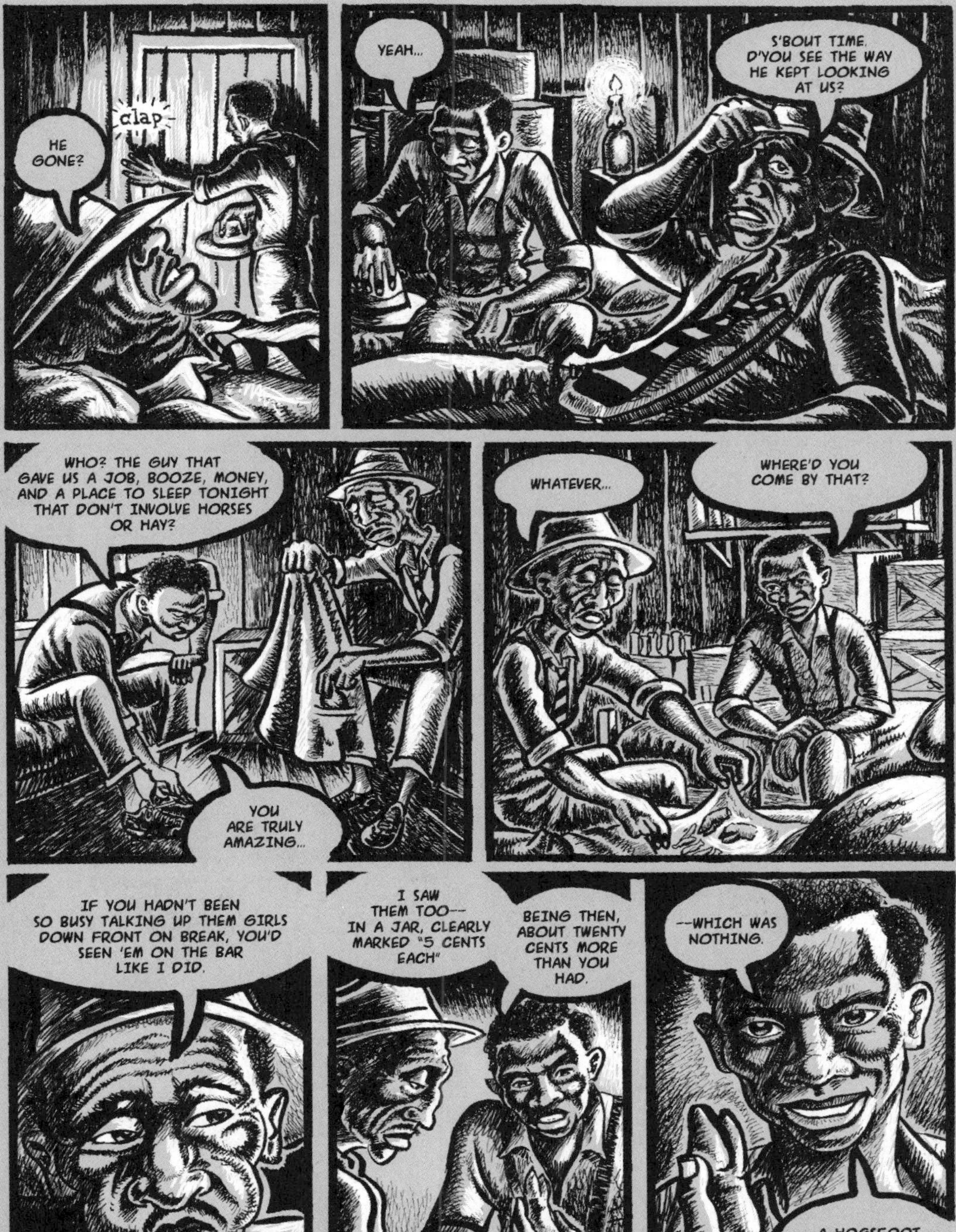
clap
HE GONE?
YEAH...
S'BOUT TIME. D'YOU SEE THE WAY HE KEPT LOOKING AT US?
WHO? THE GUY THAT GAVE US A JOB, BOOZE, MONEY, AND A PLACE TO SLEEP TONIGHT THAT DON'T INVOLVE HORSES OR HAY?
YOU ARE TRULY AMAZING...
WHATEVER...
WHERE'D YOU COME BY THAT?
IF YOU HADN'T BEEN SO BUSY TALKING UP THEM GIRLS DOWN FRONT ON BREAK, YOU'D SEEN 'EM ON THE BAR LIKE I DID.
I SAW THEM TOO-- IN A JAR, CLEARLY MARKED "5 CENTS EACH"
BEING THEN, ABOUT TWENTY CENTS MORE THAN YOU HAD.
--WHICH WAS NOTHING.
A HOGSFOOT BUYS YOU MY SILENCE.

32

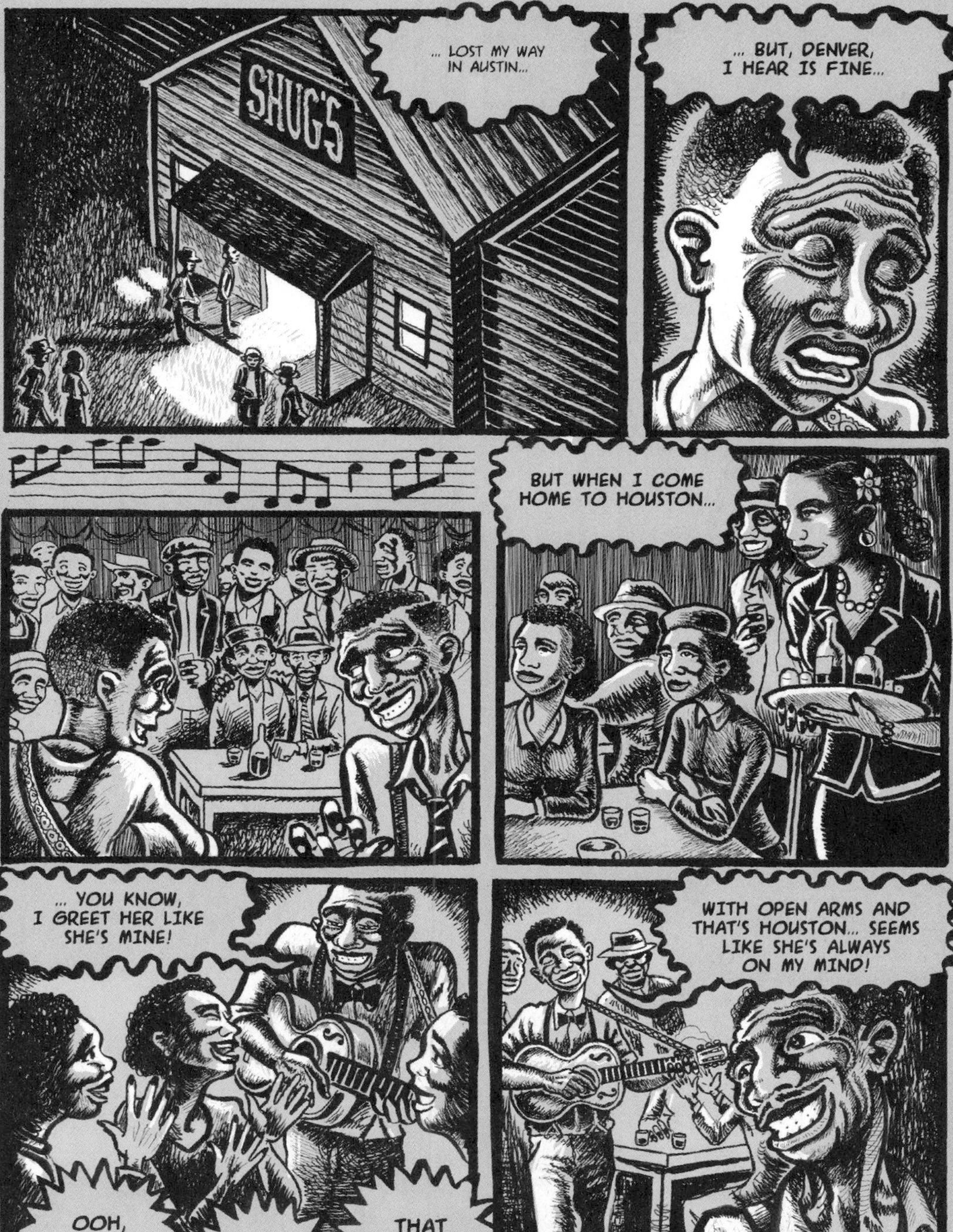
SHUG'S
... LOST MY WAY IN AUSTIN...
... BUT, DENVER, I HEAR IS FINE...
BUT WHEN I COME HOME TO HOUSTON...
... YOU KNOW, I GREET HER LIKE SHE'S MINE!
OOH, BABY!
WHOOO!
THAT MAN!
WITH OPEN ARMS AND THAT'S HOUSTON... SEEMS LIKE SHE'S ALWAYS ON MY MIND!

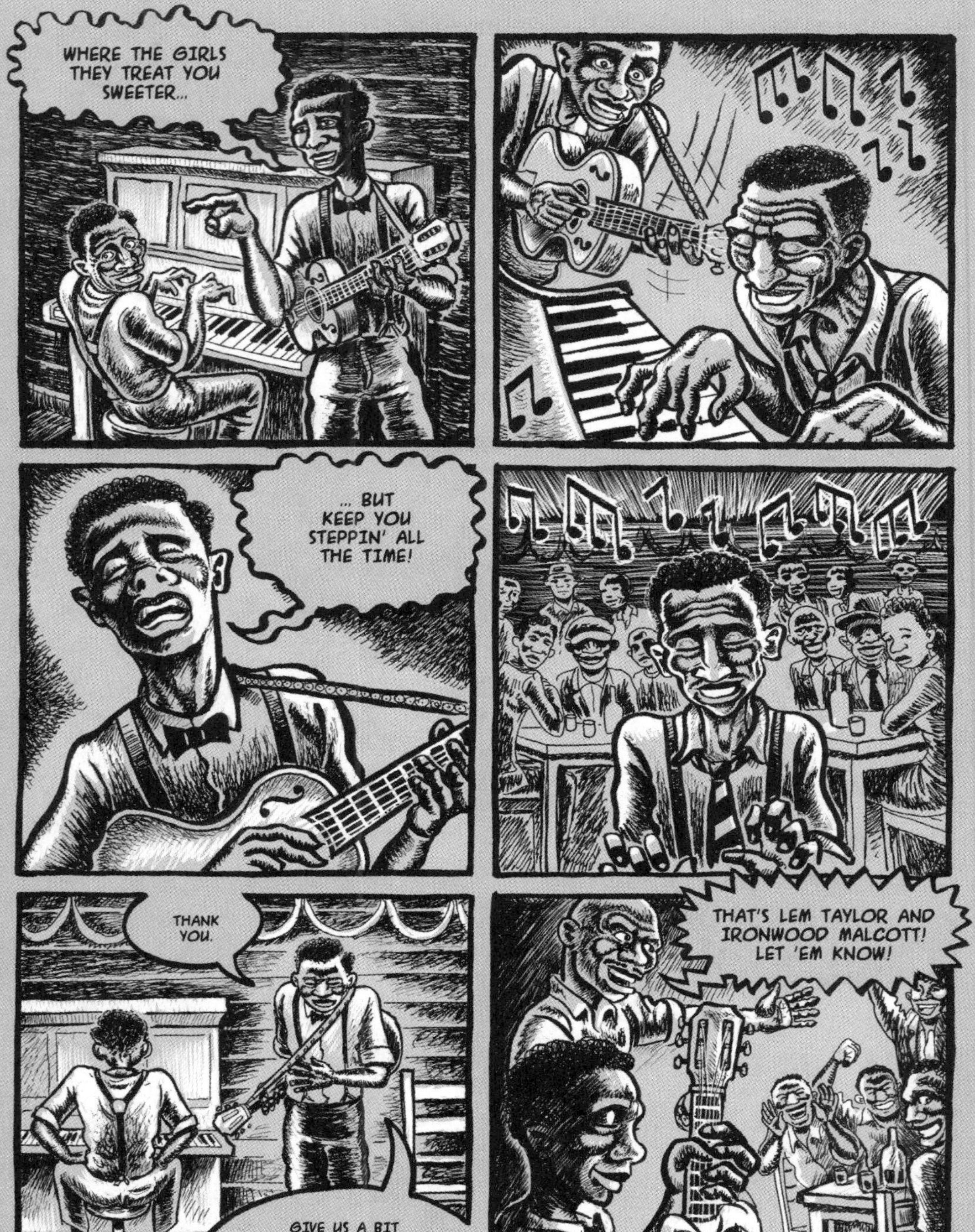
WHERE THE GIRLS THEY TREAT YOU SWEETER...
... BUT KEEP YOU STEPPIN' ALL THE TIME!
THANK YOU.
GIVE US A BIT TO GET WHERE YOU AT AND WE'LL MEET YA'LL BACK HERE IN TWENTY.
THAT'S LEM TAYLOR AND IRONWOOD MALCOTT! LET 'EM KNOW!

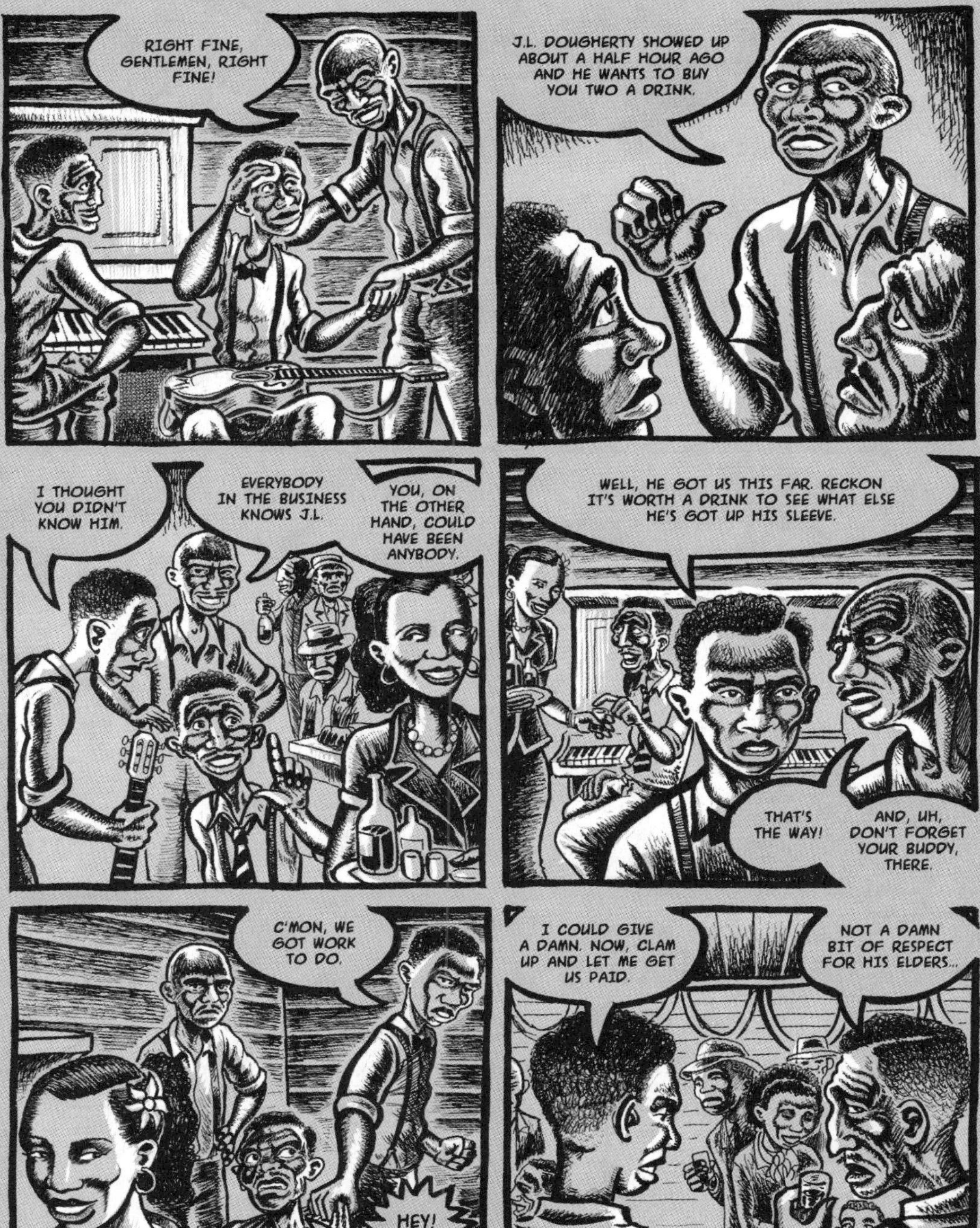

RIGHT FINE, GENTLEMEN, RIGHT FINE!
J.L. DOUGHERTY SHOWED UP ABOUT A HALF HOUR AGO AND HE WANTS TO BUY YOU TWO A DRINK.
I THOUGHT YOU DIDN'T KNOW HIM.
EVERYBODY IN THE BUSINESS KNOWS J.L.
YOU, ON THE OTHER HAND, COULD HAVE BEEN ANYBODY.
WELL, HE GOT US THIS FAR. RECKON IT'S WORTH A DRINK TO SEE WHAT ELSE HE'S GOT UP HIS SLEEVE.
THAT'S THE WAY!
AND, UH, DON'T FORGET YOUR BUDDY, THERE.
C'MON, WE GOT WORK TO DO.
HEY!
WHAT DID I SAY ABOUT PUTTING YOUR HANDS ON ME?
I COULD GIVE A DAMN. NOW, CLAM UP AND LET ME GET US PAID.
NOT A DAMN BIT OF RESPECT FOR HIS ELDERS...

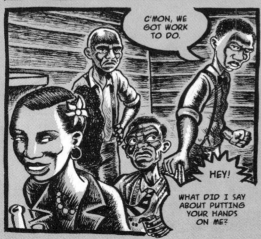

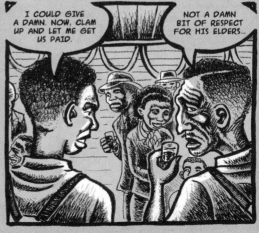

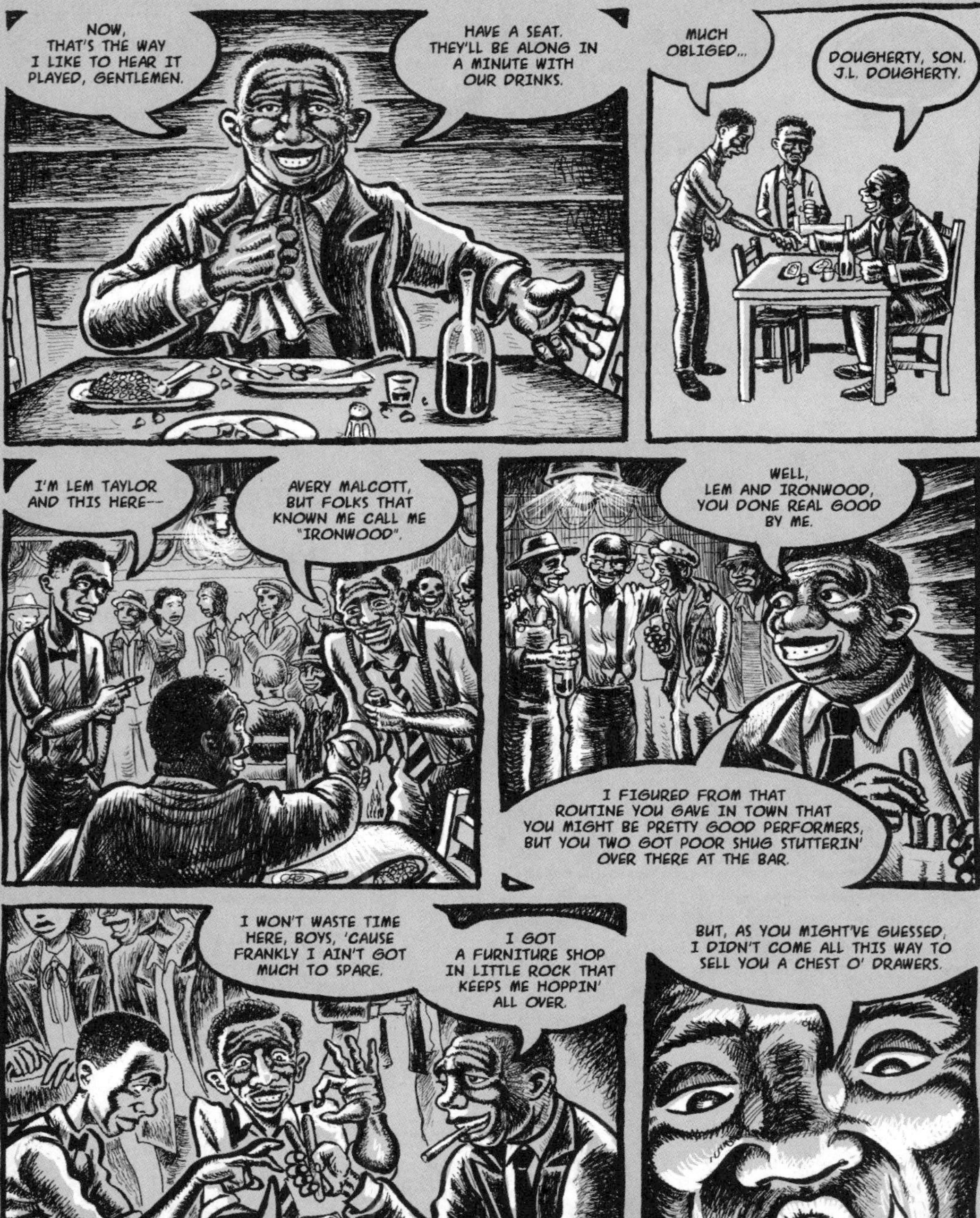
NOW, THAT'S THE WAY I LIKE TO HEAR IT PLAYED, GENTLEMEN.
HAVE A SEAT. THEY'LL BE ALONG IN A MINUTE WITH OUR DRINKS.
MUCH OBLIGED...
DOUGHERTY, SON. J.L. DOUGHERTY.
I'M LEM TAYLOR AND THIS HERE--
AVERY MALCOTT, BUT FOLKS THAT KNOWN ME CALL ME "IRONWOOD".
WELL, LEM AND IRONWOOD, YOU DONE REAL GOOD BY ME.
I FIGURED FROM THAT ROUTINE YOU GAVE IN TOWN THAT YOU MIGHT BE PRETTY GOOD PERFORMERS, BUT YOU TWO GOT POOR SHUG STUTTERIN' OVER THERE AT THE BAR.
I WON'T WASTE TIME HERE, BOYS, 'CAUSE FRANKLY I AIN'T GOT MUCH TO SPARE.
I GOT A FURNITURE SHOP IN LITTLE ROCK THAT KEEPS ME HOPPIN' ALL OVER.
DON'T MIND IF I DO, J.L.
BUT, AS YOU MIGHT'VE GUESSED, I DIDN'T COME ALL THIS WAY TO SELL YOU A CHEST O' DRAWERS.

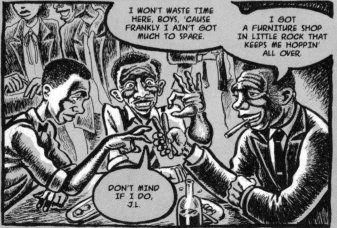

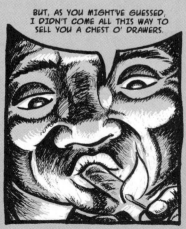

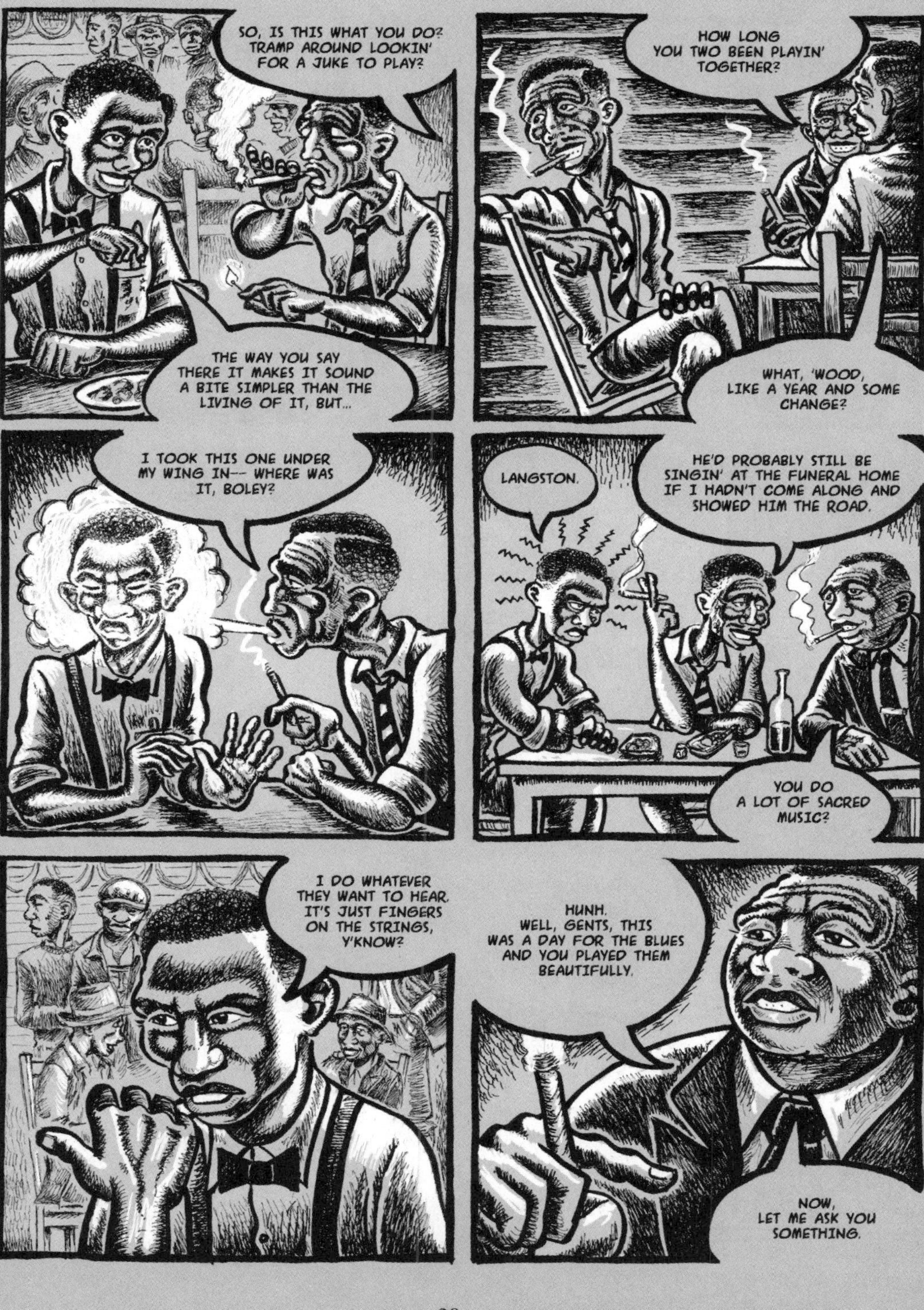
SO, IS THIS WHAT YOU DO? TRAMP AROUND LOOKIN' FOR A JUKE TO PLAY?
THE WAY YOU SAY THERE IT MAKES IT SOUND A BITE SIMPLER THAN THE LIVING OF IT, BUT...
HOW LONG YOU TWO BEEN PLAYIN' TOGETHER?
WHAT, 'WOOD, LIKE A YEAR AND SOME CHANGE?
I TOOK THIS ONE UNDER MY WING IN-- WHERE WAS IT, BOLEY?
LANGSTON.
HE'D PROBABLY STILL BE SINGIN' AT THE FUNERAL HOME IF I HADN'T COME ALONG AND SHOWED HIM THE ROAD.
YOU DO A LOT OF SACRED MUSIC?
I DO WHATEVER THEY WANT TO HEAR. IT'S JUST FINGERS ON THE STRINGS, Y'KNOW?
HUNH. WELL, GENTS, THIS WAS A DAY FOR THE BLUES AND YOU PLAYED THEM BEAUTIFULLY.
NOW, LET ME ASK YOU SOMETHING.

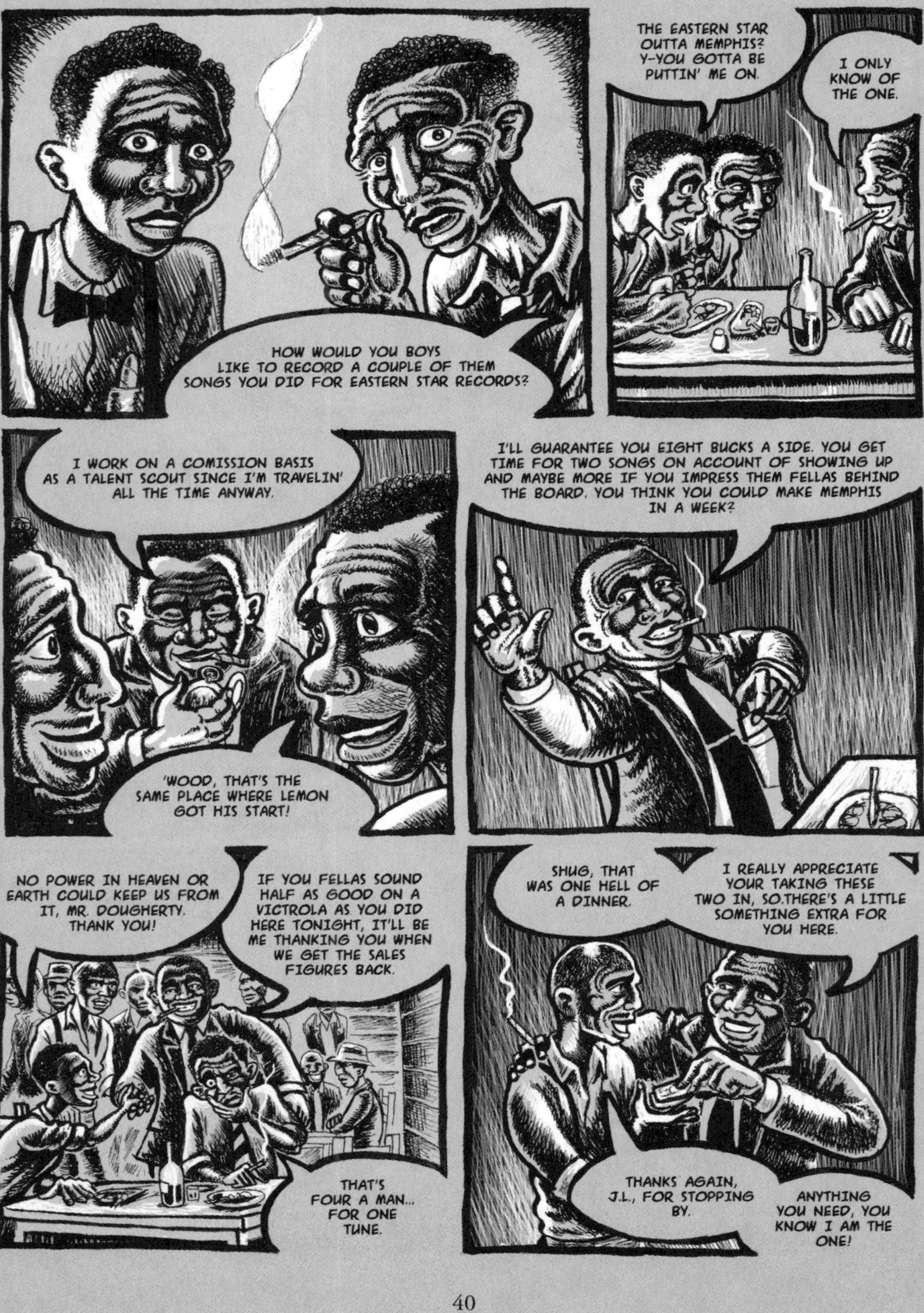
HOW WOULD YOU BOYS LIKE TO RECORD A COUPLE OF THEM SONGS YOU DID FOR EASTERN STAR RECORDS?
THE EASTERN STAR OUTTA MEMPHIS? Y-YOU GOTTA BE PUTTIN' ME ON.
I ONLY KNOW OF THE ONE.
I WORK ON A COMISSION BASIS AS A TALENT SCOUT SINCE I'M TRAVELIN' ALL THE TIME ANYWAY.
'WOOD, THAT'S THE SAME PLACE WHERE LEMON GOT HIS START!
I'LL GUARANTEE YOU EIGHT BUCKS A SIDE. YOU GET TIME FOR TWO SONGS ON ACCOUNT OF SHOWING UP AND MAYBE MORE IF YOU IMPRESS THEM FELLAS BEHIND THE BOARD. YOU THINK YOU COULD MAKE MEMPHIS IN A WEEK?
NO POWER IN HEAVEN OR EARTH COULD KEEP US FROM IT, MR. DOUGHERTY. THANK YOU!
IF YOU FELLAS SOUND HALF AS GOOD ON A VICTROLA AS YOU DID HERE TONIGHT, IT'LL BE ME THANKING YOU WHEN WE GET THE SALES FIGURES BACK.
THAT'S FOUR A MAN... FOR ONE TUNE.
SHUG, THAT WAS ONE HELL OF A DINNER.
I REALLY APPRECIATE YOUR TAKING THESE TWO IN, SO.THERE'S A LITTLE SOMETHING EXTRA FOR YOU HERE.
THANKS AGAIN, J.L., FOR STOPPING BY.
ANYTHING YOU NEED, YOU KNOW I AM THE ONE!

41

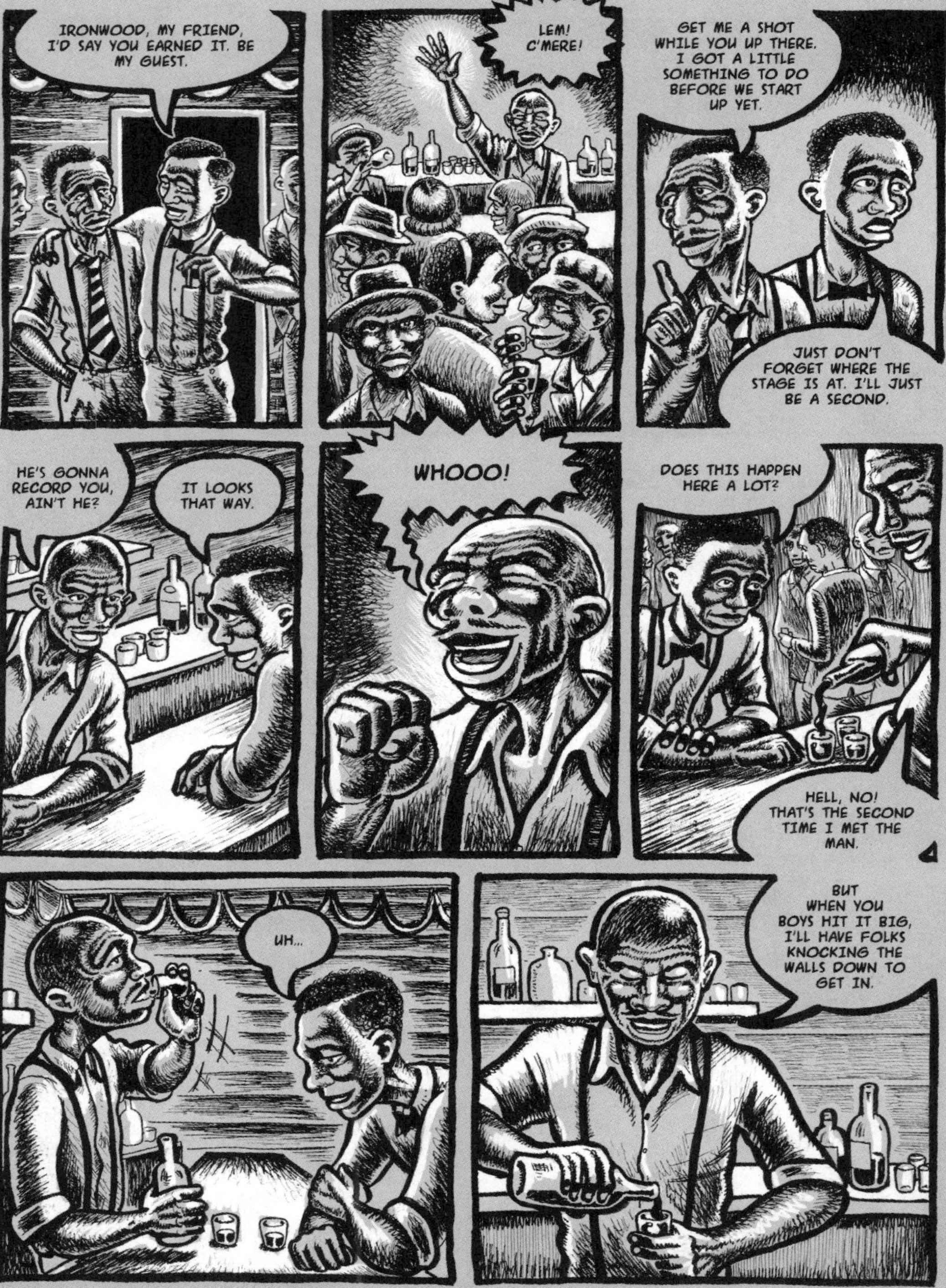
IRONWOOD, MY FRIEND, I'D SAY YOU EARNED IT. BE MY GUEST.
LEM! C'MERE!
GET ME A SHOT WHILE YOU UP THERE. I GOT A LITTLE SOMETHING TO DO BEFORE WE START UP YET.
JUST DON'T FORGET WHERE THE STAGE IS AT. I'LL JUST BE A SECOND.
HE'S GONNA RECORD YOU, AIN'T HE?
IT LOOKS THAT WAY.
WHOOO!
DOES THIS HAPPEN HERE A LOT?
HELL, NO! THAT'S THE SECOND TIME I MET THE MAN.
UH...
BUT WHEN YOU BOYS HIT IT BIG, I'LL HAVE FOLKS KNOCKING THE WALLS DOWN TO GET IN.

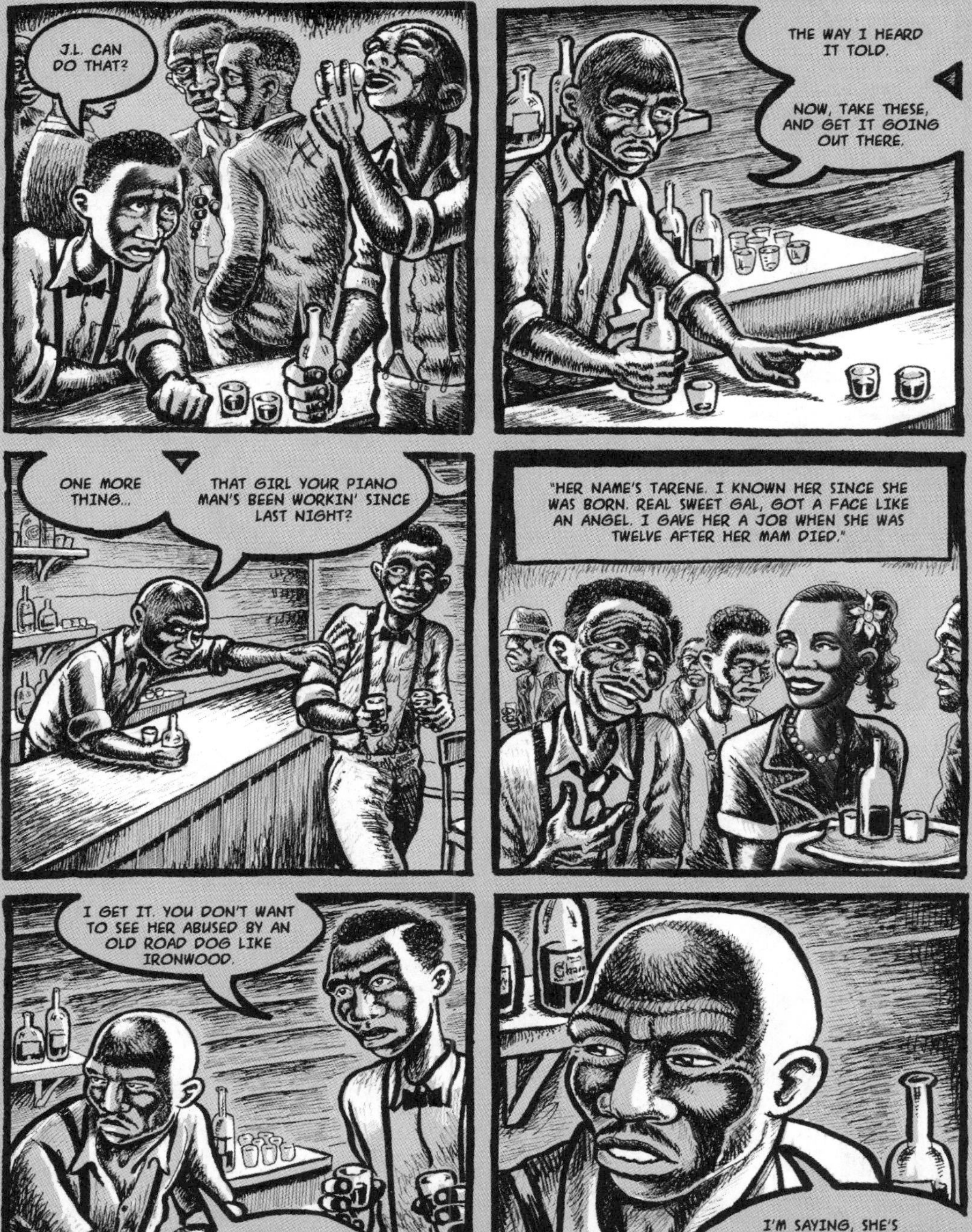
J.L. CAN DO THAT?
THE WAY I HEARD IT TOLD.
NOW, TAKE THESE, AND GET IT GOING OUT THERE.
ONE MORE THING...
THAT GIRL YOUR PIANO MAN'S BEEN WORKIN' SINCE LAST NIGHT?
"HER NAME'S TARENE. I KNOWN HER SINCE SHE WAS BORN. REAL SWEET GAL, GOT A FACE LIKE AN ANGEL. I GAVE HER A JOB WHEN SHE WAS TWELVE AFTER HER MAM DIED."
I GET IT. YOU DON'T WANT TO SEE HER ABUSED BY AN OLD ROAD DOG LIKE IRONWOOD.
NO, YOU GOT IT ALL TWISTED 'ROUND.
I'M SAYING, SHE'S A PRETTY GIRL AND YOUR BOY THERE AIN'T THE FIRST ONE TO TAKE NOTICE O' THAT.

44

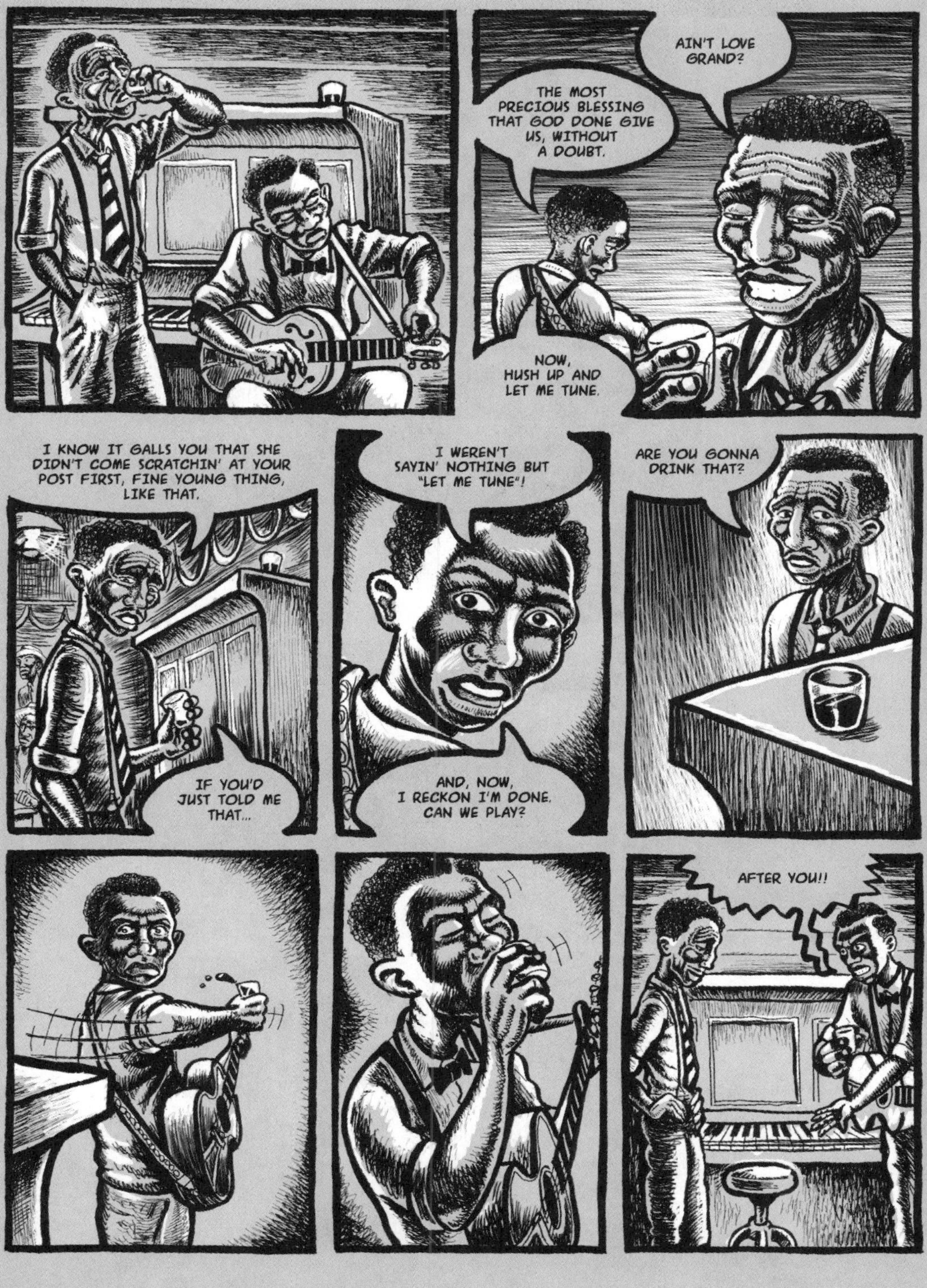
AIN'T LOVE GRAND?
THE MOST PRECIOUS BLESSING THAT GOD DONE GIVE US, WITHOUT A DOUBT.
NOW, HUSH UP AND LET ME TUNE.
I KNOW IT GALLS YOU THAT SHE DIDN'T COME SCRATCHIN' AT YOUR POST FIRST, FINE YOUNG THING, LIKE THAT.
IF YOU'D JUST TOLD ME THAT...
I WEREN'T SAYIN' NOTHING BUT "LET ME TUNE"!
AND, NOW, I RECKON I'M DONE. CAN WE PLAY?
ARE YOU GONNA DRINK THAT?
AFTER YOU!!

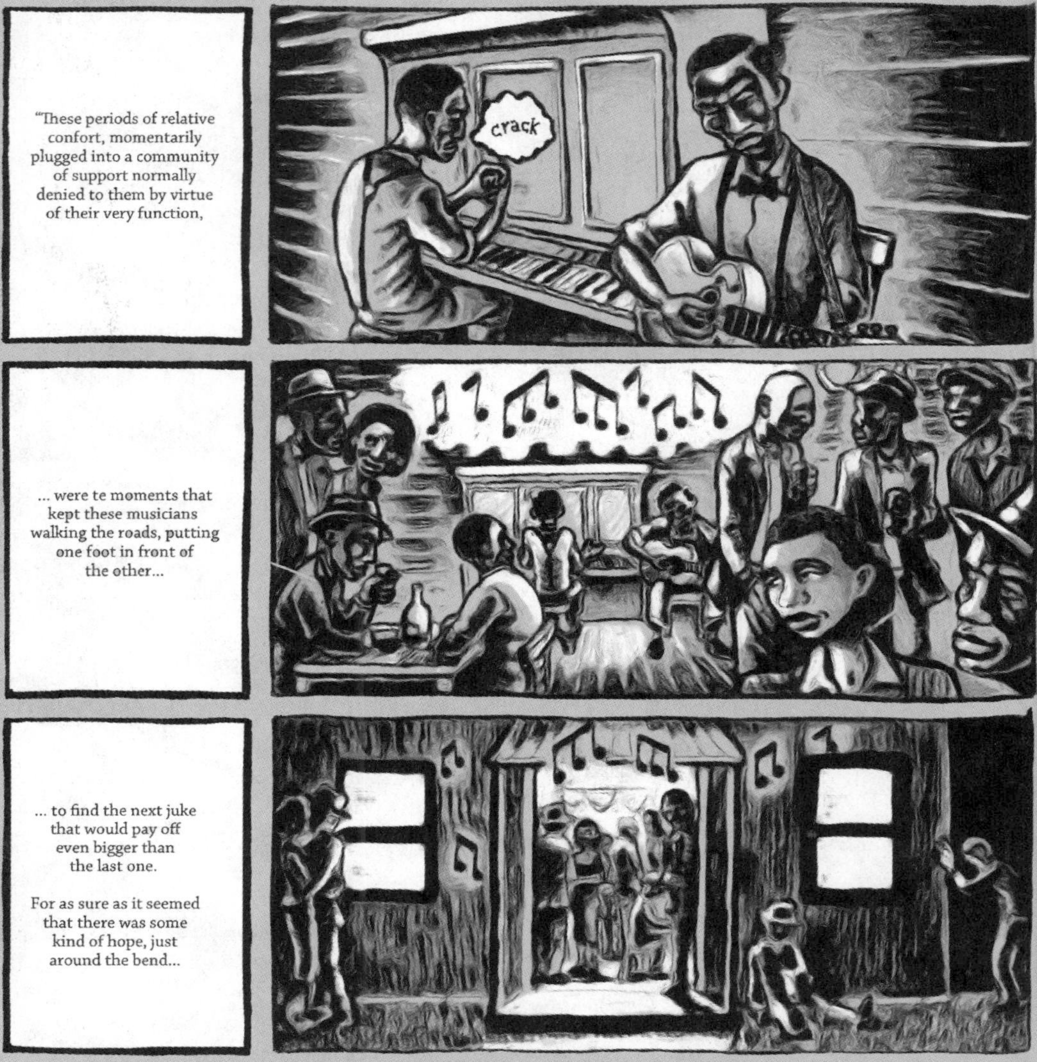
"These periods of relative confort, momentarily plugged into a community of support normally denied to them by virtue of their very function,
crack
... were te moments that kept these musicians walking the roads, putting one foot in front of the other...
... to find the next juke that would pay off even bigger than the last one.
For as sure as it seemed that there was some kind of hope, just around the bend...
... it was no secret that catastrophe was just as likely to take them before they arrived."

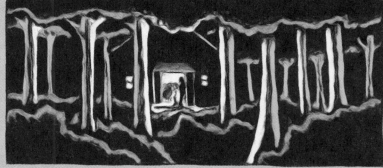

"The Roots of British R&B: Blind Lemon Jefferson to T-Bone Walker", Deldoff, Sheldon. (Early Rock Magazine #37, February 1966.)

4

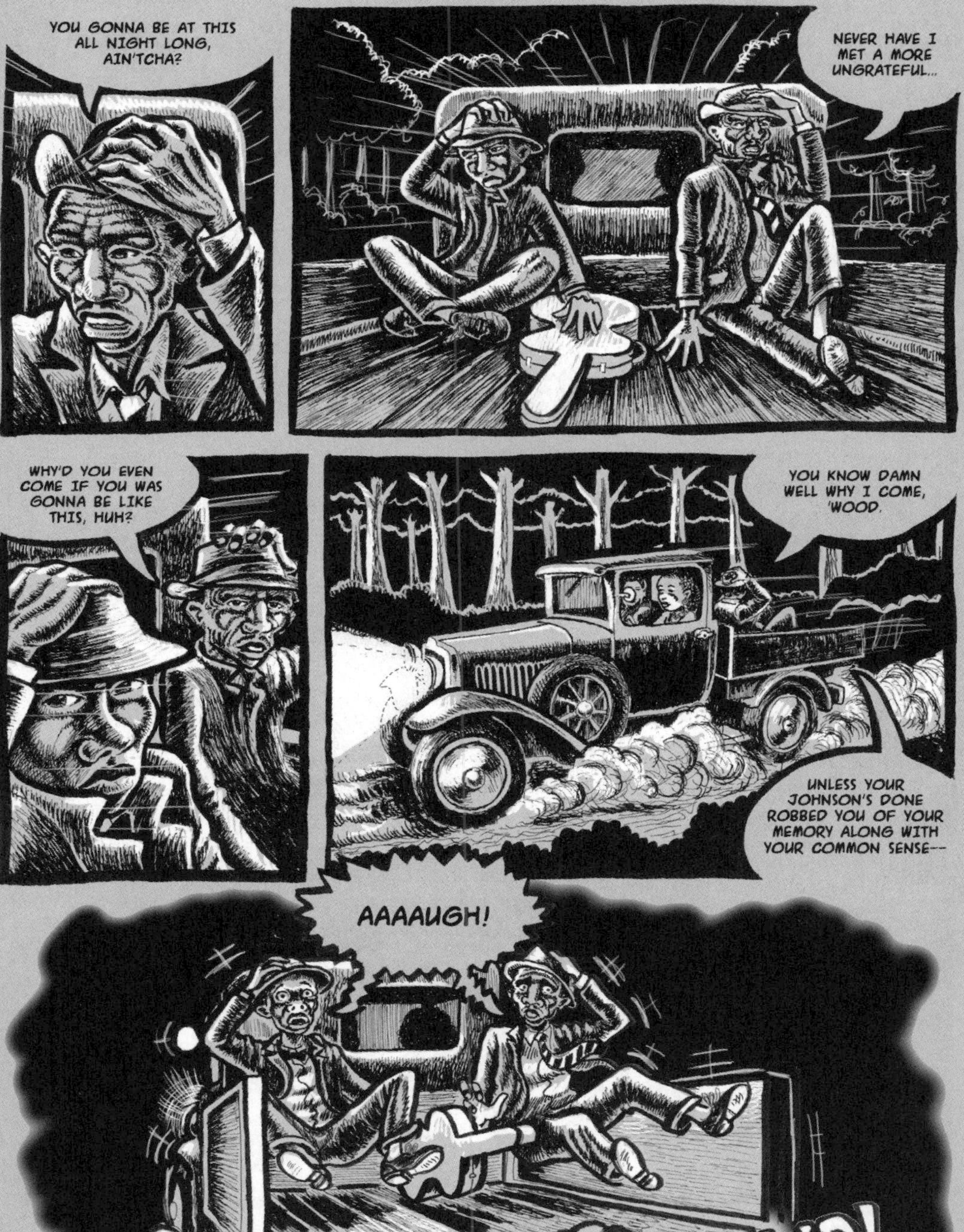
YOU GONNA BE AT THIS ALL NIGHT LONG, AIN'TCHA?
NEVER HAVE I MET A MORE UNGRATEFUL...
WHY'D YOU EVEN COME IF YOU WAS GONNA BE LIKE THIS, HUH?
YOU KNOW DAMN WELL WHY I COME, 'WOOD.
UNLESS YOUR JOHNSON'S DONE ROBBED YOU OF YOUR MEMORY ALONG WITH YOUR COMMON SENSE--
AAAAUGH!
BUMP!

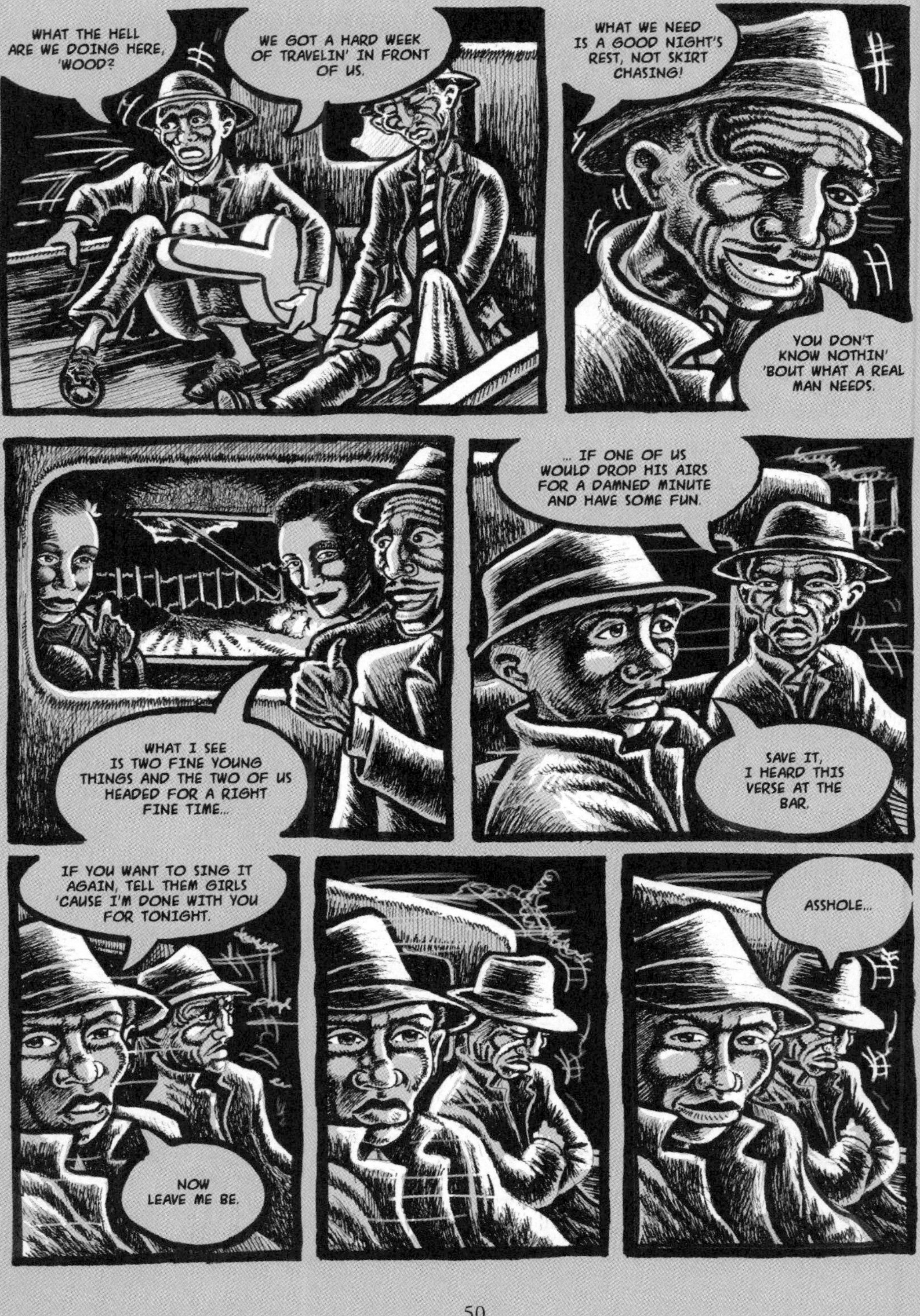
WHAT THE HELL ARE WE DOING HERE, 'WOOD?
WE GOT A HARD WEEK OF TRAVELIN' IN FRONT OF US.
WHAT WE NEED IS A GOOD NIGHT'S REST, NOT SKIRT CHASING!
YOU DON'T KNOW NOTHIN' 'BOUT WHAT A REAL MAN NEEDS.
WHAT I SEE IS TWO FINE YOUNG THINGS AND THE TWO OF US HEADED FOR A RIGHT FINE TIME...
... IF ONE OF US WOULD DROP HIS AIRS FOR A DAMNED MINUTE AND HAVE SOME FUN.
SAVE IT, I HEARD THIS VERSE AT THE BAR.
IF YOU WANT TO SING IT AGAIN, TELL THEM GIRLS 'CAUSE I'M DONE WITH YOU FOR TONIGHT.
NOW LEAVE ME BE.
ASSHOLE...

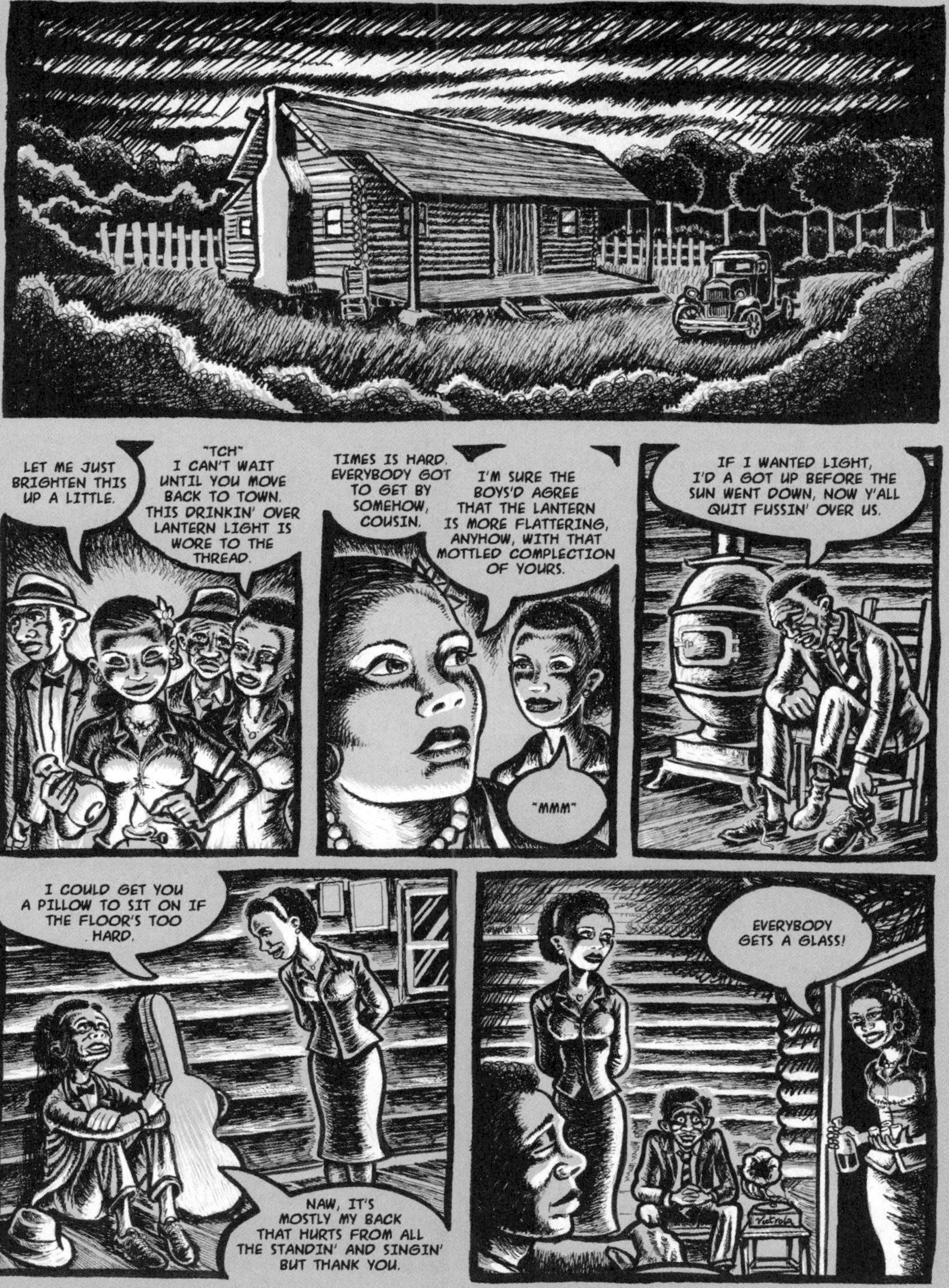
LET ME JUST BRIGHTEN THIS UP A LITTLE.
"TCH" I CAN'T WAIT UNTIL YOU MOVE BACK TO TOWN. THIS DRINKIN' OVER LANTERN LIGHT IS WORE TO THE THREAD.
TIMES IS HARD. EVERYBODY GOT TO GET BY SOMEHOW, COUSIN.
I'M SURE THE BOYS'D AGREE THAT THE LANTERN IS MORE FLATTERING, ANYHOW, WITH THAT MOTTLED COMPLECTION OF YOURS.
"MMM"
IF I WANTED LIGHT, I'D A GOT UP BEFORE THE SUN WENT DOWN, NOW Y'ALL QUIT FUSSIN' OVER US.
I COULD GET YOU A PILLOW TO SIT ON IF THE FLOOR'S TOO HARD.
NAW, IT'S MOSTLY MY BACK THAT HURTS FROM ALL THE STANDIN' AND SINGIN' BUT THANK YOU.
EVERYBODY GETS A GLASS!
Victrola

52

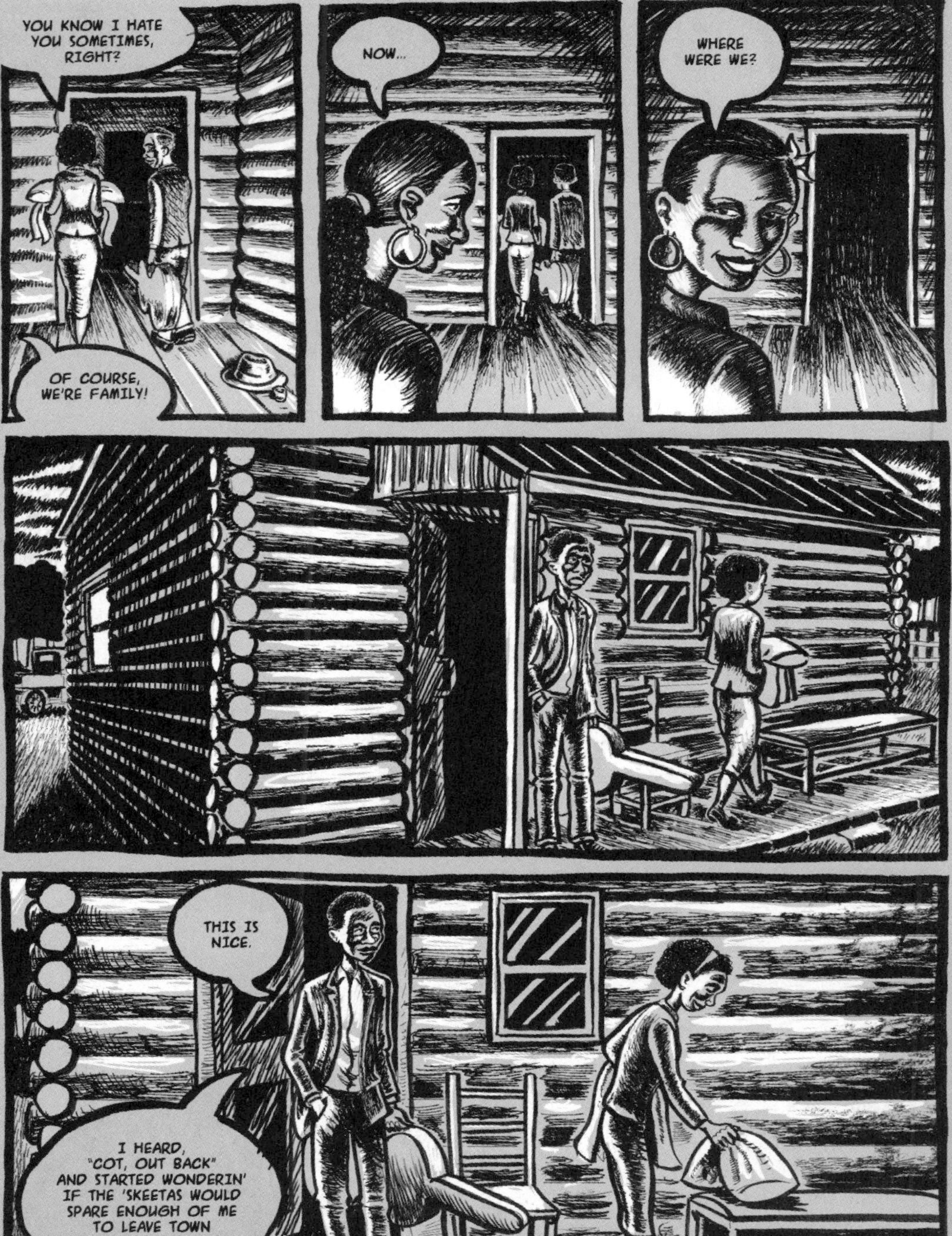
YOU KNOW I HATE YOU SOMETIMES, RIGHT?
OF COURSE, WE'RE FAMILY!
NOW...
WHERE WERE WE?
THIS IS NICE.
I HEARD, "COT, OUT BACK" AND STARTED WONDERIN' IF THE 'SKEETAS WOULD SPARE ENOUGH OF ME TO LEAVE TOWN TOMORROW.

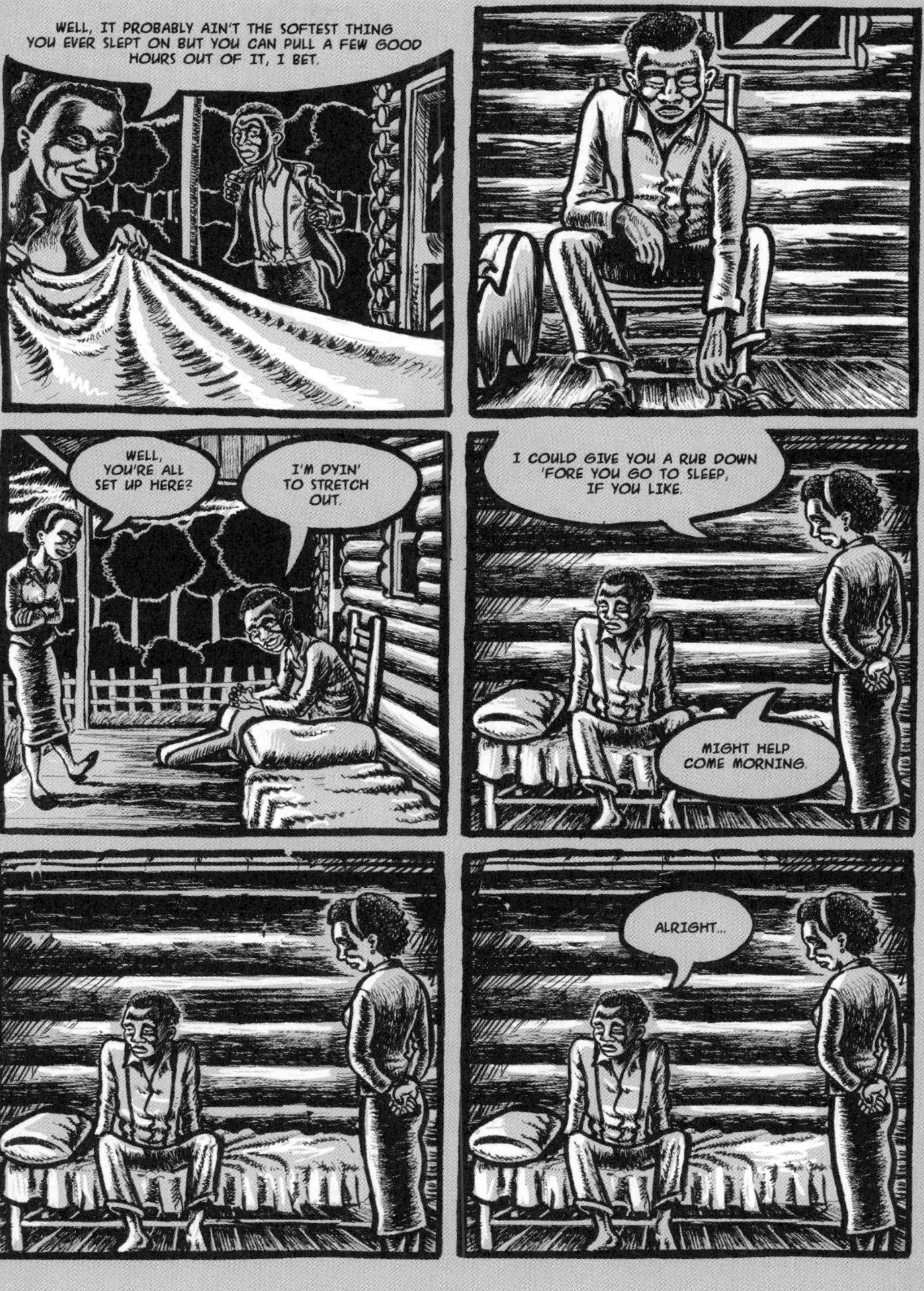
WELL, IT PROBABLY AIN'T THE SOFTEST THING YOU EVER SLEPT ON BUT YOU CAN PULL A FEW GOOD HOURS OUT OF IT, I BET.
WELL, YOU'RE ALL SET UP HERE?
I'M DYIN' TO STRETCH OUT.
I COULD GIVE YOU A RUB DOWN 'FORE YOU GO TO SLEEP, IF YOU LIKE.
MIGHT HELP COME MORNING.
ALRIGHT...

GIVE ME YOUR SHIRT AND LAY ON YOUR BELLY.
"UNNH"
YOU'RE TIGHT AS BAILIN' WIRE.
WHEN'S THE LAST TIME YOU SLEPT IN A BED?
"MMH" LAST NIGHT, BUT IT WASN'T NOTHIN' BUT BOXCARS AND BARNS FOR A MONTH OF SUNDAYS BEFORE THAT.
IT ADD UP IN A WAY THAT ONE NIGHT DON'T FIX.

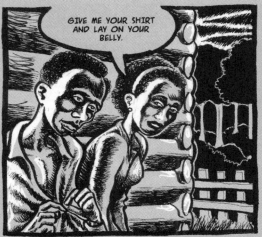

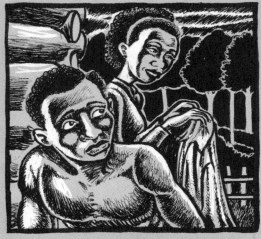

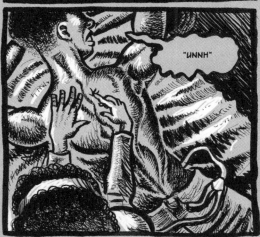

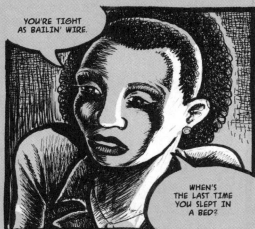

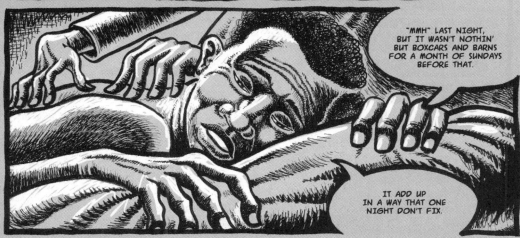

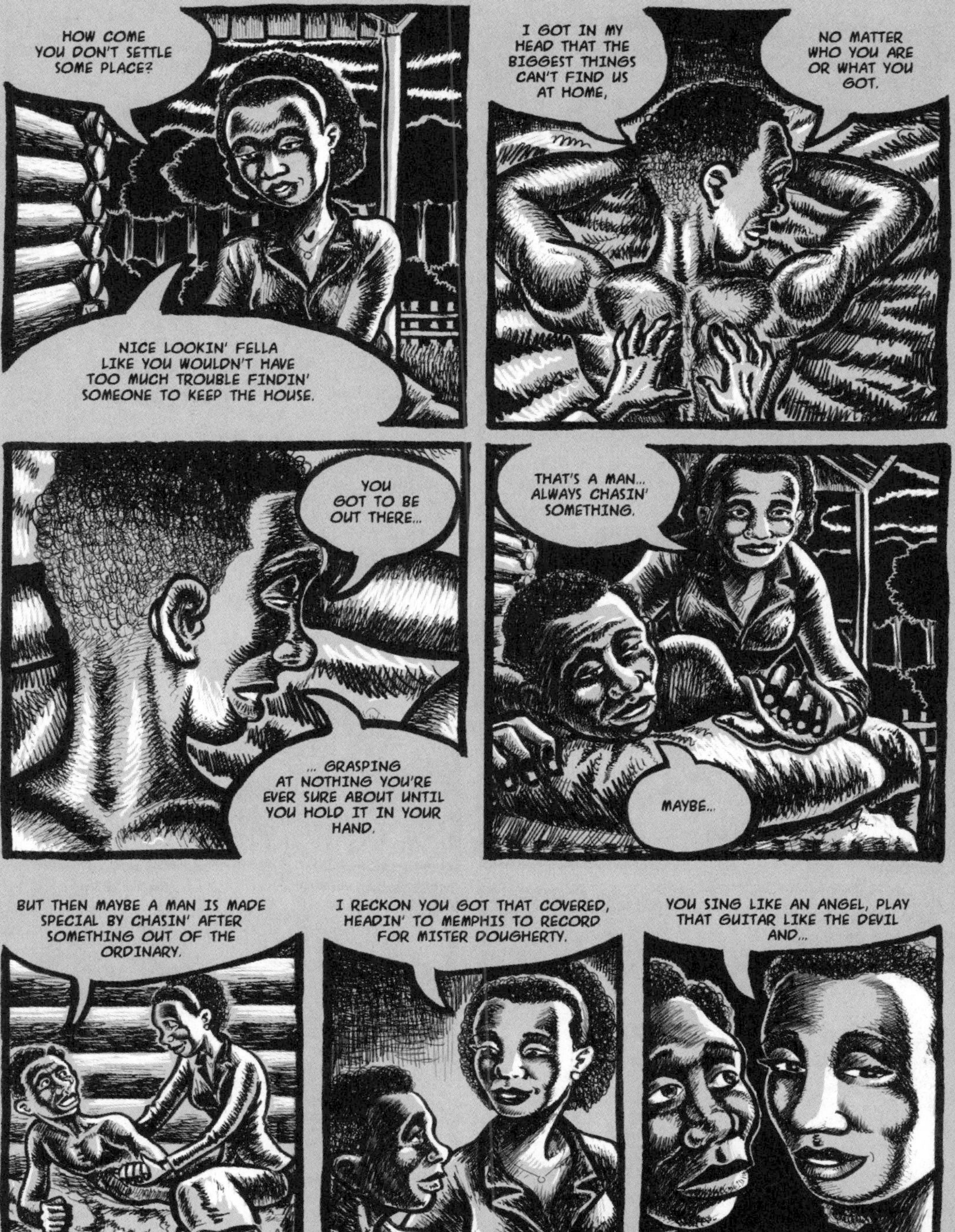
HOW COME YOU DON'T SETTLE SOME PLACE?
NICE LOOKIN' FELLA LIKE YOU WOULDN'T HAVE TOO MUCH TROUBLE FINDIN' SOMEONE TO KEEP THE HOUSE.
I GOT IN MY HEAD THAT THE BIGGEST THINGS CAN'T FIND US AT HOME,
NO MATTER WHO YOU ARE OR WHAT YOU GOT.
YOU GOT TO BE OUT THERE...
... GRASPING AT NOTHING YOU'RE EVER SURE ABOUT UNTIL YOU HOLD IT IN YOUR HAND.
THAT'S A MAN... ALWAYS CHASIN' SOMETHING.
MAYBE...
BUT THEN MAYBE A MAN IS MADE SPECIAL BY CHASIN' AFTER SOMETHING OUT OF THE ORDINARY.
I RECKON YOU GOT THAT COVERED, HEADIN' TO MEMPHIS TO RECORD FOR MISTER DOUGHERTY.
YOU SING LIKE AN ANGEL, PLAY THAT GUITAR LIKE THE DEVIL AND...

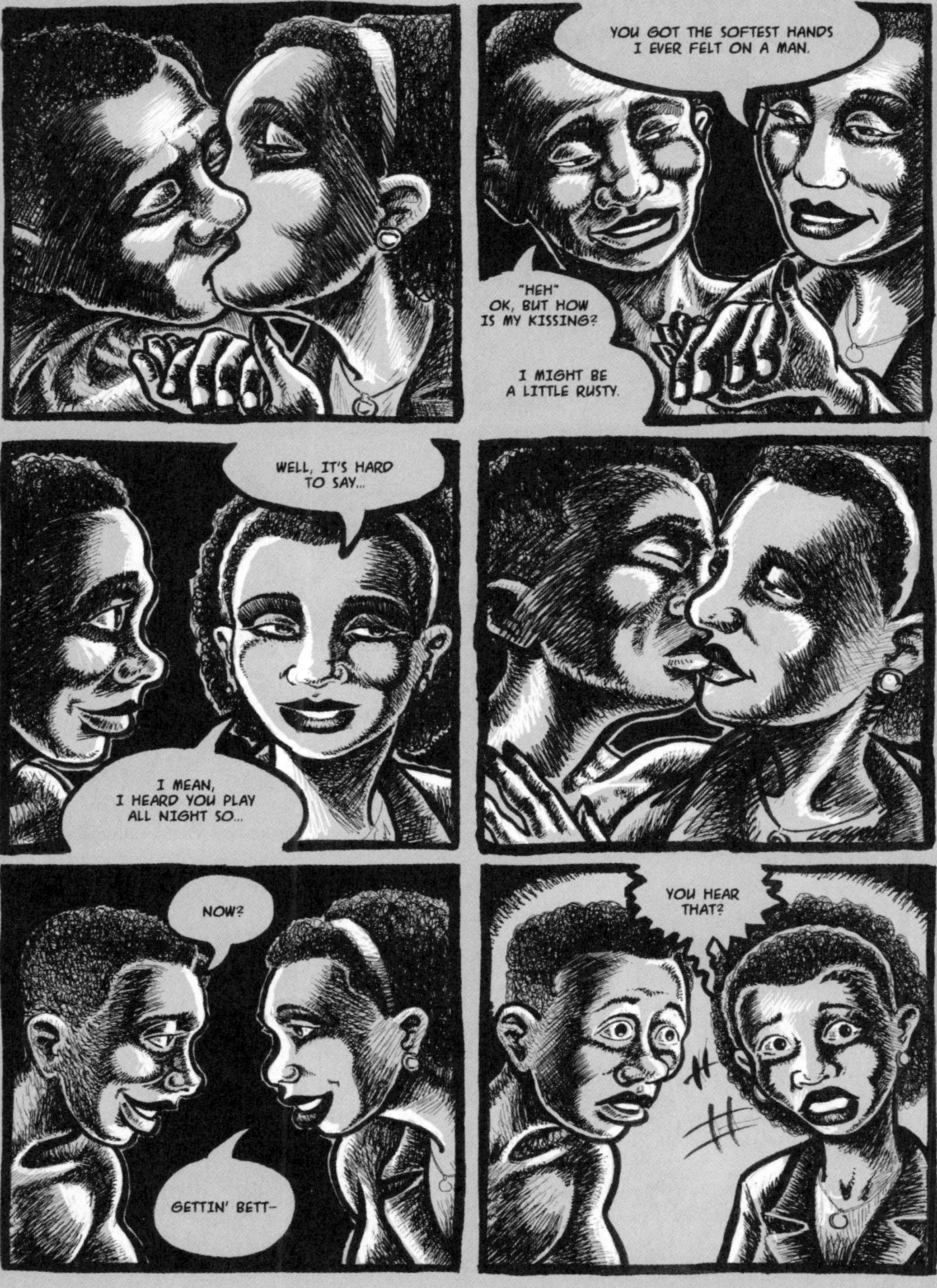
YOU GOT THE SOFTEST HANDS I EVER FELT ON A MAN.
"HEH" OK, BUT HOW IS MY KISSING?
I MIGHT BE A LITTLE RUSTY.
WELL, IT'S HARD TO SAY...
I MEAN, I HEARD YOU PLAY ALL NIGHT SO...
NOW?
GETTIN' BETT-
YOU HEAR THAT?

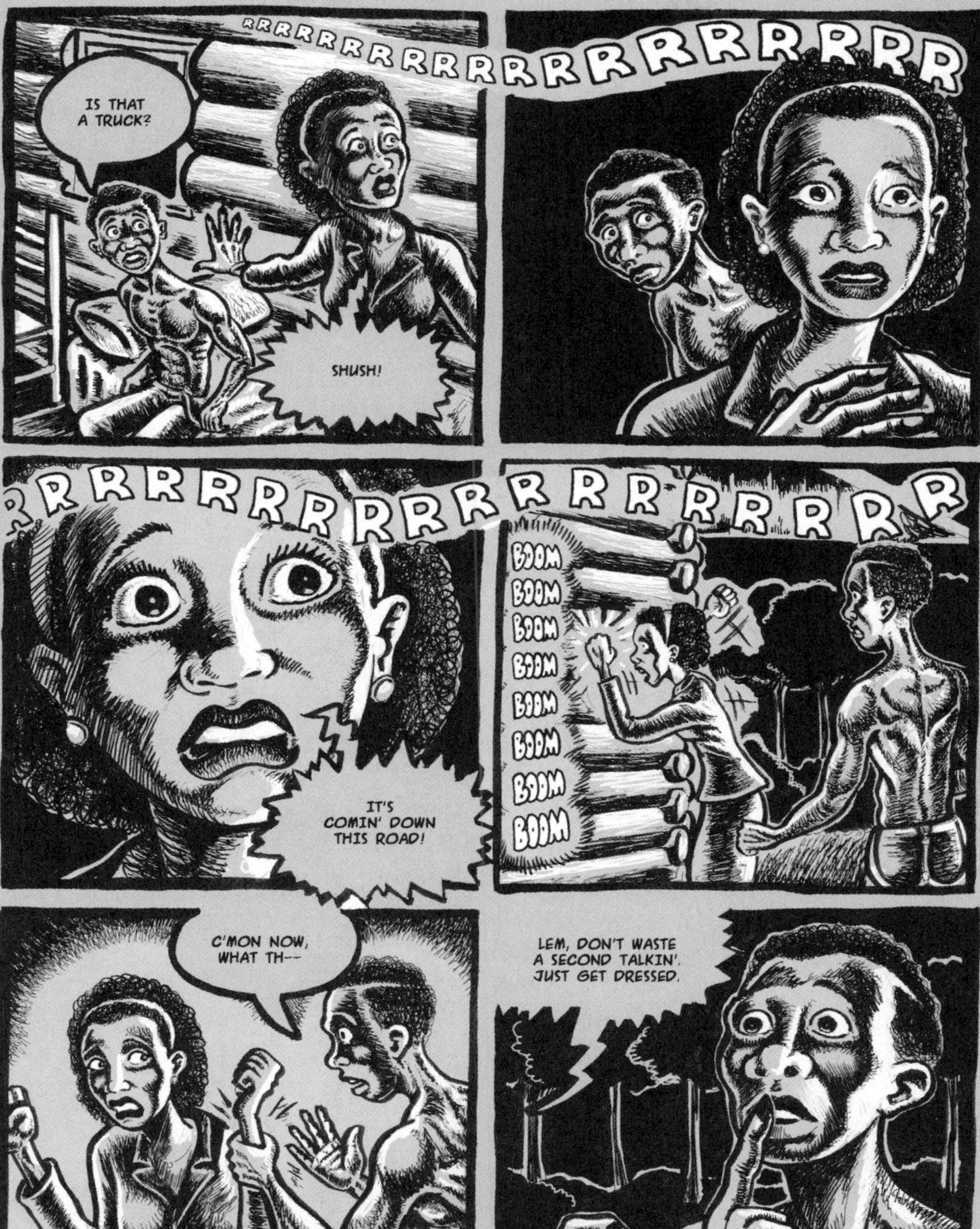
RRRRRRRRRRRRRRRRRR
IS THAT A TRUCK?
SHUSH!
RRRRRRRRRRRRRRRRRR
IT'S COMIN' DOWN THIS ROAD!
BOOM
BOOM
BOOM
BOOM
BOOM
BOOM
BOOM
BOOM
C'MON NOW, WHAT TH--
LEM, DON'T WASTE A SECOND TALKIN', JUST GET DRESSED.

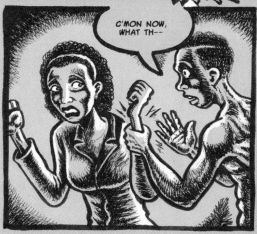

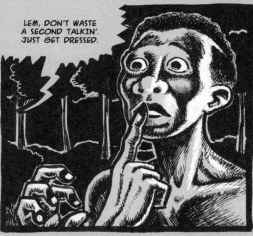

60

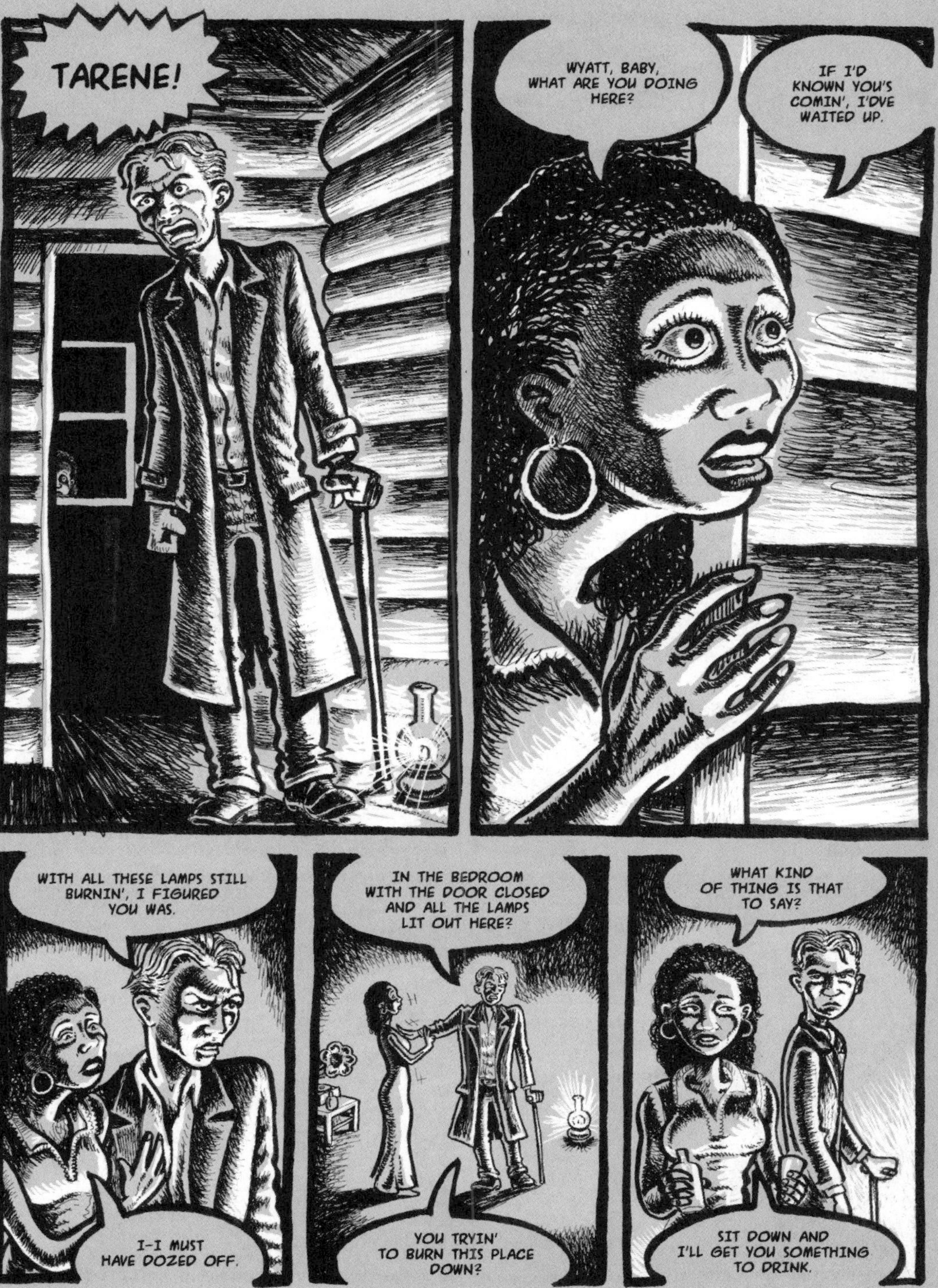
TARENE!
WYATT, BABY, WHAT ARE YOU DOING HERE?
IF I'D KNOWN YOU'S COMIN', I'DVE WAITED UP.
WITH ALL THESE LAMPS STILL BURNIN', I FIGURED YOU WAS.
I-I MUST HAVE DOZED OFF.
IN THE BEDROOM WITH THE DOOR CLOSED AND ALL THE LAMPS LIT OUT HERE?
YOU TRYIN' TO BURN THIS PLACE DOWN?
WHAT KIND OF THING IS THAT TO SAY?
SIT DOWN AND I'LL GET YOU SOMETHING TO DRINK.

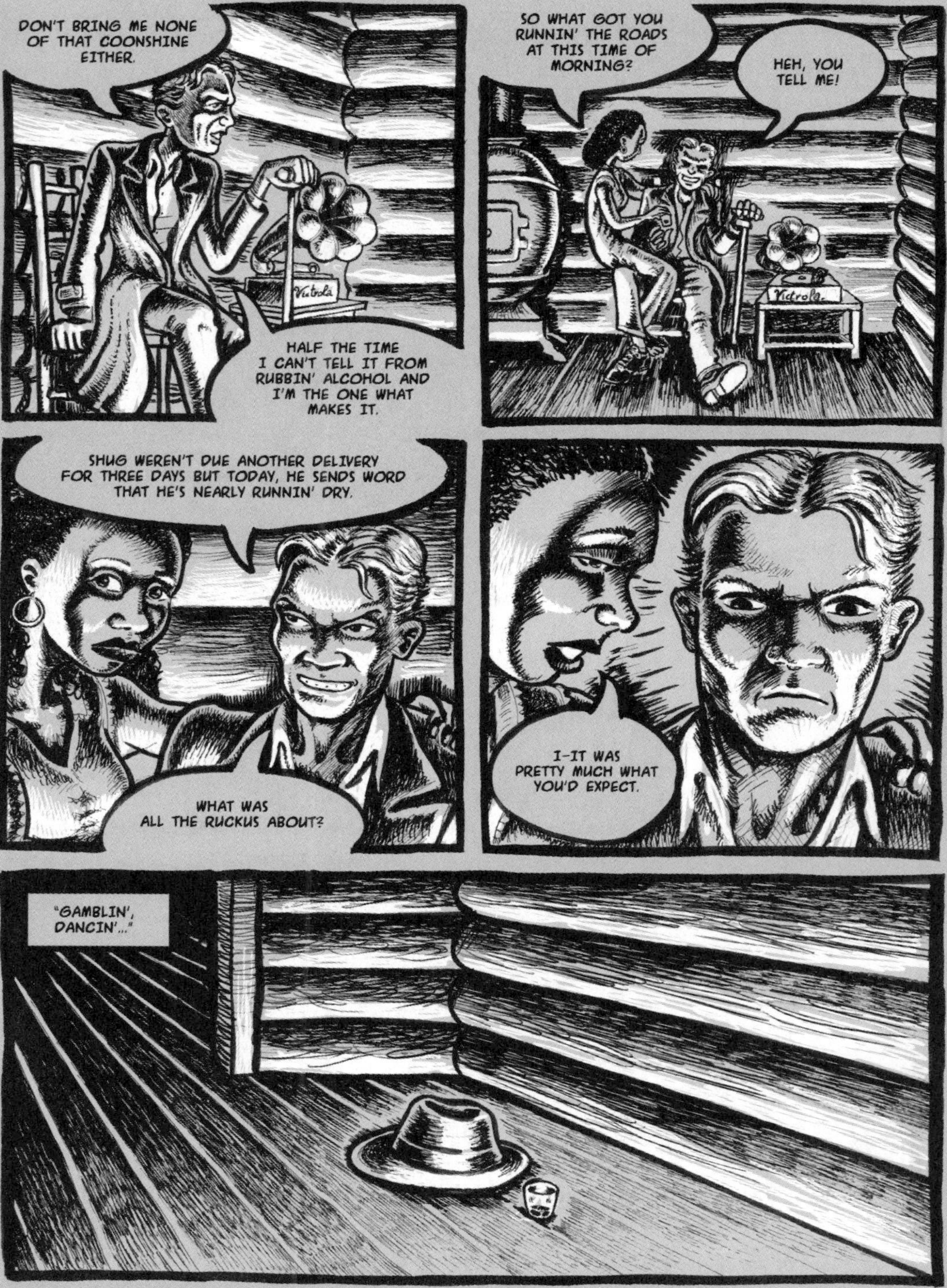
DON'T BRING ME NONE OF THAT COONSHINE EITHER.
HALF THE TIME I CAN'T TELL IT FROM RUBBIN' ALCOHOL AND I'M THE ONE WHAT MAKES IT.
Victrola
SO WHAT GOT YOU RUNNIN' THE ROADS AT THIS TIME OF MORNING?
HEH, YOU TELL ME!
Victrola
SHUG WEREN'T DUE ANOTHER DELIVERY FOR THREE DAYS BUT TODAY, HE SENDS WORD THAT HE'S NEARLY RUNNIN' DRY.
WHAT WAS ALL THE RUCKUS ABOUT?
I-IT WAS PRETTY MUCH WHAT YOU'D EXPECT.
"GAMBLIN', DANCIN'..."

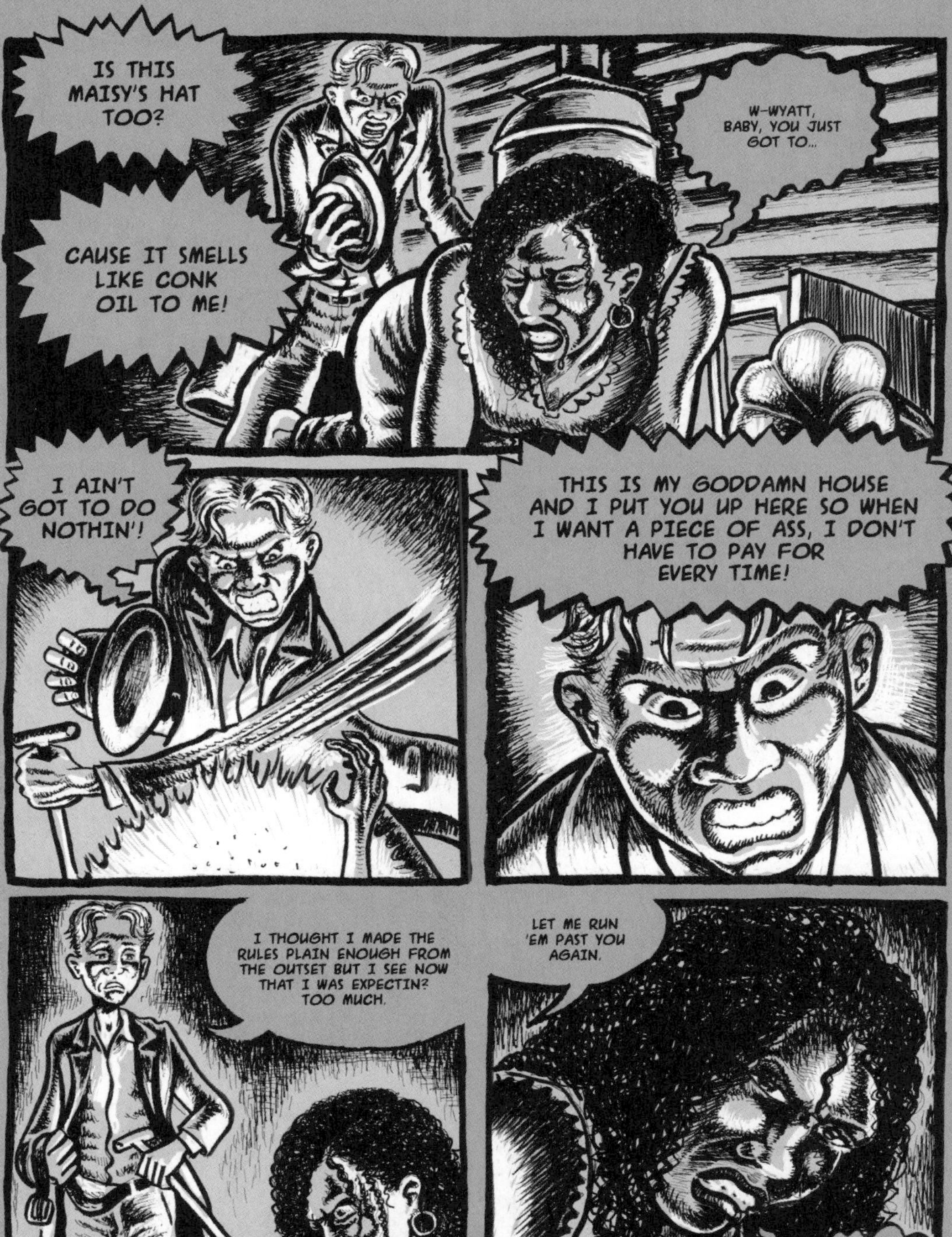

IS THIS MAISY'S HAT TOO?
CAUSE IT SMELLS LIKE CONK OIL TO ME!
W-WYATT, BABY, YOU JUST GOT TO...
I AIN'T GOT TO DO NOTHIN'!
THIS IS MY GODDAMN HOUSE AND I PUT YOU UP HERE SO WHEN I WANT A PIECE OF ASS, I DON'T HAVE TO PAY FOR EVERY TIME!
I THOUGHT I MADE THE RULES PLAIN ENOUGH FROM THE OUTSET BUT I SEE NOW THAT I WAS EXPECTIN' TOO MUCH.
LET ME RUN 'EM PAST YOU AGAIN.
WYATT... BABY...

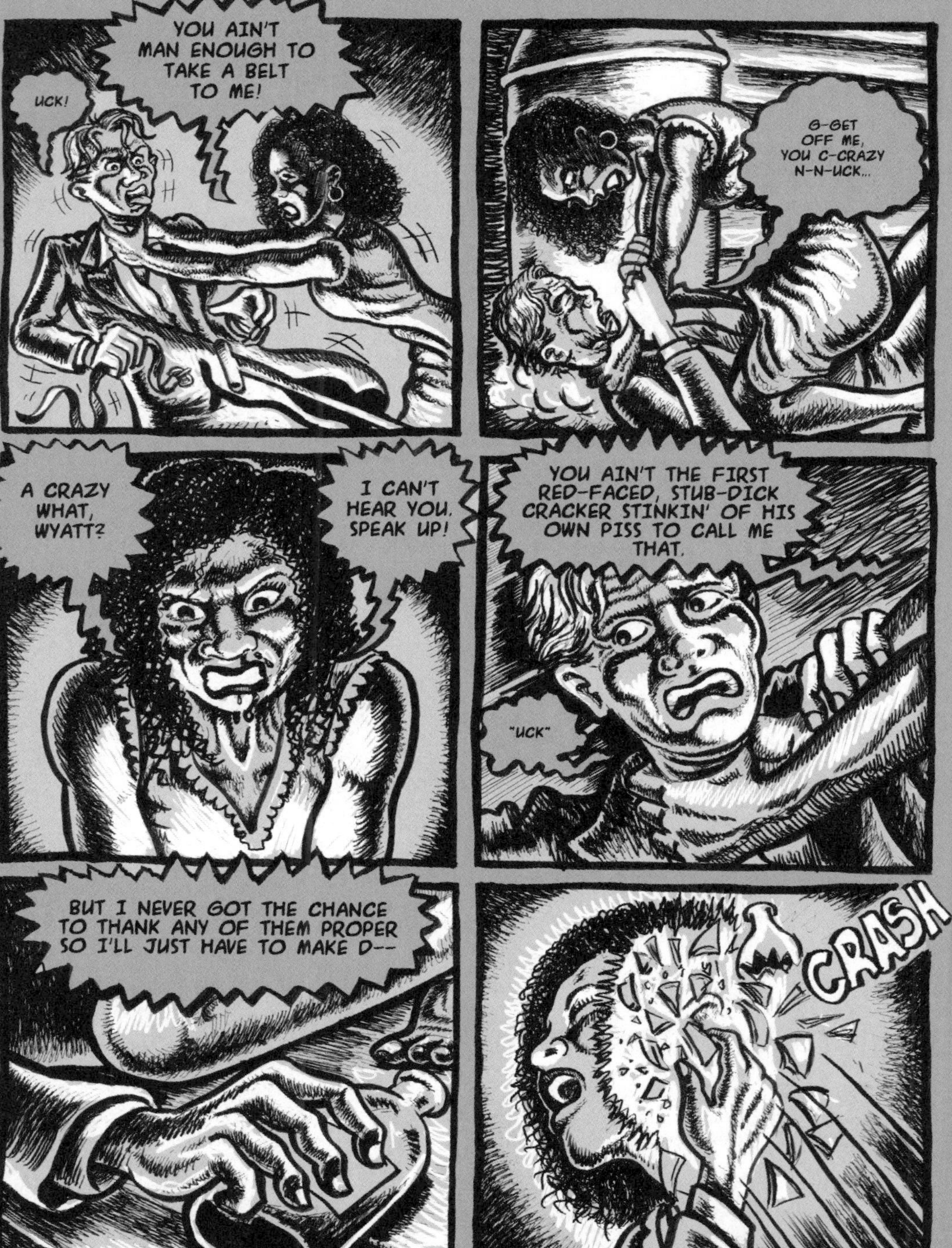

YOU AIN'T MAN ENOUGH TO TAKE A BELT TO ME!
UCK!
G-GET OFF ME, YOU C-CRAZY N-N-UCK...
A CRAZY WHAT, WYATT?
I CAN'T HEAR YOU. SPEAK UP!
YOU AIN'T THE FIRST RED-FACED, STUB-DICK CRACKER STINKIN' OF HIS OWN PISS TO CALL ME THAT.
"UCK"
BUT I NEVER GOT THE CHANCE TO THANK ANY OF THEM PROPER SO I'LL JUST HAVE TO MAKE D--
CRASH

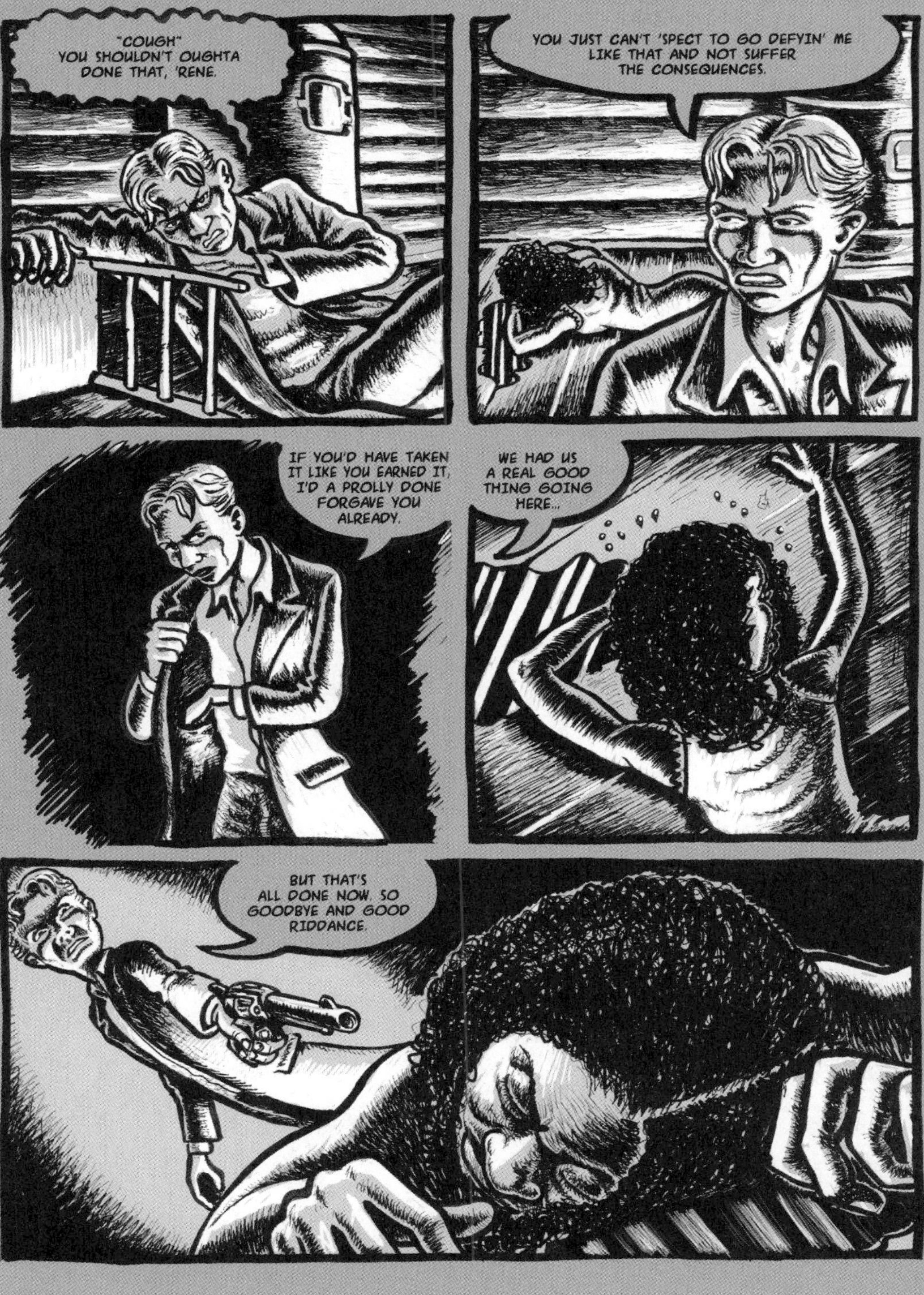
"COUGH"
YOU SHOULDN'T OUGHTA DONE THAT, 'RENE.
YOU JUST CAN'T 'SPECT TO GO DEFYIN' ME LIKE THAT AND NOT SUFFER THE CONSEQUENCES.
IF YOU'D HAVE TAKEN IT LIKE YOU EARNED IT, I'D A PROLLY DONE FORGAVE YOU ALREADY.
WE HAD US A REAL GOOD THING GOING HERE...
BUT THAT'S ALL DONE NOW. SO GOODBYE AND GOOD RIDDANCE.

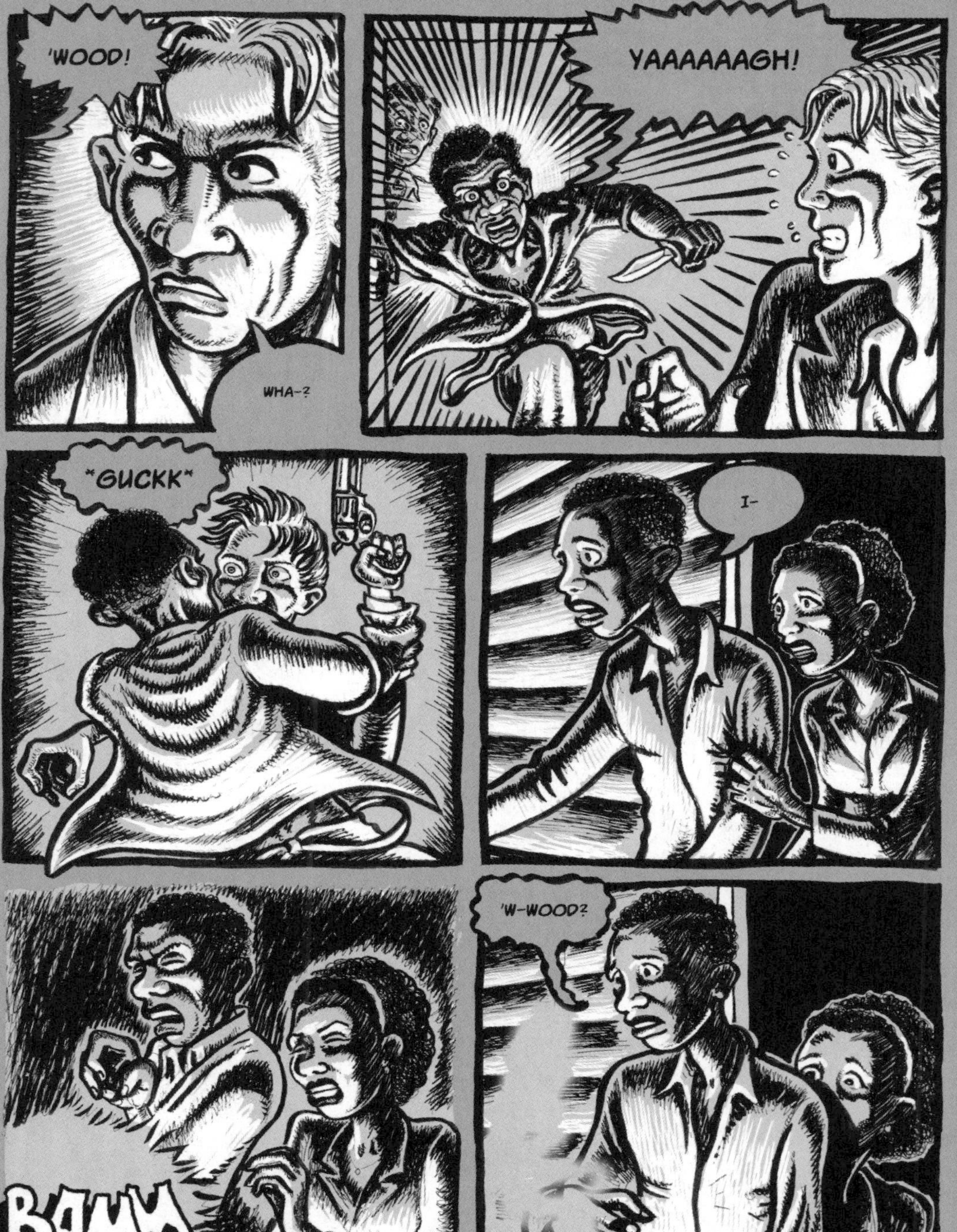

'WOOD!
WHA-?
YAAAAAAGH!
"GUCKK"
I-
BAMM
'W-WOOD?

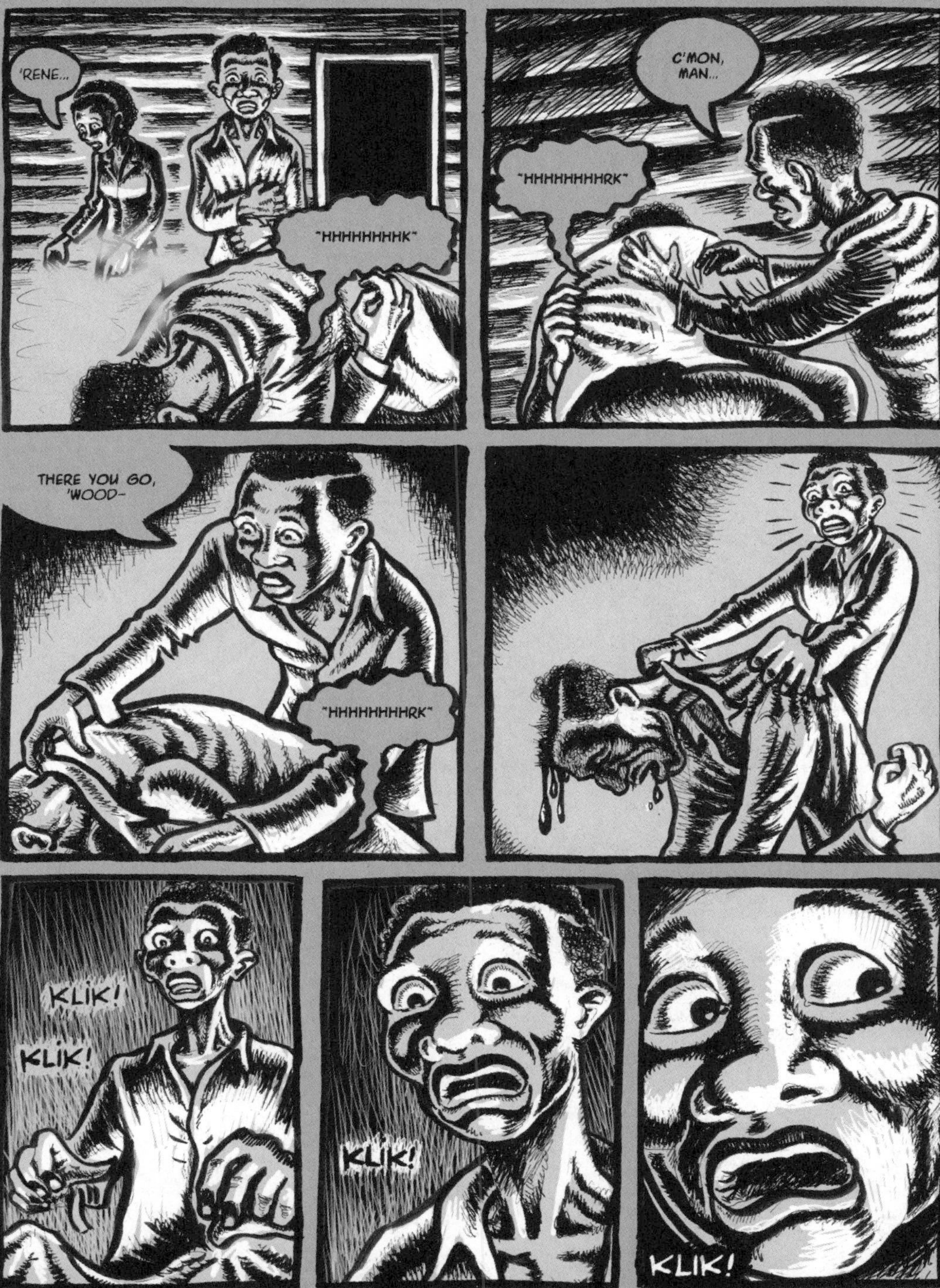
'RENE...
"HHHHHHHHK"
C'MON, MAN...
"HHHHHHHHRK"
THERE YOU GO, 'WOOD-
"HHHHHHHHRK"
KLIK!
KLIK!
KLIK!
KLIK!

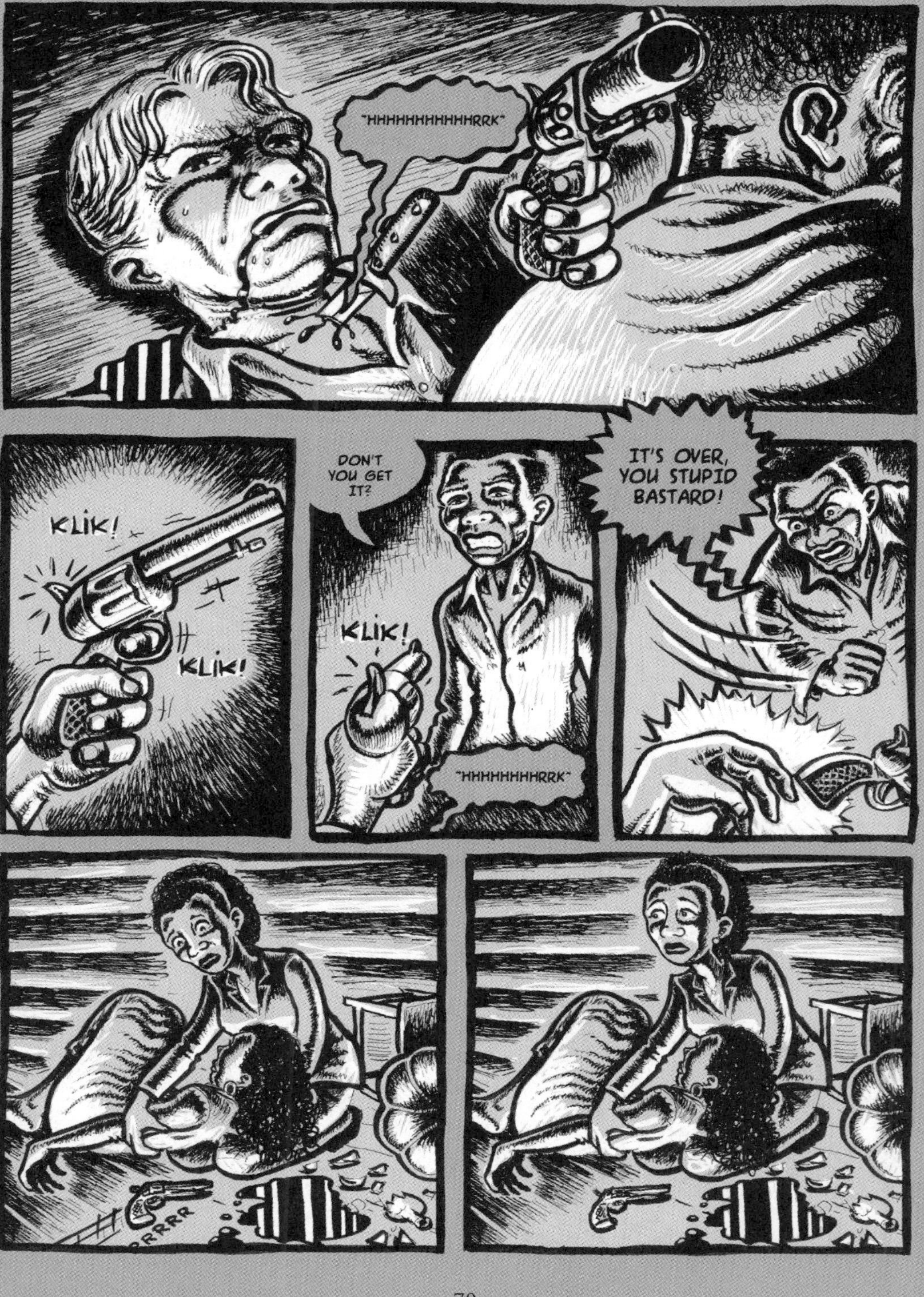
"HHHHHHHHHHHHRRK"
KLIK!
KLIK!
DON'T YOU GET IT?
KLIK!
"HHHHHHHHRRK"
IT'S OVER, YOU STUPID BASTARD!
RRRR

71

5

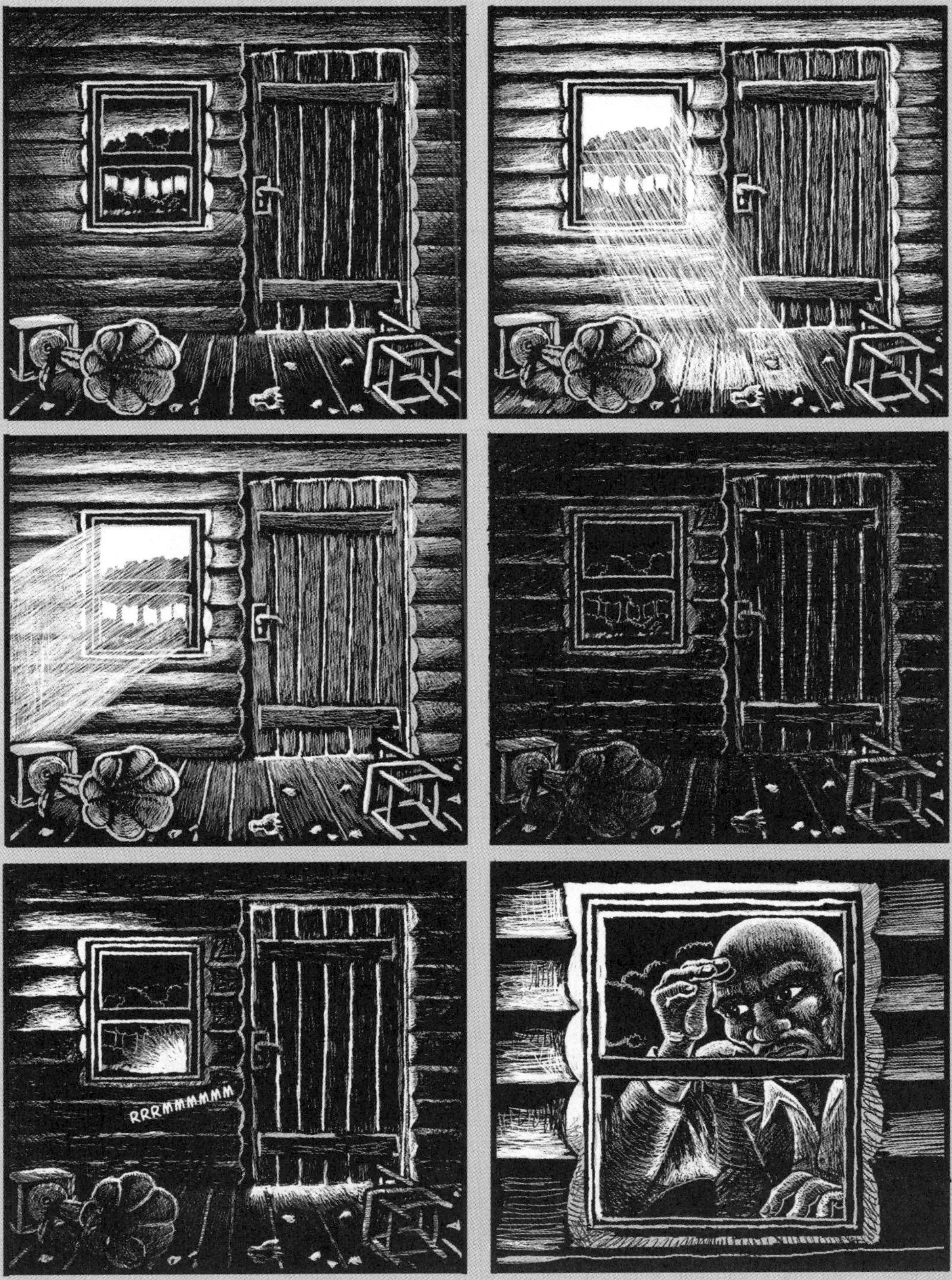
RRRMMMMMMM

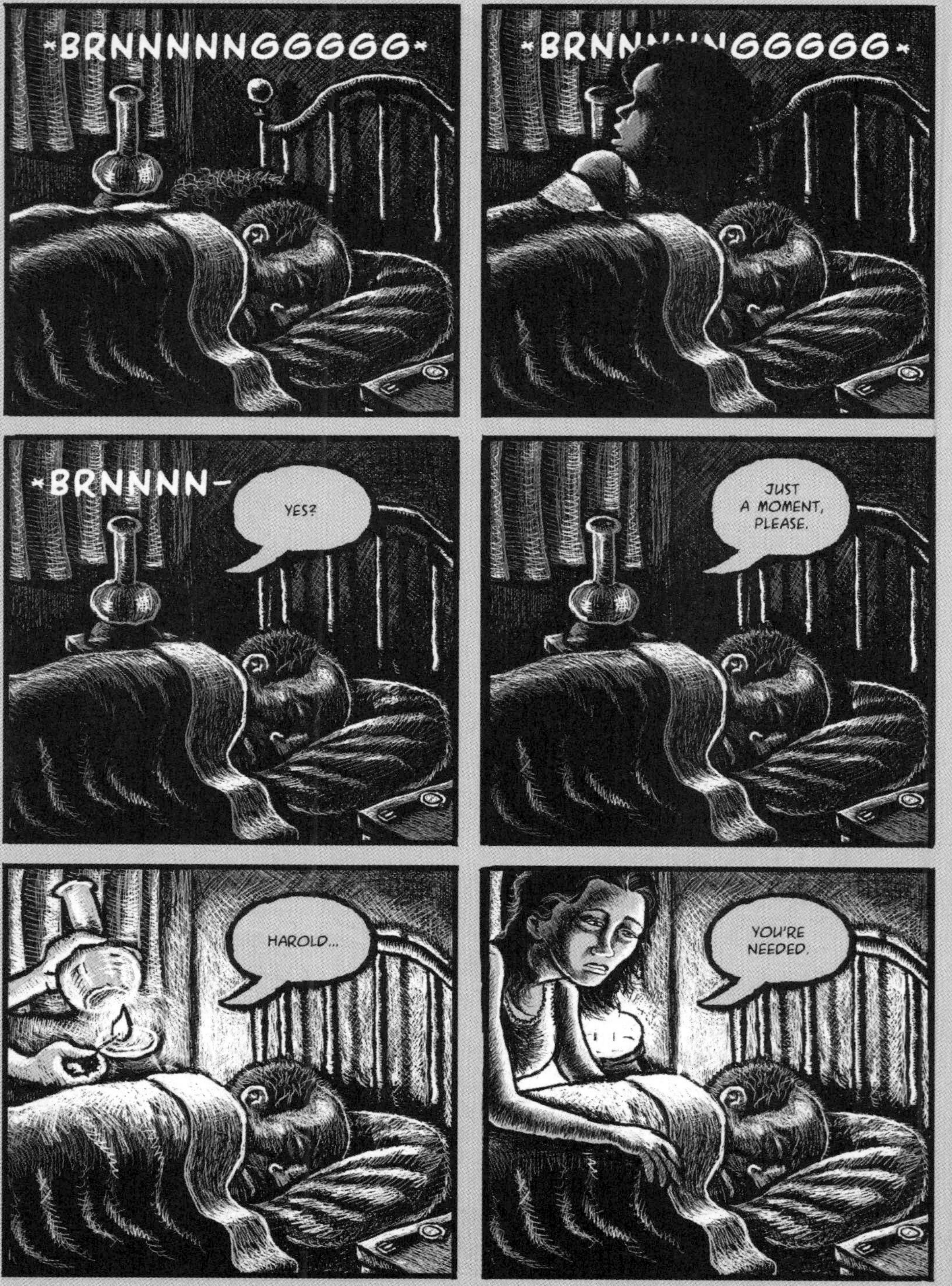
BRNNNNNGGGGG
BRNNNNNGGGGG
*BRNNNN-
YES?
JUST A MOMENT, PLEASE.
HAROLD...
YOU'RE NEEDED.

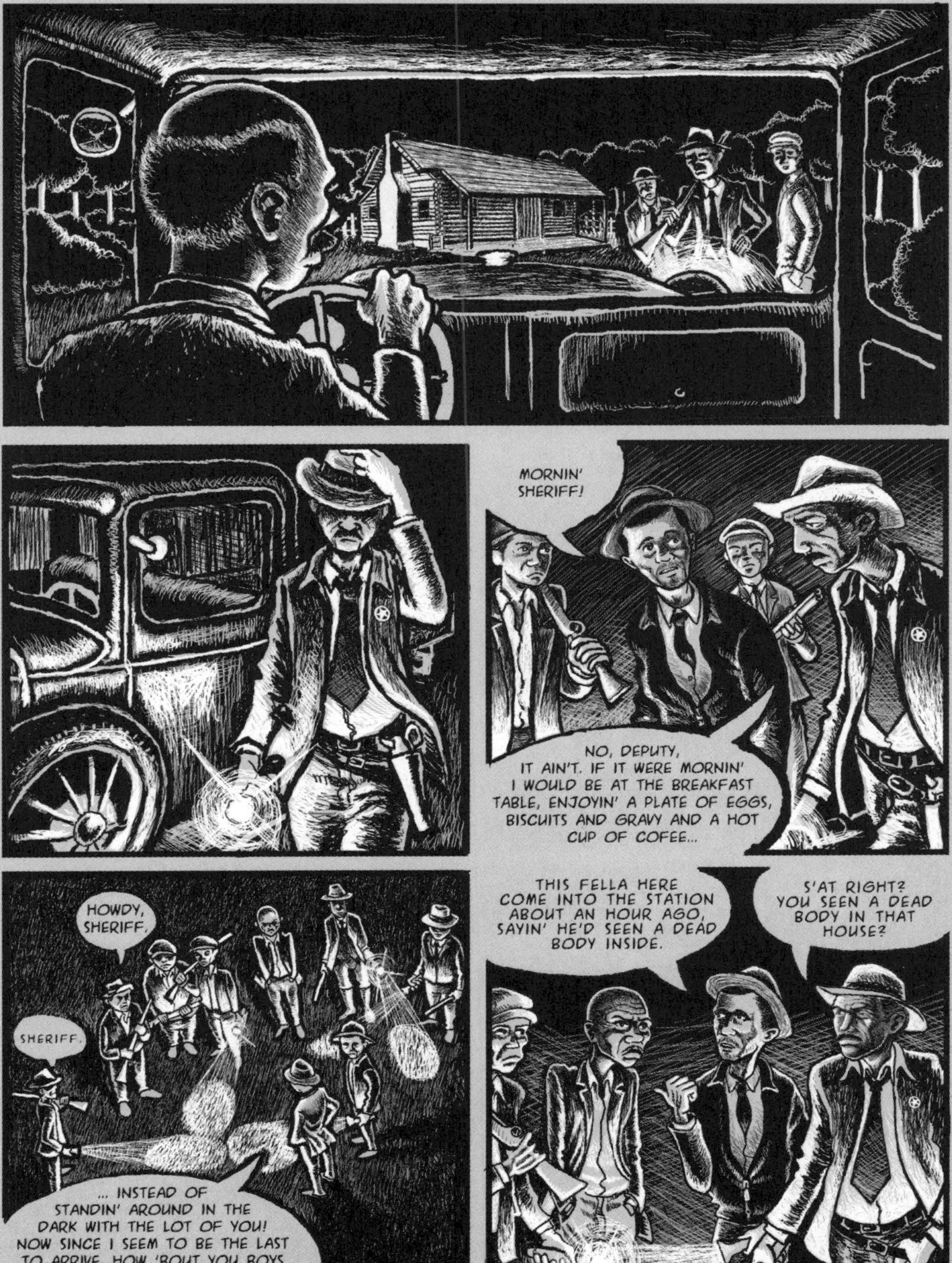
MORNIN' SHERIFF!
NO, DEPUTY, IT AIN'T. IF IT WERE MORNIN' I WOULD BE AT THE BREAKFAST TABLE, ENJOYIN' A PLATE OF EGGS, BISCUITS AND GRAVY AND A HOT CUP OF COFEE...
HOWDY, SHERIFF.
SHERIFF.
... INSTEAD OF STANDIN' AROUND IN THE DARK WITH THE LOT OF YOU! NOW SINCE I SEEM TO BE THE LAST TO ARRIVE, HOW 'BOUT YOU BOYS FILL ME IN?
THIS FELLA HERE COME INTO THE STATION ABOUT AN HOUR AGO, SAYIN' HE'D SEEN A DEAD BODY INSIDE.
S'AT RIGHT? YOU SEEN A DEAD BODY IN THAT HOUSE?

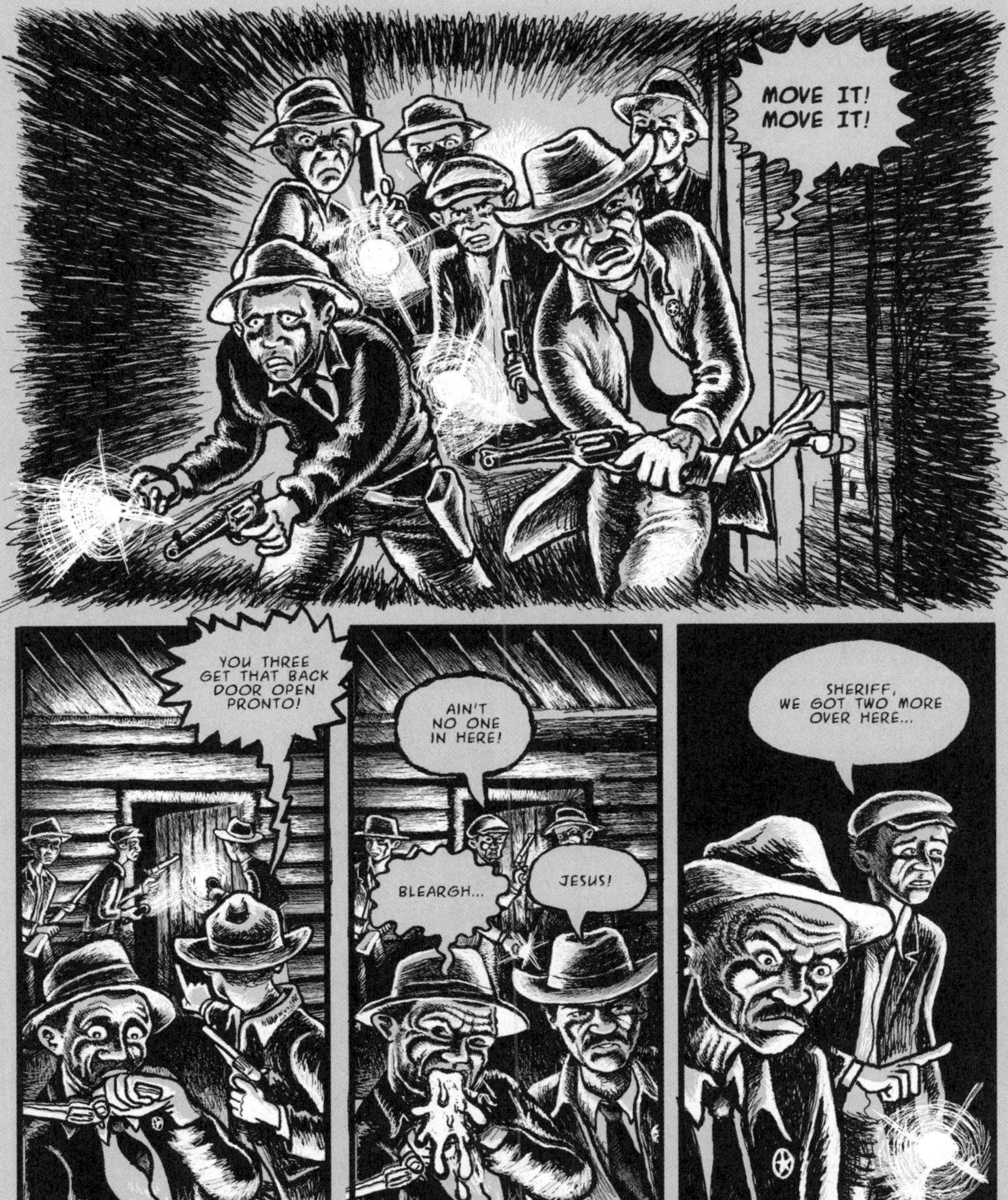
MOVE IT! MOVE IT!
YOU THREE GET THAT BACK DOOR OPEN PRONTO!
AIN'T NO ONE IN HERE!
BLEARGH...
JESUS!
SHERIFF, WE GOT TWO MORE OVER HERE...

80

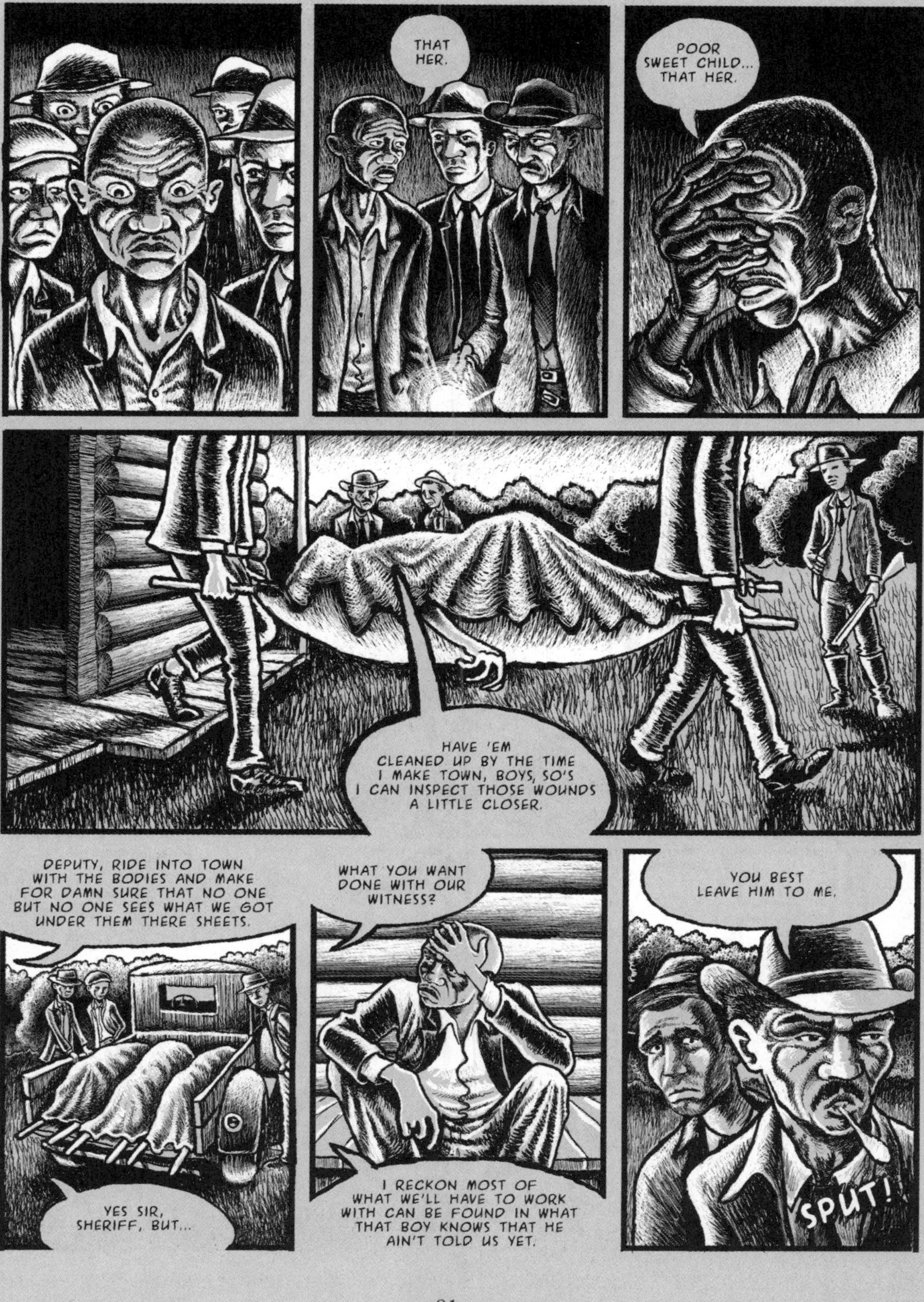
THAT HER.
POOR SWEET CHILD... THAT HER.
HAVE 'EM CLEANED UP BY THE TIME I MAKE TOWN, BOYS, SO'S I CAN INSPECT THOSE WOUNDS A LITTLE CLOSER.
DEPUTY, RIDE INTO TOWN WITH THE BODIES AND MAKE FOR DAMN SURE THAT NO ONE BUT NO ONE SEES WHAT WE GOT UNDER THEM THERE SHEETS.
YES SIR, SHERIFF, BUT...
WHAT YOU WANT DONE WITH OUR WITNESS?
I RECKON MOST OF WHAT WE'LL HAVE TO WORK WITH CAN BE FOUND IN WHAT THAT BOY KNOWS THAT HE AIN'T TOLD US YET.
YOU BEST LEAVE HIM TO ME.
SPUT!

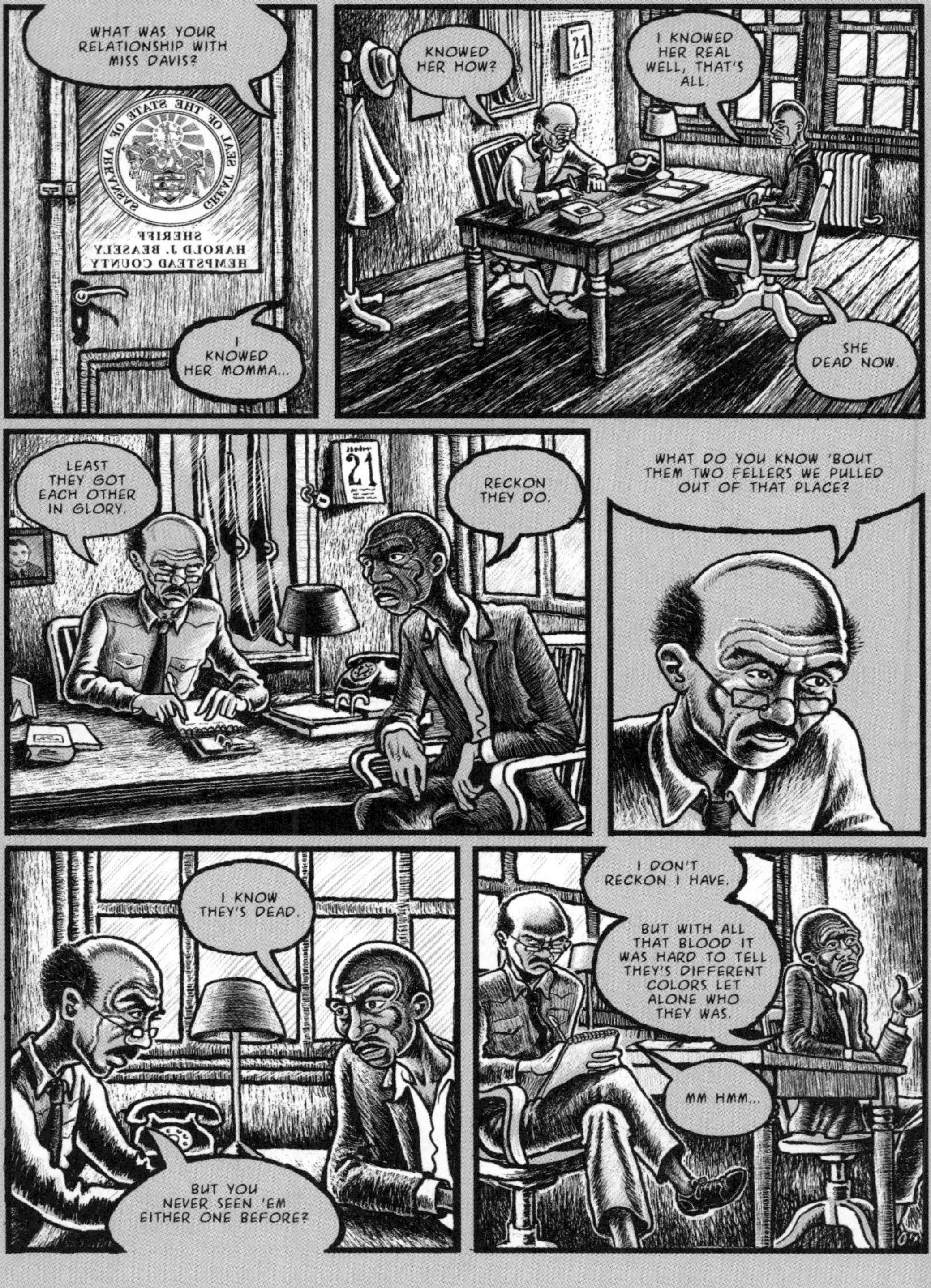
WHAT WAS YOUR RELATIONSHIP WITH MISS DAVIS?
SHERIFF
HAROLD J. BEASELY
HEMPSTEAD COUNTY
I KNOWED HER MOMMA...
KNOWED HER HOW?
I KNOWED HER REAL WELL, THAT'S ALL.
SHE DEAD NOW.
LEAST THEY GOT EACH OTHER IN GLORY.
RECKON THEY DO.
WHAT DO YOU KNOW 'BOUT THEM TWO FELLERS WE PULLED OUT OF THAT PLACE?
I KNOW THEY'S DEAD.
BUT YOU NEVER SEEN 'EM EITHER ONE BEFORE?
I DON'T RECKON I HAVE.
BUT WITH ALL THAT BLOOD IT WAS HARD TO TELL THEY'S DIFFERENT COLORS LET ALONE WHO THEY WAS.
MM HMM...

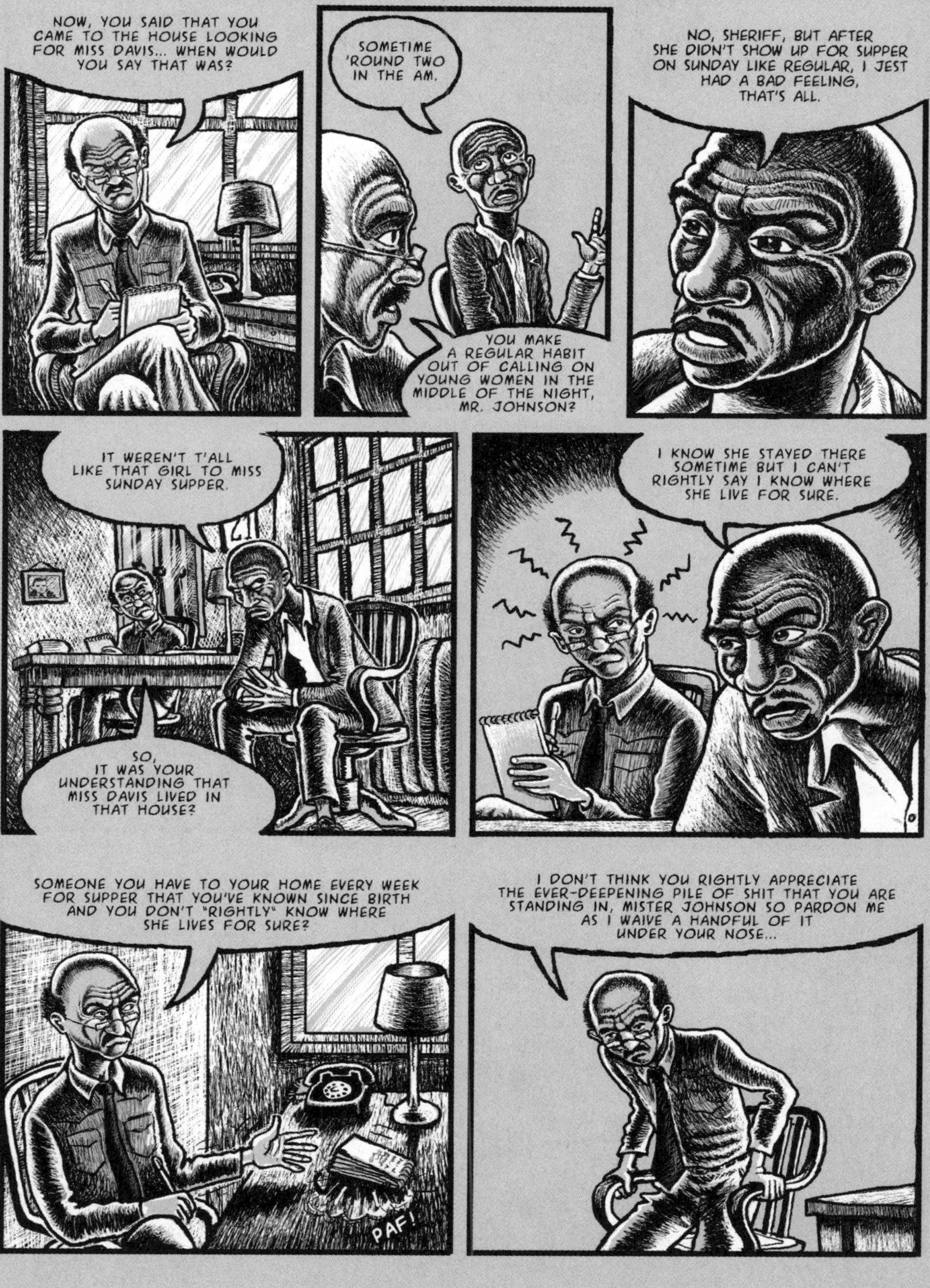
NOW, YOU SAID THAT YOU CAME TO THE HOUSE LOOKING FOR MISS DAVIS... WHEN WOULD YOU SAY THAT WAS?
SOMETIME 'ROUND TWO IN THE AM.
YOU MAKE A REGULAR HABIT OUT OF CALLING ON YOUNG WOMEN IN THE MIDDLE OF THE NIGHT, MR. JOHNSON?
NO, SHERIFF, BUT AFTER SHE DIDN'T SHOW UP FOR SUPPER ON SUNDAY LIKE REGULAR, I JEST HAD A BAD FEELING, THAT'S ALL.
IT WEREN'T T'ALL LIKE THAT GIRL TO MISS SUNDAY SUPPER.
SO, IT WAS YOUR UNDERSTANDING THAT MISS DAVIS LIVED IN THAT HOUSE?
I KNOW SHE STAYED THERE SOMETIME BUT I CAN'T RIGHTLY SAY I KNOW WHERE SHE LIVE FOR SURE.
SOMEONE YOU HAVE TO YOUR HOME EVERY WEEK FOR SUPPER THAT YOU'VE KNOWN SINCE BIRTH AND YOU DON'T "RIGHTLY" KNOW WHERE SHE LIVES FOR SURE?
PAF!
I DON'T THINK YOU RIGHTLY APPRECIATE THE EVER-DEEPENING PILE OF SHIT THAT YOU ARE STANDING IN, MISTER JOHNSON SO PARDON ME AS I WAIVE A HANDFUL OF IT UNDER YOUR NOSE...

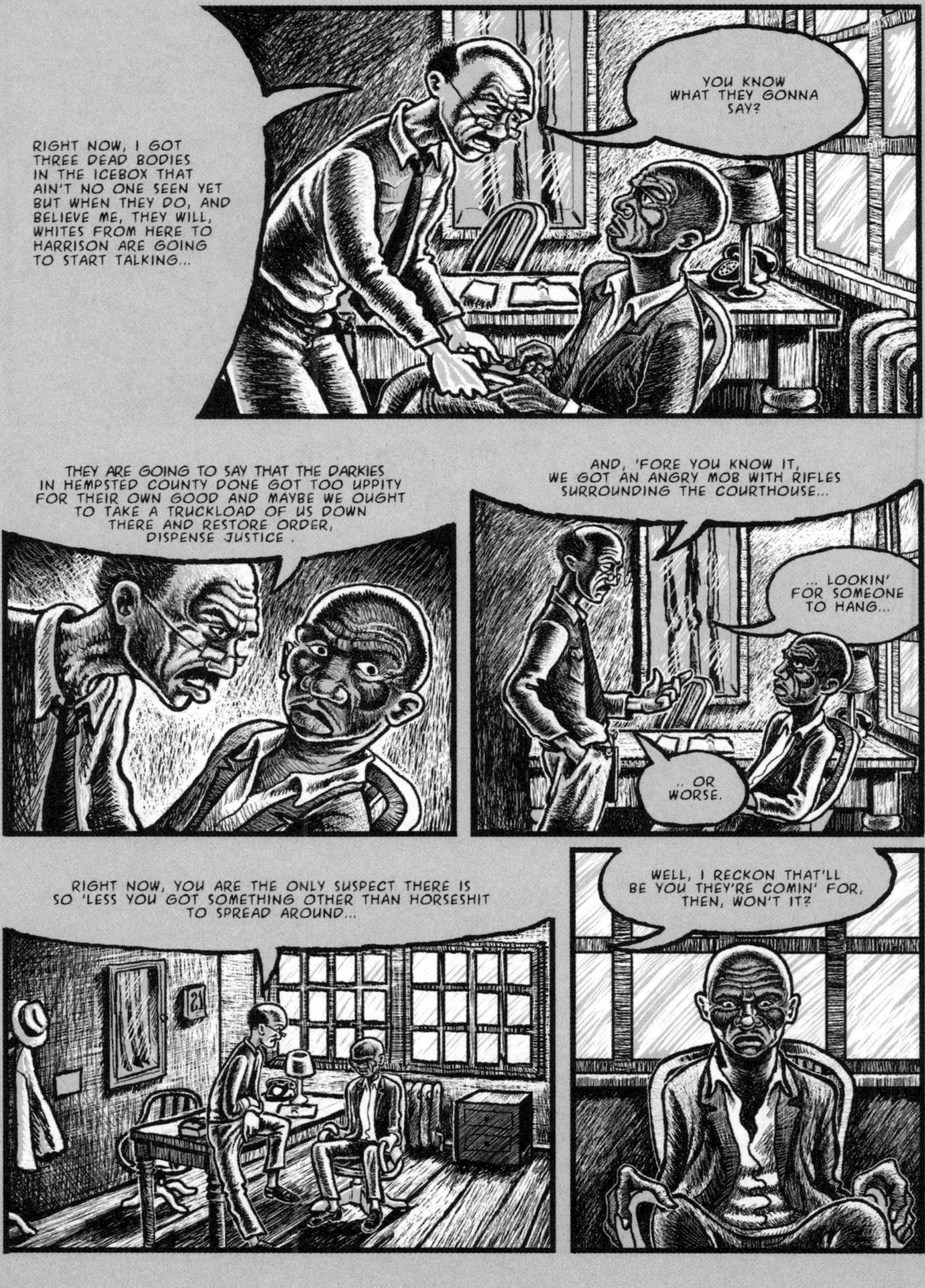
RIGHT NOW, I GOT THREE DEAD BODIES IN THE ICEBOX THAT AIN'T NO ONE SEEN YET BUT WHEN THEY DO, AND BELIEVE ME, THEY WILL, WHITES FROM HERE TO HARRISON ARE GOING TO START TALKING...
YOU KNOW WHAT THEY GONNA SAY?
THEY ARE GOING TO SAY THAT THE DARKIES IN HEMPSTED COUNTY DONE GOT TOO UPPITY FOR THEIR OWN GOOD AND MAYBE WE OUGHT TO TAKE A TRUCKLOAD OF US DOWN THERE AND RESTORE ORDER, DISPENSE JUSTICE .
AND, 'FORE YOU KNOW IT, WE GOT AN ANGRY MOB WITH RIFLES SURROUNDING THE COURTHOUSE...
... LOOKIN' FOR SOMEONE TO HANG...
...OR WORSE.
RIGHT NOW, YOU ARE THE ONLY SUSPECT THERE IS SO 'LESS YOU GOT SOMETHING OTHER THAN HORSESHIT TO SPREAD AROUND...
WELL, I RECKON THAT'LL BE YOU THEY'RE COMIN' FOR, THEN, WON'T IT?

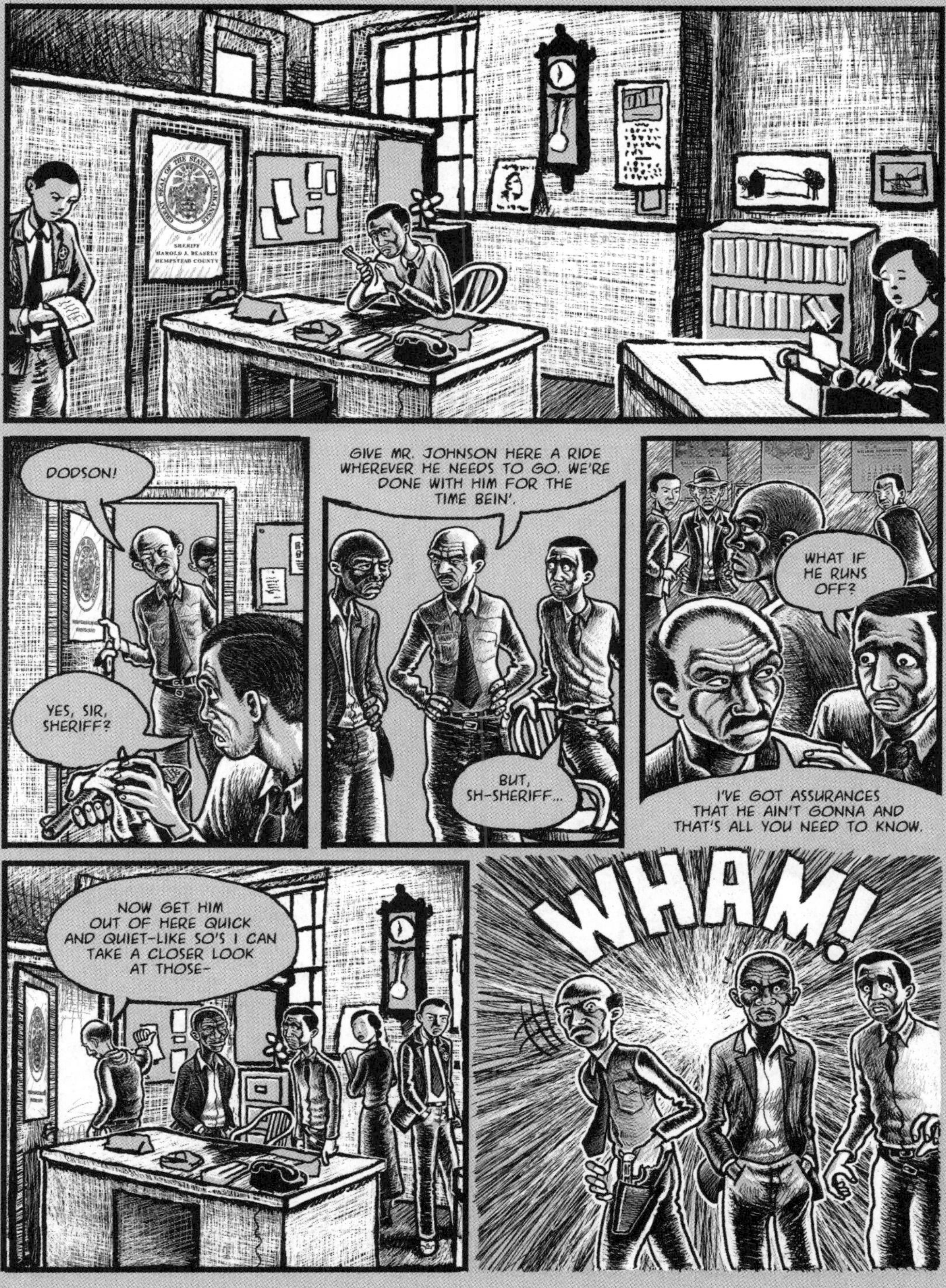
GREAT SEAL OF THE STATE OF ARKANSAS
SHERIFF
HAROLD J. BEASELY
HEMPSTEAD COUNTY
DODSON!
YES, SIR, SHERIFF?
GIVE MR. JOHNSON HERE A RIDE WHEREVER HE NEEDS TO GO. WE'RE DONE WITH HIM FOR THE TIME BEIN'.
BUT, SH-SHERIFF...
WHAT IF HE RUNS OFF?
I'VE GOT ASSURANCES THAT HE AIN'T GONNA AND THAT'S ALL YOU NEED TO KNOW.
NOW GET HIM OUT OF HERE QUICK AND QUIET-LIKE SO'S I CAN TAKE A CLOSER LOOK AT THOSE-
WHAM!

86

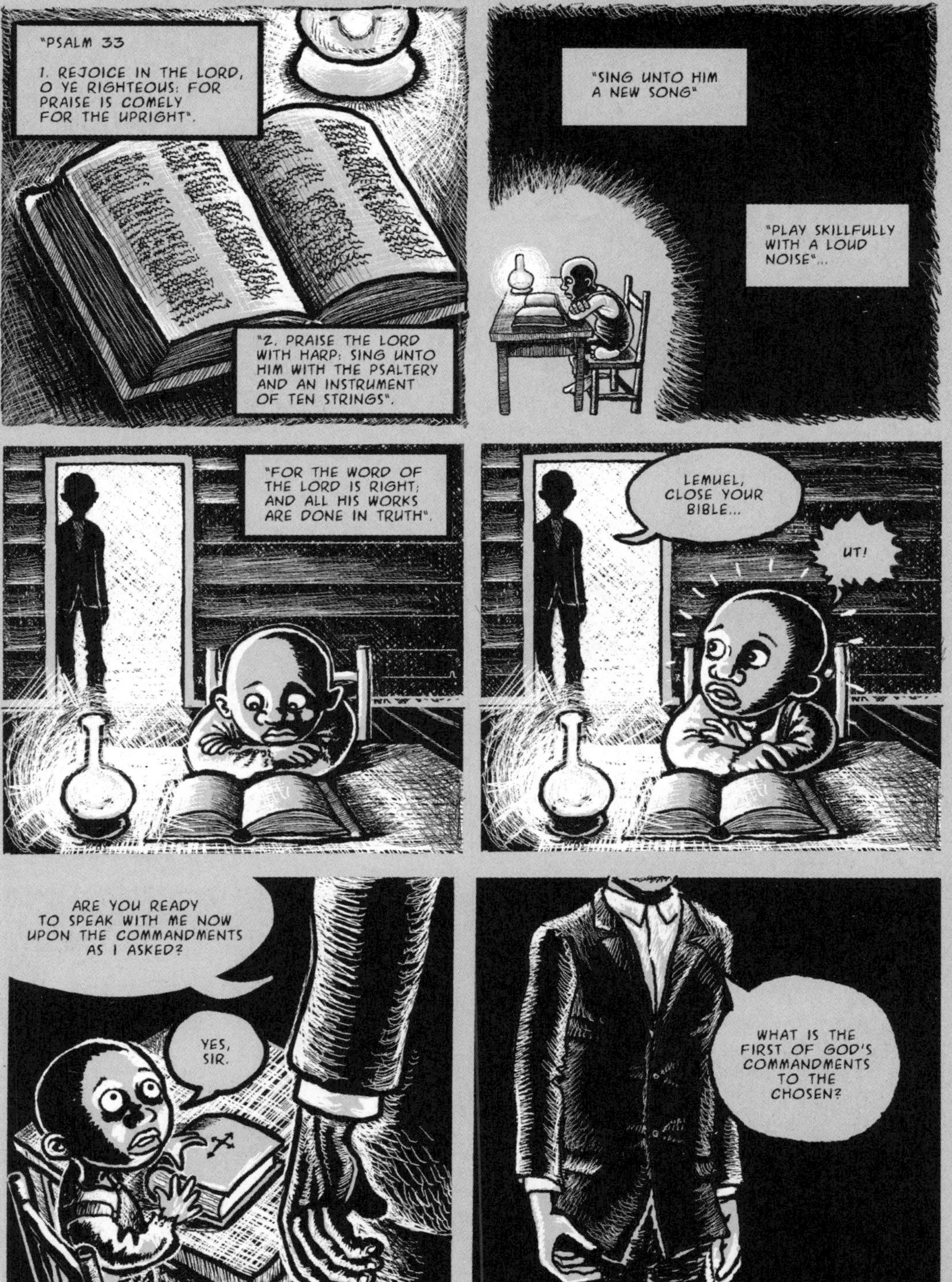
"PSALM 33
1. REJOICE IN THE LORD, O YE RIGHTEOUS: FOR PRAISE IS COMELY FOR THE UPRIGHT".
"2. PRAISE THE LORD WITH HARP: SING UNTO HIM WITH THE PSALTERY AND AN INSTRUMENT OF TEN STRINGS".
"SING UNTO HIM A NEW SONG"
"PLAY SKILLFULLY WITH A LOUD NOISE"...
"FOR THE WORD OF THE LORD IS RIGHT; AND ALL HIS WORKS ARE DONE IN TRUTH".
LEMUEL, CLOSE YOUR BIBLE...
UT!
ARE YOU READY TO SPEAK WITH ME NOW UPON THE COMMANDMENTS AS I ASKED?
YES, SIR.
WHAT IS THE FIRST OF GOD'S COMMANDMENTS TO THE CHOSEN?

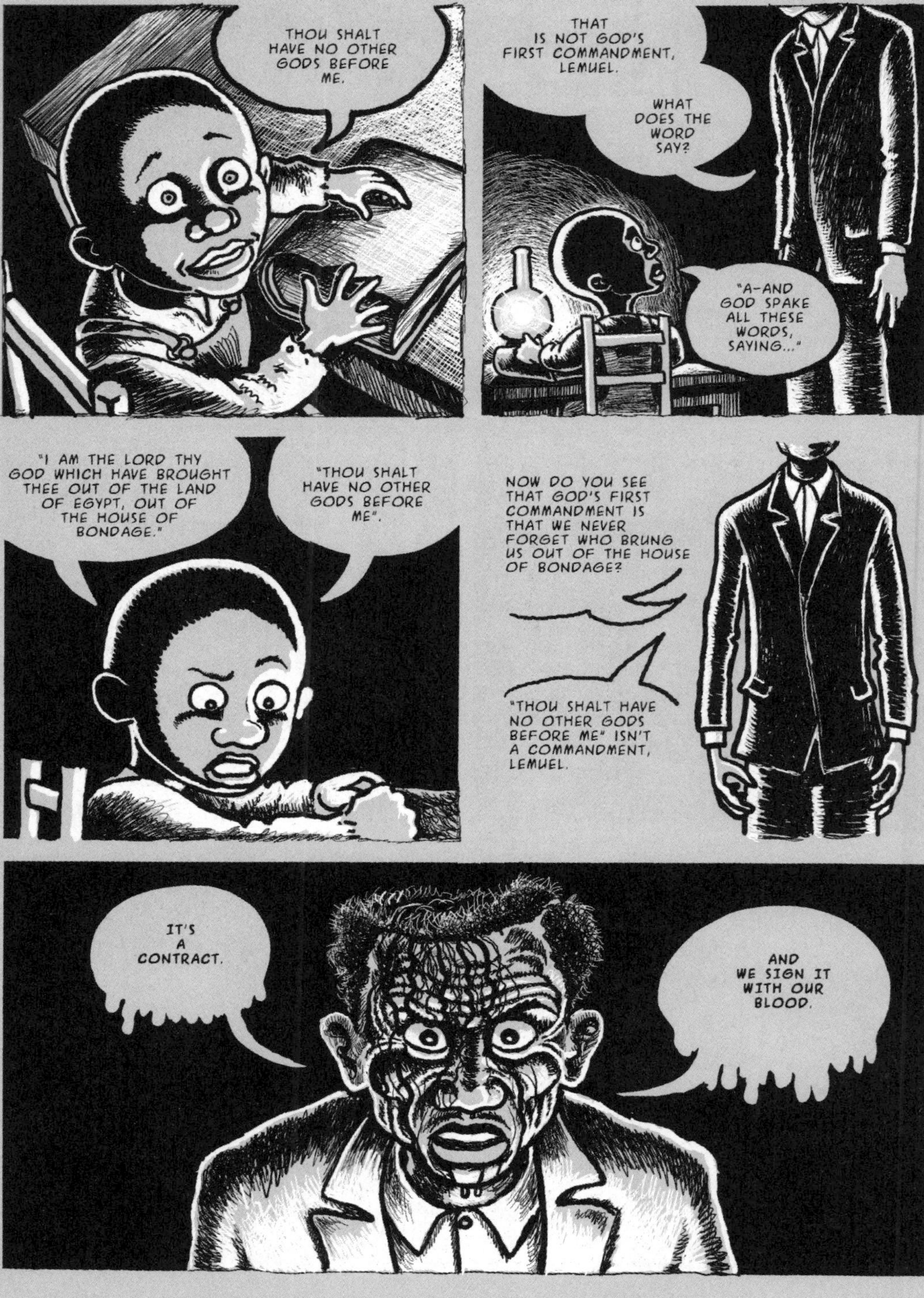
THOU SHALT HAVE NO OTHER GODS BEFORE ME.
THAT IS NOT GOD'S FIRST COMMANDMENT, LEMUEL.
WHAT DOES THE WORD SAY?
"A-AND GOD SPAKE ALL THESE WORDS, SAYING..."
"I AM THE LORD THY GOD WHICH HAVE BROUGHT THEE OUT OF THE LAND OF EGYPT, OUT OF THE HOUSE OF BONDAGE."
"THOU SHALT HAVE NO OTHER GODS BEFORE ME".
NOW DO YOU SEE THAT GOD'S FIRST COMMANDMENT IS THAT WE NEVER FORGET WHO BRUNG US OUT OF THE HOUSE OF BONDAGE?
"THOU SHALT HAVE NO OTHER GODS BEFORE ME" ISN'T A COMMANDMENT, LEMUEL.
IT'S A CONTRACT.
AND WE SIGN IT WITH OUR BLOOD.

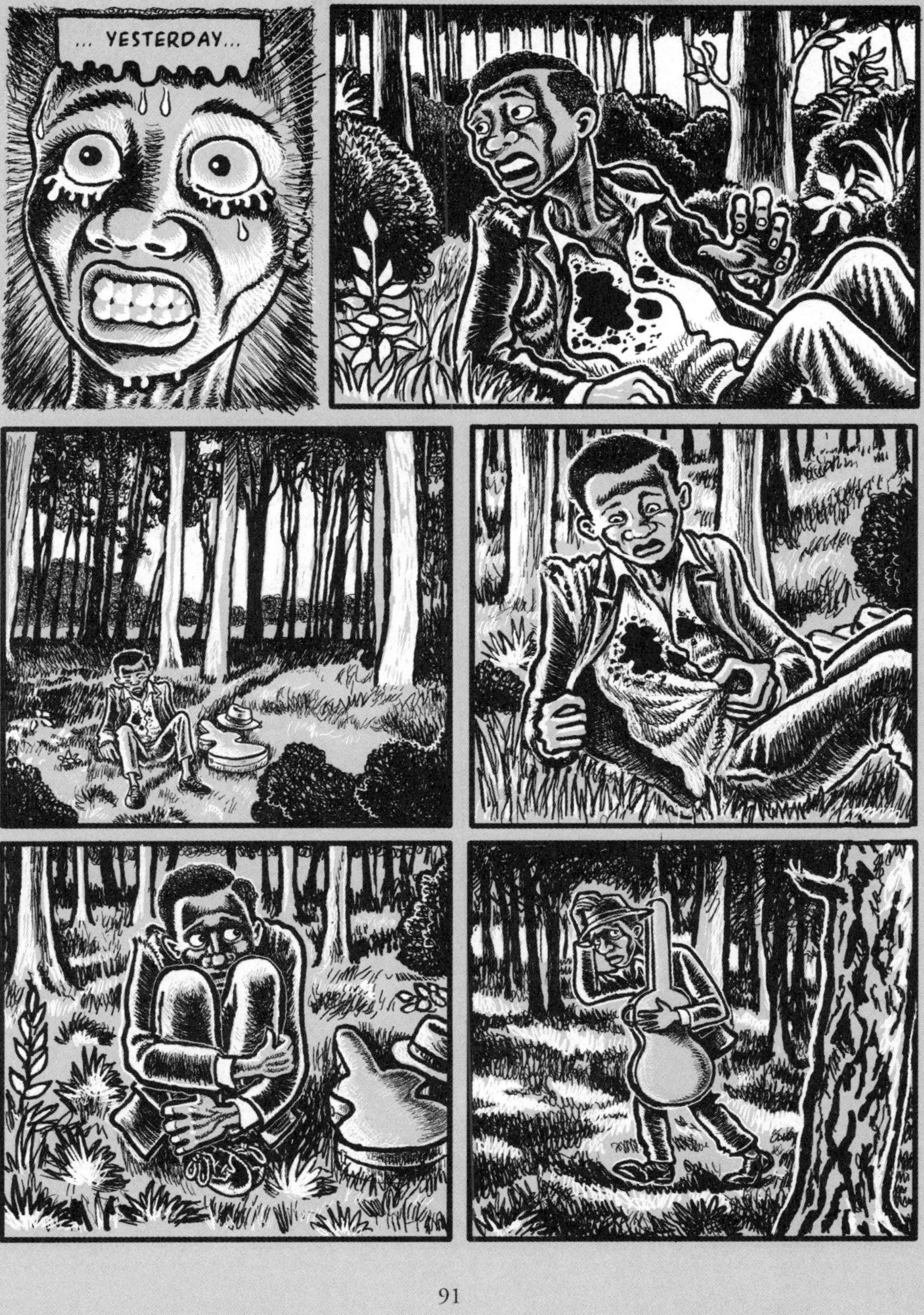
... YESTERDAY...

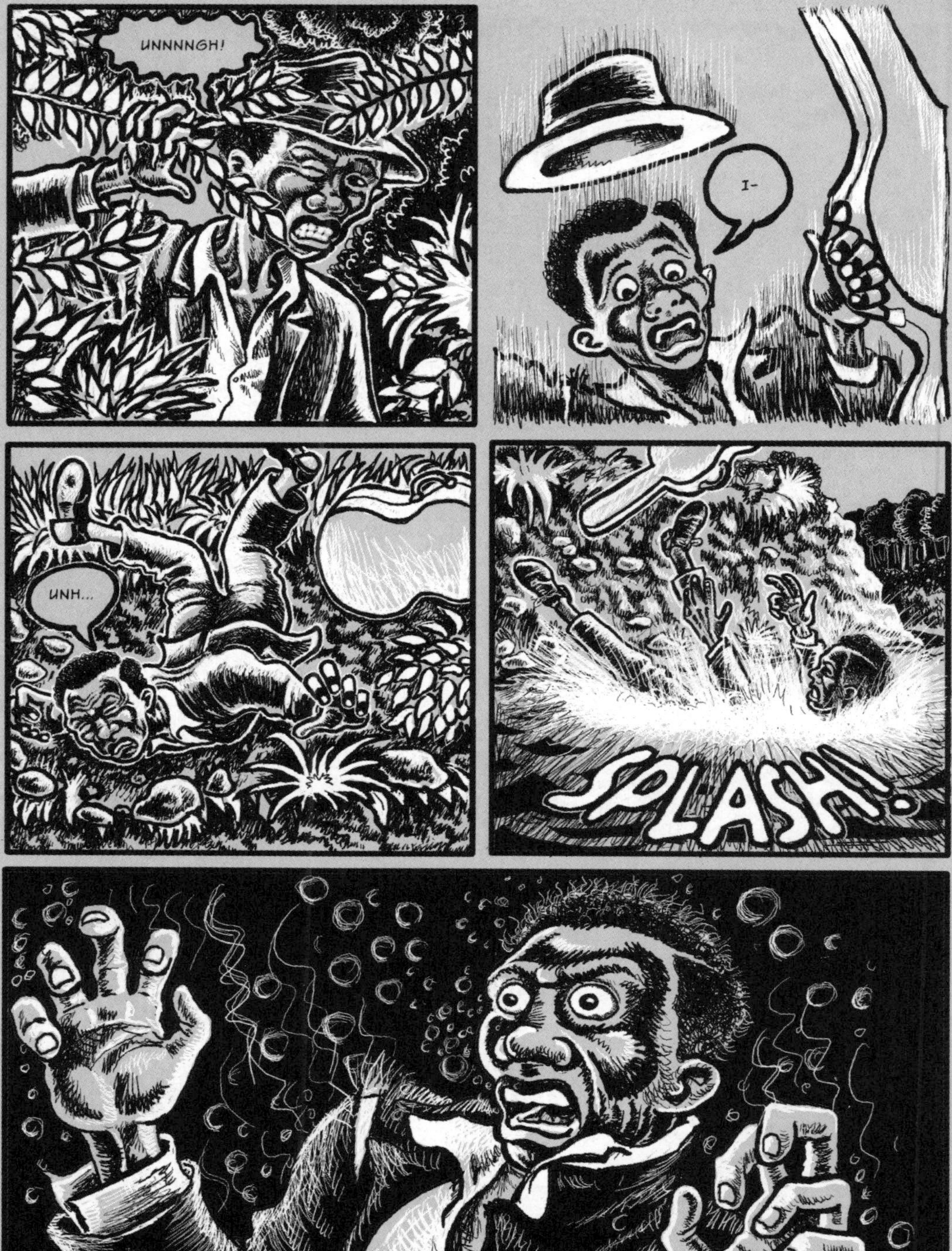
UNNNNGH!
I-
UNH...
SPLASH!

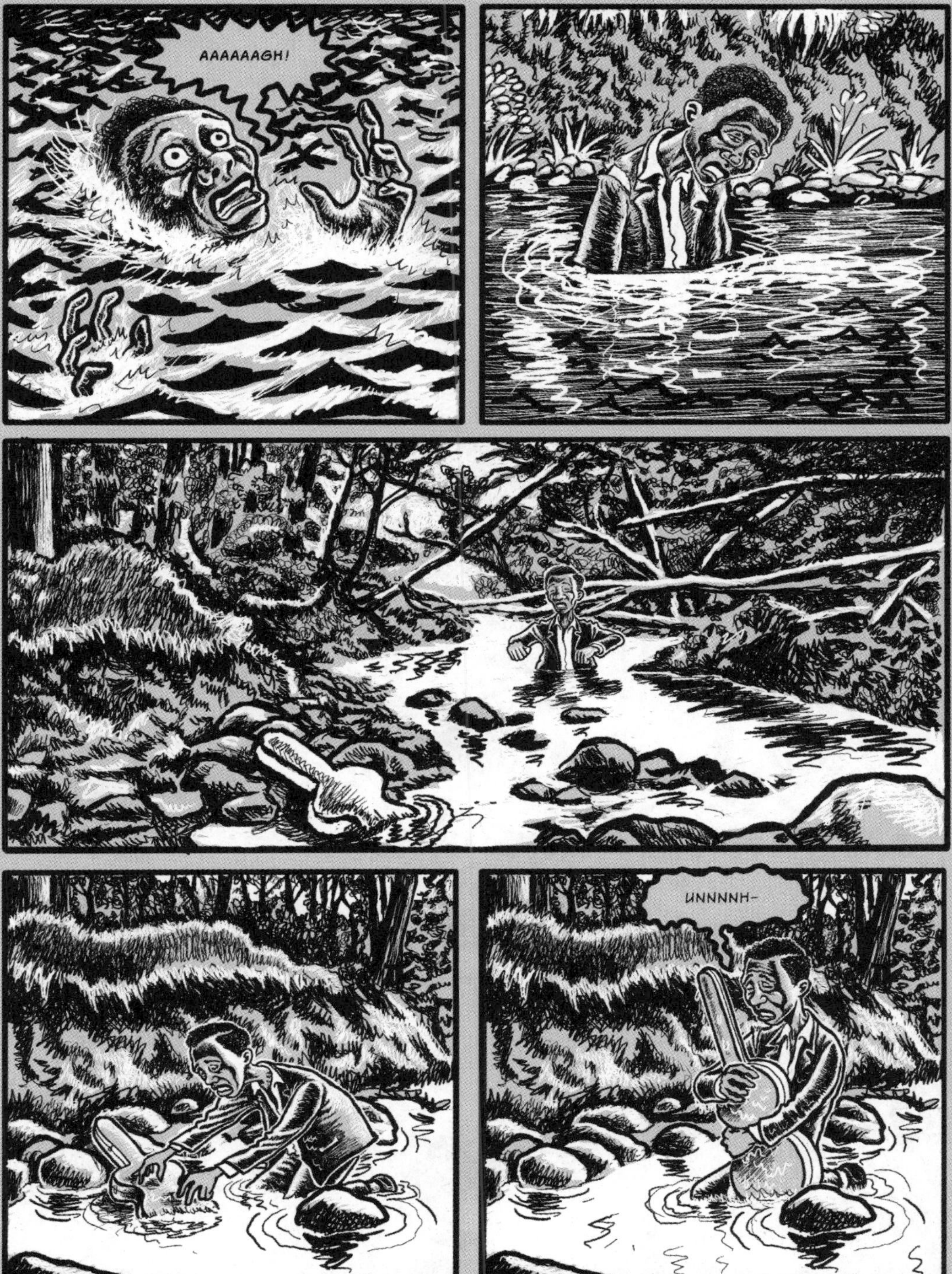
AAAAAAGH!
UNNNNH-

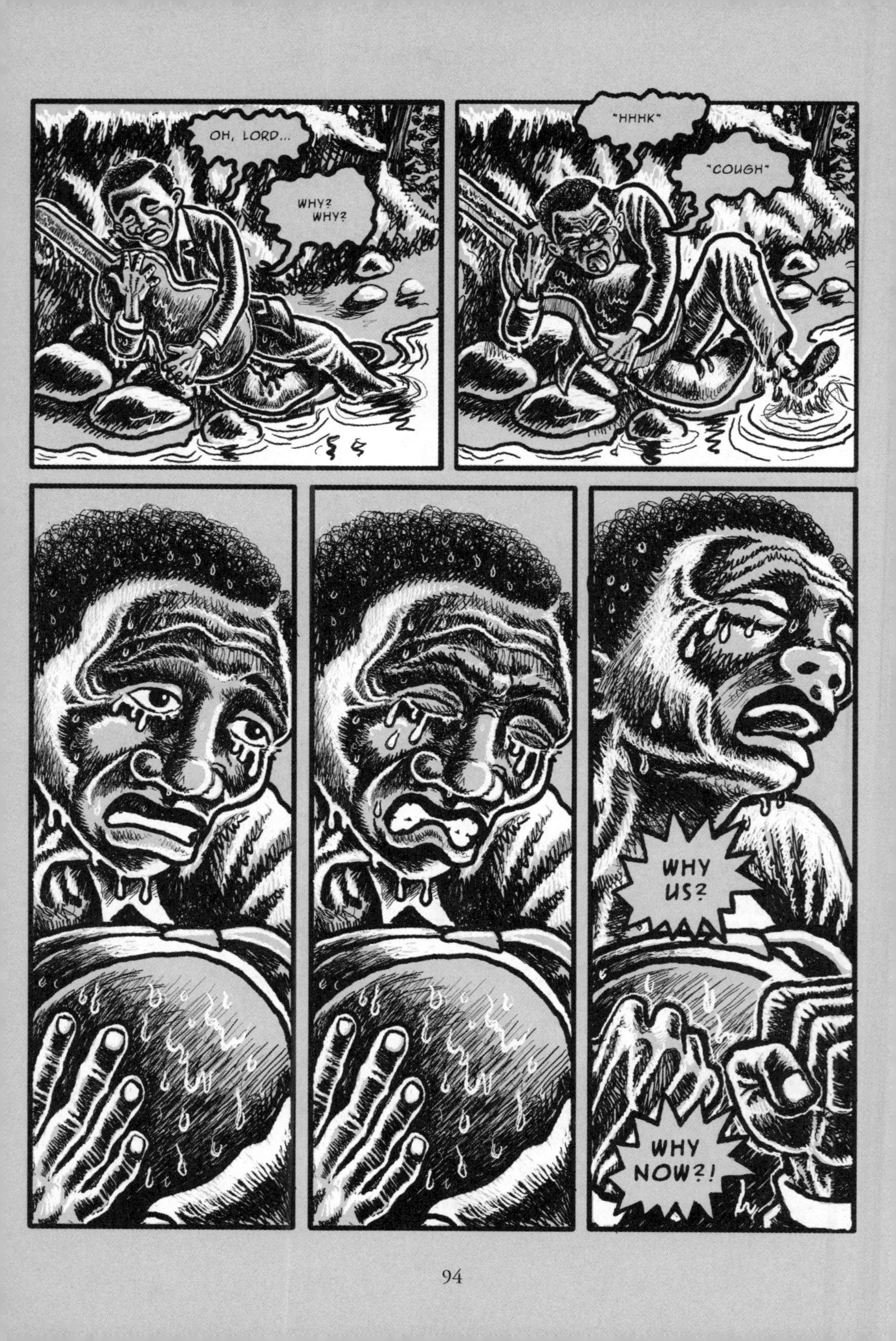
OH, LORD...
WHY? WHY?
"HHHK"
"COUGH"
WHY US?
WHY NOW?!

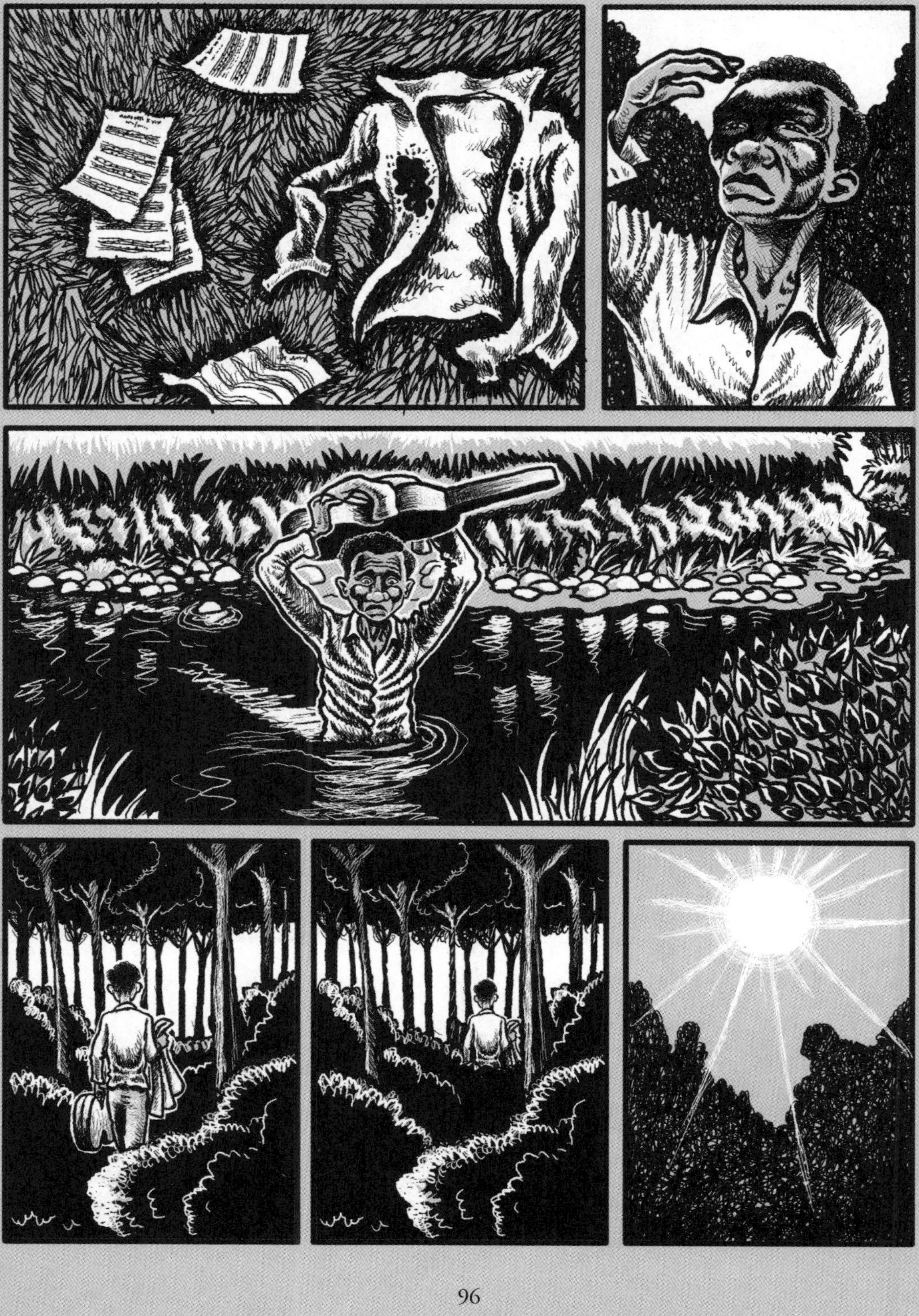

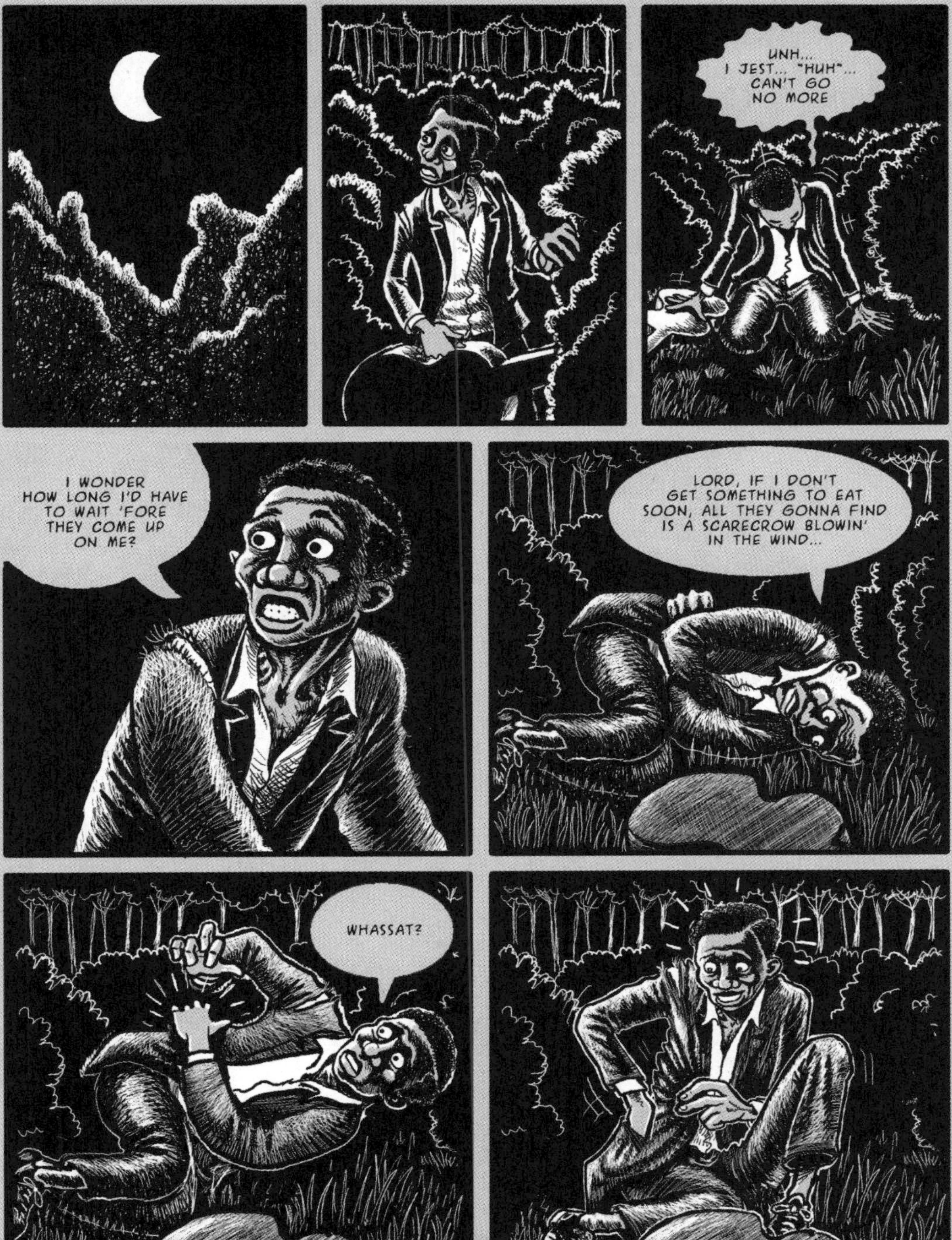
UNH...
I JEST... "HUH"...
CAN'T GO
NO MORE
I WONDER
HOW LONG I'D HAVE
TO WAIT 'FORE
THEY COME UP
ON ME?
LORD, IF I DON'T
GET SOMETHING TO EAT
SOON, ALL THEY GONNA FIND
IS A SCARECROW BLOWIN'
IN THE WIND...
WHASSAT?

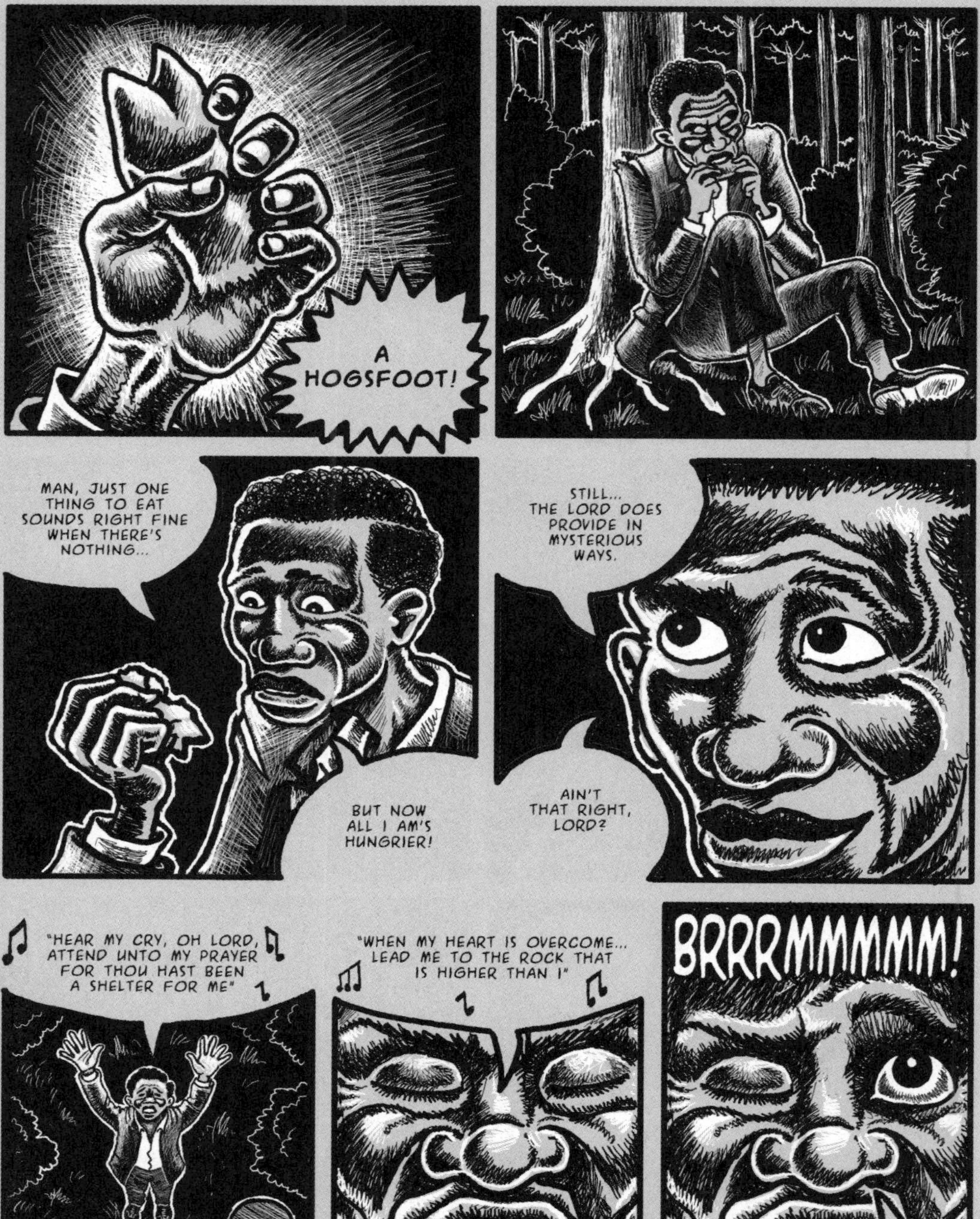
A HOGSFOOT!
MAN, JUST ONE THING TO EAT SOUNDS RIGHT FINE WHEN THERE'S NOTHING...
BUT NOW ALL I AM'S HUNGRIER!
STILL... THE LORD DOES PROVIDE IN MYSTERIOUS WAYS.
AIN'T THAT RIGHT, LORD?
"HEAR MY CRY, OH LORD, ATTEND UNTO MY PRAYER FOR THOU HAST BEEN A SHELTER FOR ME"
"WHEN MY HEART IS OVERCOME... LEAD ME TO THE ROCK THAT IS HIGHER THAN I"
BRRRMMMMM!
AMEN?

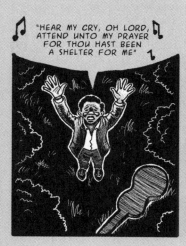

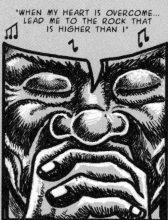

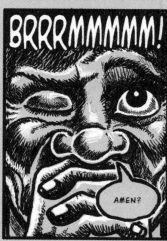

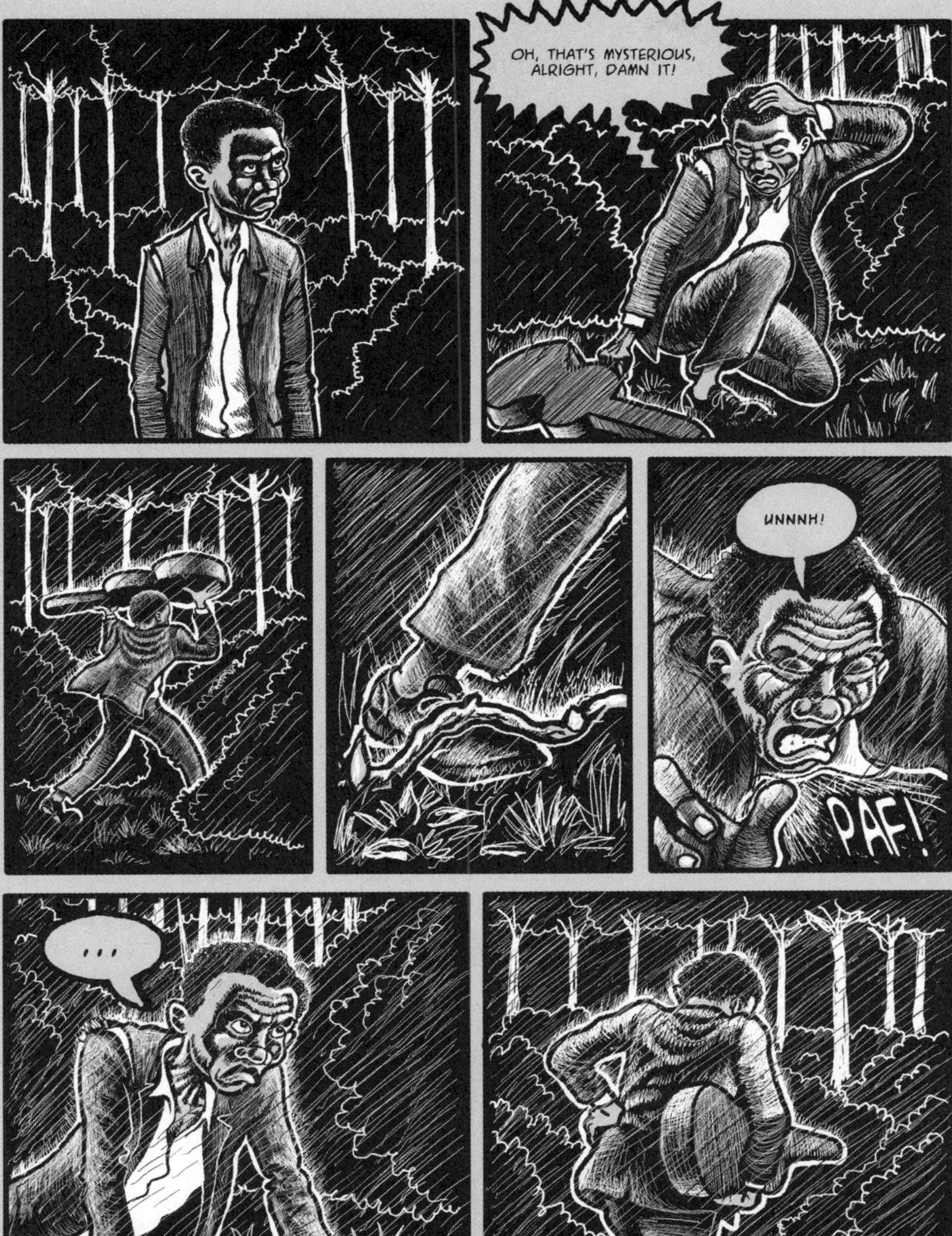
OH, THAT'S MYSTERIOUS, ALRIGHT, DAMN IT!
UNNNH!
PAF!
...

100

7

WE...
"AHEM"

SORRY...
THE OFFICERS, ARRIVED
AT APPROXIMATELY
10:30 AM.

UPON ENTERING THE HOUSE AT 312 "A" STREET,
OFFICERS VERIFIED EARLIER REPORTS OF ONE
MAISY ABRAMS, AGED 20 YRS AND LOCAL
TO HOPE, DEAD IN HER HOME.

Goodman
Funeral home
12 West End
Hope

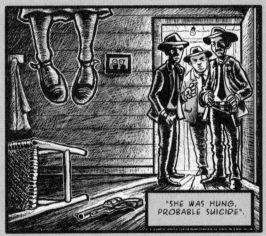

"SHE WAS HUNG,
PROBABLE SUICIDE".

"SHE WAS COVERED IN BLOOD
THAT WASN'T HER OWN AND HAIR
THAT MATCHED OUR WHITE VICTIM
IN THE OTHER MURDER"...

... "ALONG WITH A BROKEN
PISTOL, COVERED IN BLOOD
AND THAT SAME HAIR, AT
HER FEET."

WE FOUND OUT BY TALKING TO LOCAL RESIDENTS
THAT ABRAMS WAS OF DEFINITE RELATION TO TARENE
DAVIS, OUR OTHER KNOWN VICTIM
AT THIS TIME.

THIS BRINGS
THE TOTAL NUMBER OF DEAD BODIES
TO TURN UP WITHOUT WARNING IN
THE LAST 48 HOURS TO FOUR.

104

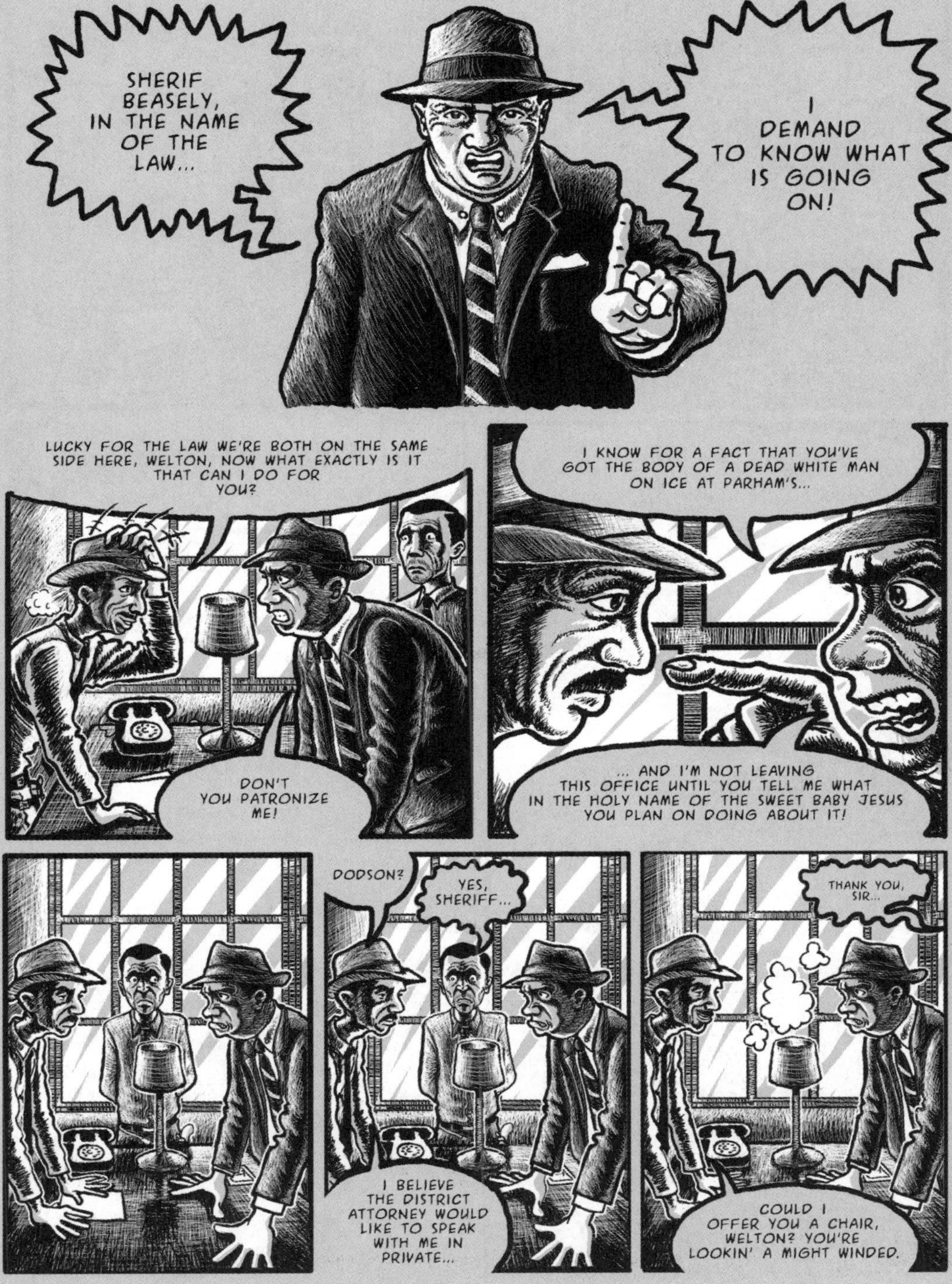
SHERIF BEASELY, IN THE NAME OF THE LAW...
I DEMAND TO KNOW WHAT IS GOING ON!
LUCKY FOR THE LAW WE'RE BOTH ON THE SAME SIDE HERE, WELTON, NOW WHAT EXACTLY IS IT THAT CAN I DO FOR YOU?
DON'T YOU PATRONIZE ME!
I KNOW FOR A FACT THAT YOU'VE GOT THE BODY OF A DEAD WHITE MAN ON ICE AT PARHAM'S...
... AND I'M NOT LEAVING THIS OFFICE UNTIL YOU TELL ME WHAT IN THE HOLY NAME OF THE SWEET BABY JESUS YOU PLAN ON DOING ABOUT IT!
DODSON?
YES, SHERIFF...
I BELIEVE THE DISTRICT ATTORNEY WOULD LIKE TO SPEAK WITH ME IN PRIVATE...
THANK YOU, SIR...
COULD I OFFER YOU A CHAIR, WELTON? YOU'RE LOOKIN' A MIGHT WINDED.

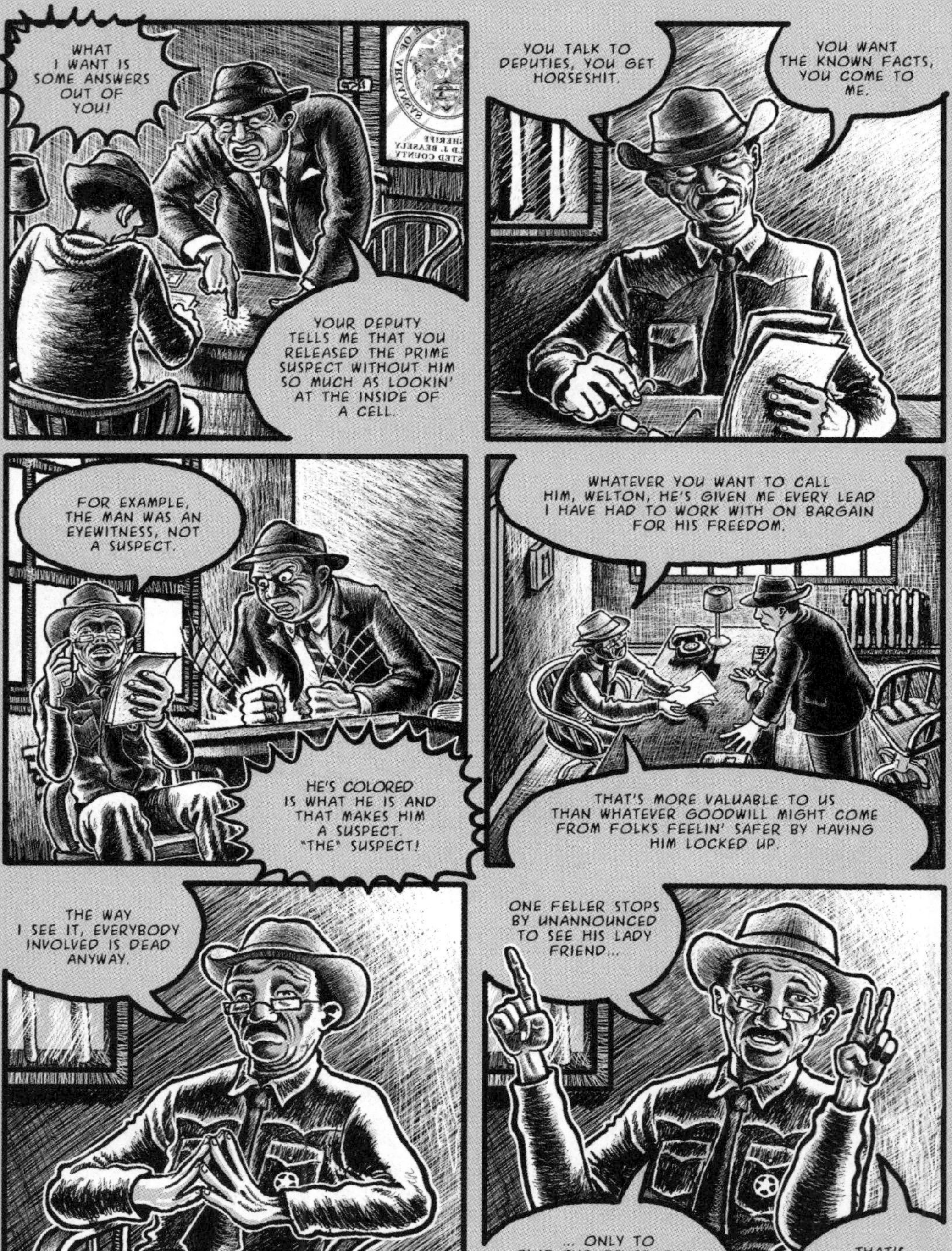
WHAT I WANT IS SOME ANSWERS OUT OF YOU!
YOUR DEPUTY TELLS ME THAT YOU RELEASED THE PRIME SUSPECT WITHOUT HIM SO MUCH AS LOOKIN' AT THE INSIDE OF A CELL.
YOU TALK TO DEPUTIES, YOU GET HORSESHIT.
YOU WANT THE KNOWN FACTS, YOU COME TO ME.
FOR EXAMPLE, THE MAN WAS AN EYEWITNESS, NOT A SUSPECT.
HE'S COLORED IS WHAT HE IS AND THAT MAKES HIM A SUSPECT. "THE" SUSPECT!
WHATEVER YOU WANT TO CALL HIM, WELTON, HE'S GIVEN ME EVERY LEAD I HAVE HAD TO WORK WITH ON BARGAIN FOR HIS FREEDOM.
THAT'S MORE VALUABLE TO US THAN WHATEVER GOODWILL MIGHT COME FROM FOLKS FEELIN' SAFER BY HAVING HIM LOCKED UP.
THE WAY I SEE IT, EVERYBODY INVOLVED IS DEAD ANYWAY.
ONE FELLER STOPS BY UNANNOUNCED TO SEE HIS LADY FRIEND...
... ONLY TO FIND THE OTHER ONE THERE WITH HER INSTEAD.
THAT'S ALWAYS BIG TROUBLE...

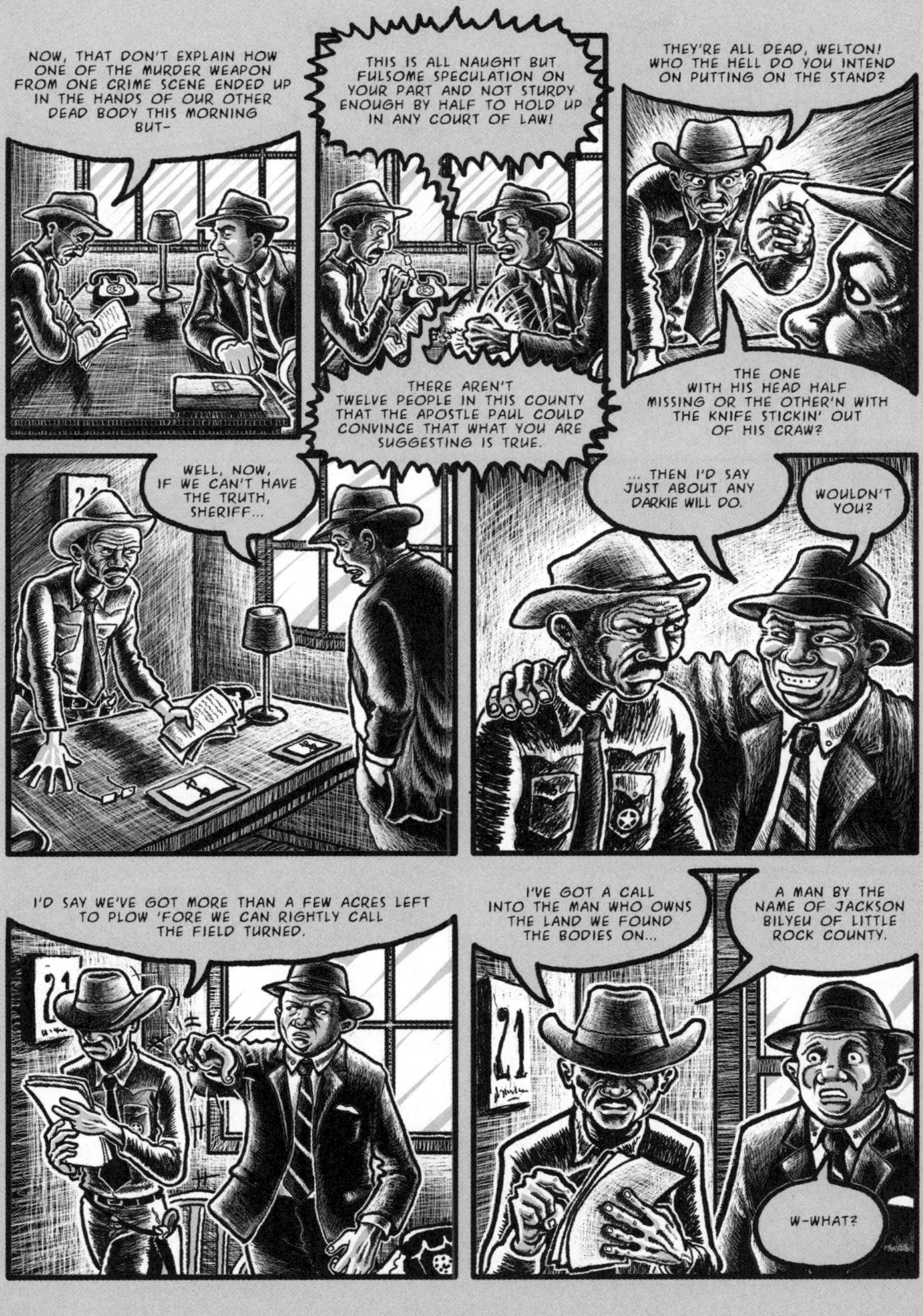
NOW, THAT DON'T EXPLAIN HOW ONE OF THE MURDER WEAPON FROM ONE CRIME SCENE ENDED UP IN THE HANDS OF OUR OTHER DEAD BODY THIS MORNING BUT-
THIS IS ALL NAUGHT BUT FULSOME SPECULATION ON YOUR PART AND NOT STURDY ENOUGH BY HALF TO HOLD UP IN ANY COURT OF LAW!
THERE AREN'T TWELVE PEOPLE IN THIS COUNTY THAT THE APOSTLE PAUL COULD CONVINCE THAT WHAT YOU ARE SUGGESTING IS TRUE.
THEY'RE ALL DEAD, WELTON! WHO THE HELL DO YOU INTEND ON PUTTING ON THE STAND?
THE ONE WITH HIS HEAD HALF MISSING OR THE OTHER'N WITH THE KNIFE STICKIN' OUT OF HIS CRAW?
WELL, NOW, IF WE CAN'T HAVE THE TRUTH, SHERIFF...
... THEN I'D SAY JUST ABOUT ANY DARKIE WILL DO.
WOULDN'T YOU?
I'D SAY WE'VE GOT MORE THAN A FEW ACRES LEFT TO PLOW 'FORE WE CAN RIGHTLY CALL THE FIELD TURNED.
I'VE GOT A CALL INTO THE MAN WHO OWNS THE LAND WE FOUND THE BODIES ON...
A MAN BY THE NAME OF JACKSON BILYEU OF LITTLE ROCK COUNTY.
W-WHAT?

JACKSON BILYEU. THAT MEAN SOMETHING TO YOU?

WELL, OF COURSE NOT.

IT'S NOT LIKE I KNOW EVERY PERSON WHO OWNS LAND IN THIS COUNTY!

I RECKON YOU DON'T...

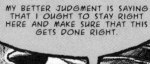

MY BETTER JUDGMENT IS SAYING THAT I OUGHT TO STAY RIGHT HERE AND MAKE SURE THAT THIS GETS DONE RIGHT.

BUT MY ITINERARY WON'T ALLOW IT.

CONSIDER YOURSELF WARNED, SIR.

THE GOOD CITIZENS OF HEMPSTEAD COUNTY WHO BROUGHT YOU IN HERE TO KEEP PEACE WILL NOT LONG TOLERATE THE IDEA OF A MURDERER IN THEIR MIDST WHO GOES UNPUNISHED.

SUFFICE IT TO SAY, 'WE'RE WAITING...

SHERIFF?

THEY GOT AHOLD OF SOMEBODY ON THE PHONE THERE IN LITTLE ROCK AND THEY SAY MR. BILYEU IS ALREADY ON HIS WAY DOWN HERE!

I RECKON THAT MEANS HE KNOWS SOMETHING WE DON'T

WAY THIS DAY HAS GONE...

... I'D WAGER HE'S JUST BRIMMIN' WITH GOOD NEWS...

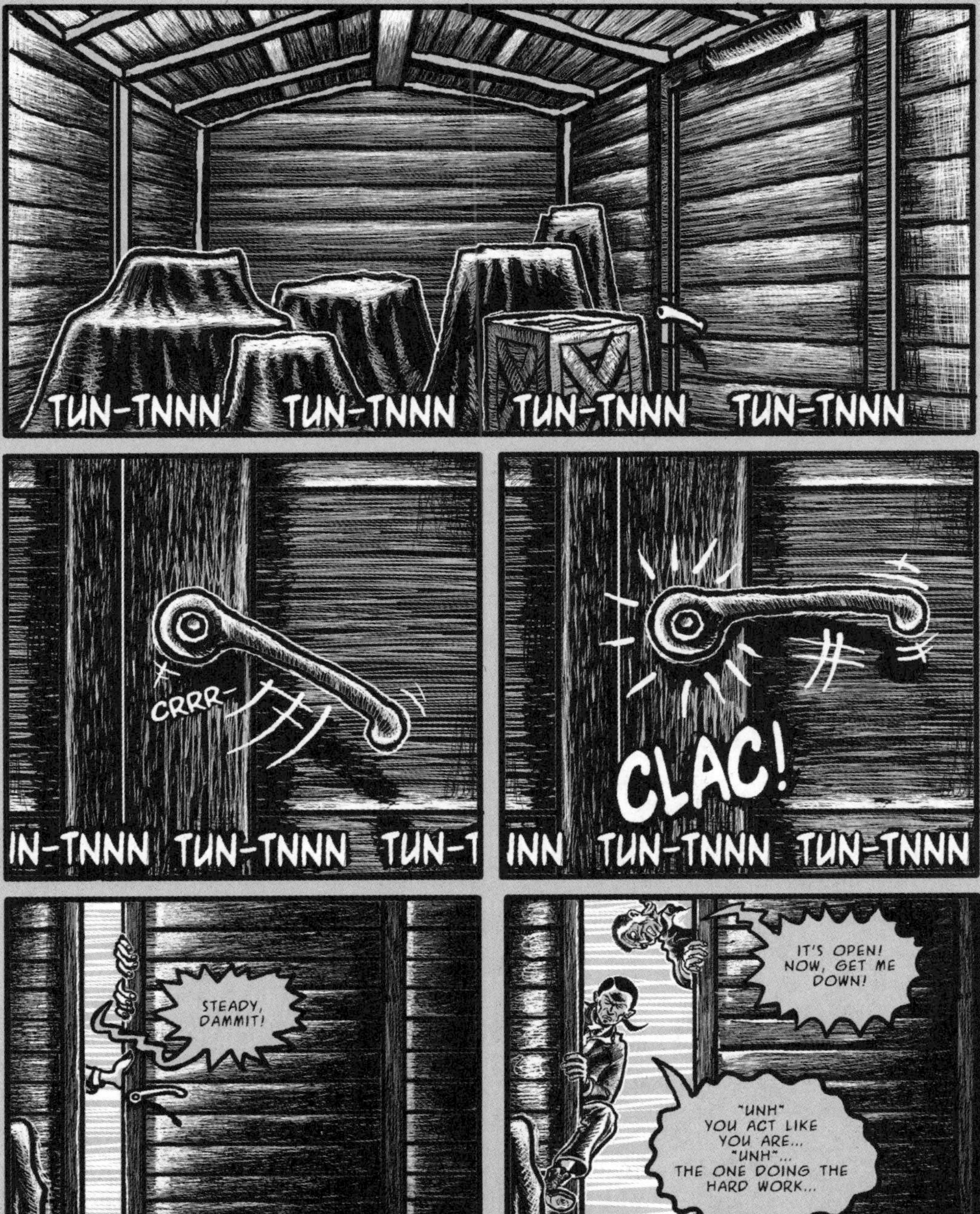
TUN-TNNN TUN-TNNN TUN-TNNN TUN-TNNN
CRRR-
IN-TNNN TUN-TNNN TUN-T
CLAC!
INN TUN-TNNN TUN-TNNN
STEADY, DAMMIT!
TUN-TNNN TUN-TNNN TUN
IT'S OPEN! NOW, GET ME DOWN!
"UNH" YOU ACT LIKE YOU ARE... "UNH"... THE ONE DOING THE HARD WORK...
TNNN TUN-TNNN TUN-TN

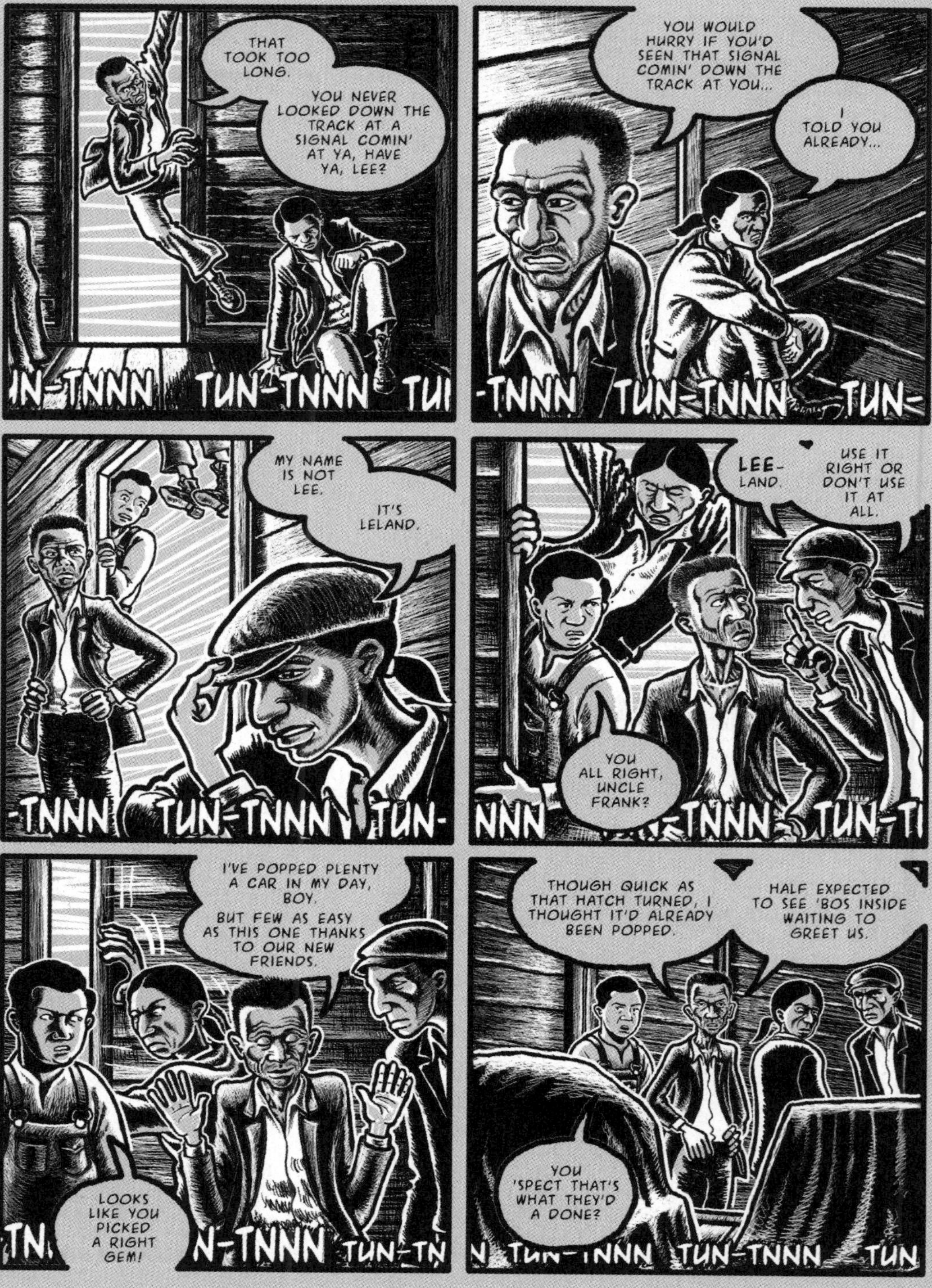
THAT TOOK TOO LONG.
YOU NEVER LOOKED DOWN THE TRACK AT A SIGNAL COMIN' AT YA, HAVE YA, LEE?
N-TNNN TUN-TNNN TU
YOU WOULD HURRY IF YOU'D SEEN THAT SIGNAL COMIN' DOWN THE TRACK AT YOU...
I TOLD YOU ALREADY...
-TNNN TUN-TNNN TUN-
MY NAME IS NOT LEE.
IT'S LELAND.
-TNNN TUN-TNNN TUN-
LEE-LAND.
USE IT RIGHT OR DON'T USE IT AT ALL.
YOU ALL RIGHT, UNCLE FRANK?
NNN -TNNN TUN-T
I'VE POPPED PLENTY A CAR IN MY DAY, BOY.
BUT FEW AS EASY AS THIS ONE THANKS TO OUR NEW FRIENDS.
LOOKS LIKE YOU PICKED A RIGHT GEM!
TN N-TNNN TUN-TN
THOUGH QUICK AS THAT HATCH TURNED, I THOUGHT IT'D ALREADY BEEN POPPED.
HALF EXPECTED TO SEE 'BOS INSIDE WAITING TO GREET US.
YOU 'SPECT THAT'S WHAT THEY'D A DONE?
N TUN-TNNN TUN-TNNN TUN

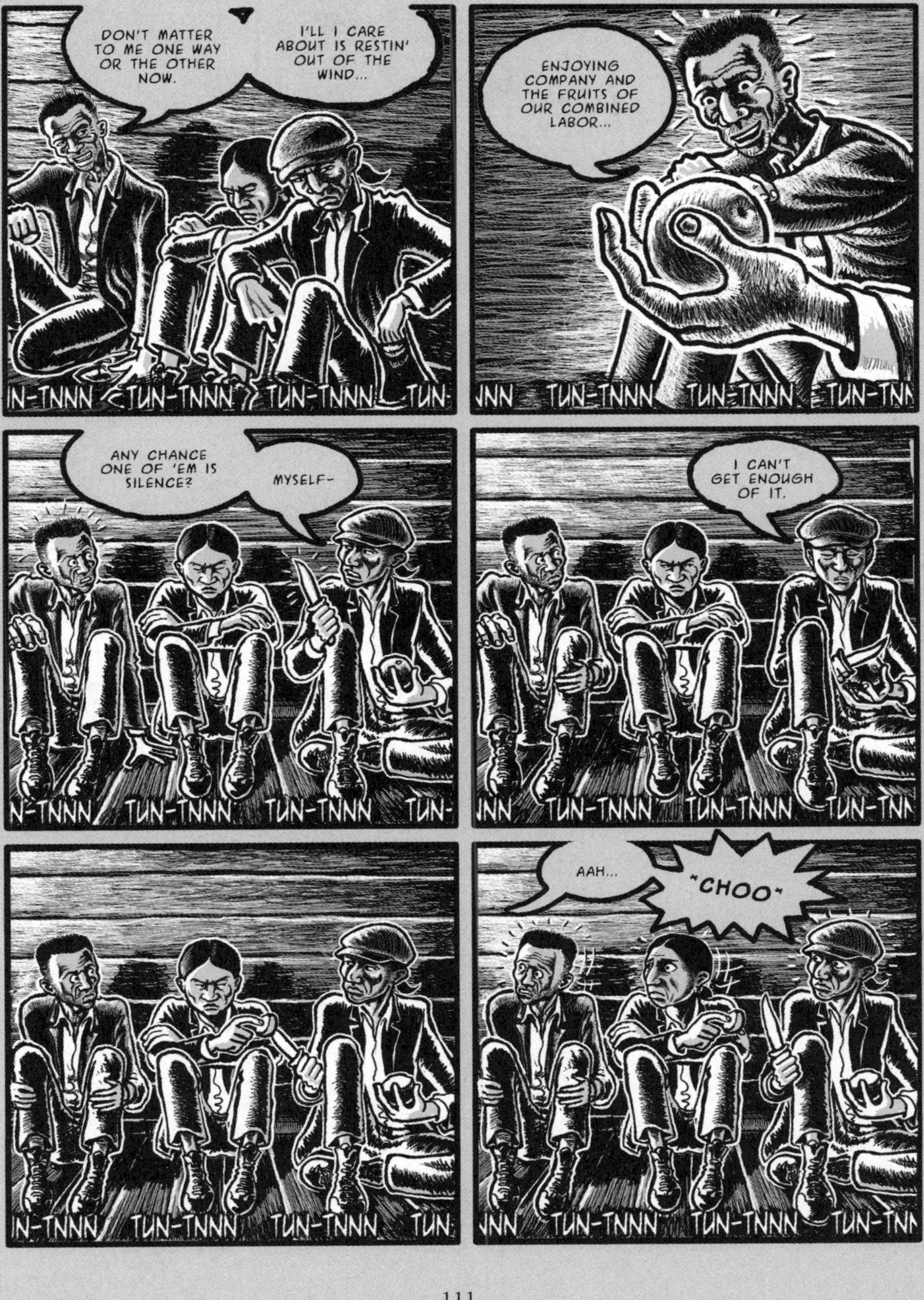
DON'T MATTER TO ME ONE WAY OR THE OTHER NOW.
I'LL I CARE ABOUT IS RESTIN' OUT OF THE WIND...
IN-TNNN TUN-TNNN TUN-TNNN TUN-
ENJOYING COMPANY AND THE FRUITS OF OUR COMBINED LABOR...
NN TUN-TNNN TUN-TNNN TUN-TN
ANY CHANCE ONE OF 'EM IS SILENCE?
MYSELF-
N-TNNN TUN-TNNN TUN-TNNN TUN-
I CAN'T GET ENOUGH OF IT.
NN TUN-TNNN TUN-TNNN TUN-TN
N-TNNN TUN-TNNN TUN-TNNN TUN-
AAH...
CHOO
NN TUN-TNNN TUN-TNNN TUN-TN

THAT WASN'T ME!
N-TNNN TUN-T
-TNNN TUN-TNNN
YOU GET ONE WARNING.
N TUN
WE'RE PULLING THIS TARP OFF.
YOU SO MUCH AS BAT AN EYELASH...
N - TNNN TUN - TNNN TU
... AND I SWEAR I'LL GUT YOU LIKE A MUDCAT.
- TNNN TUN - TNNN TUN
TNNN TUN - TN N TUN
TNNN TUN - TNNN TUN

113

114

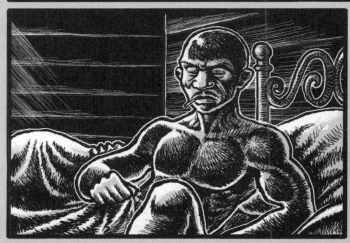

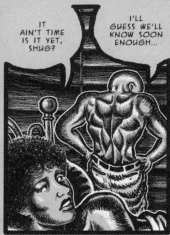

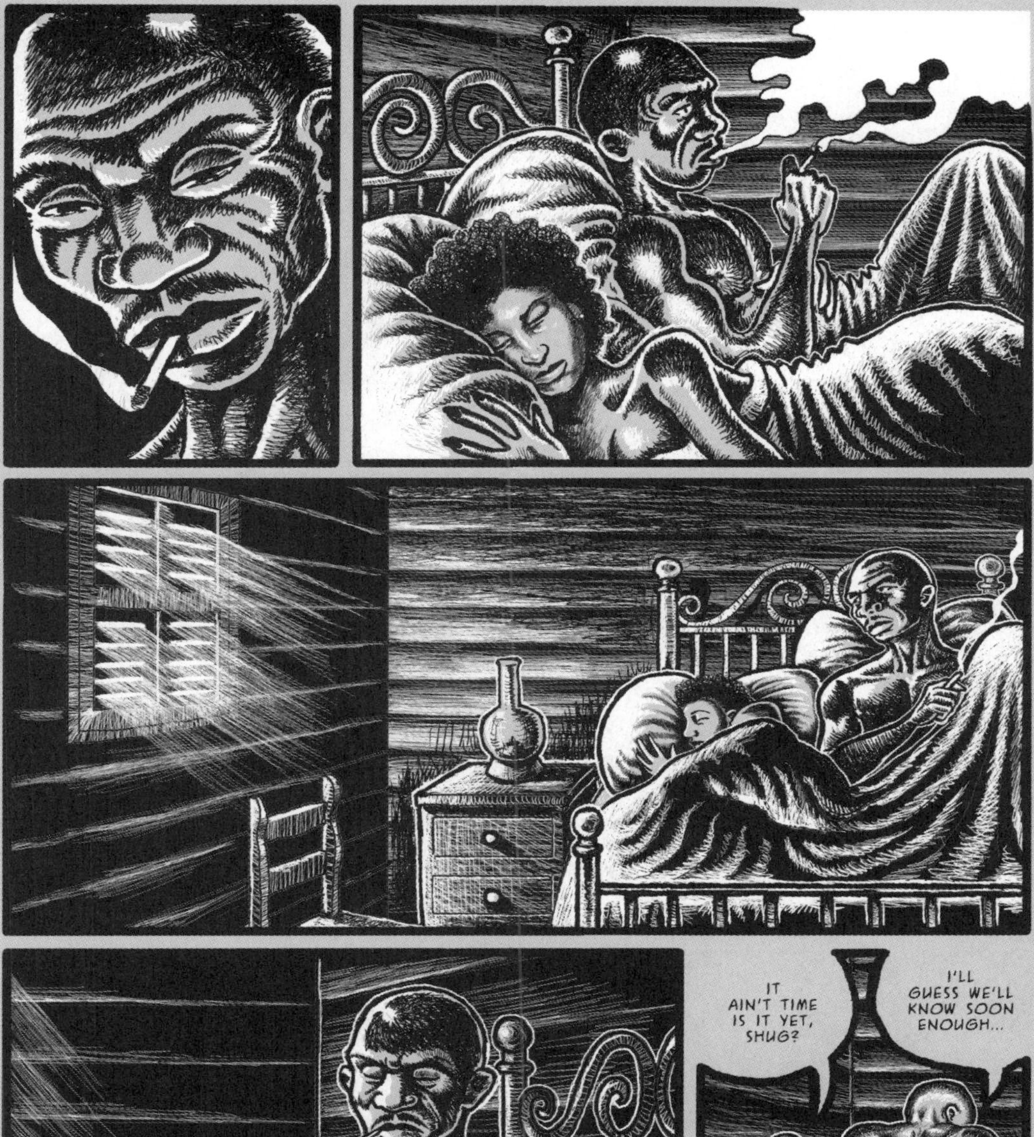
IT AIN'T TIME IS IT YET, SHUG?
I'LL GUESS WE'LL KNOW SOON ENOUGH...

121

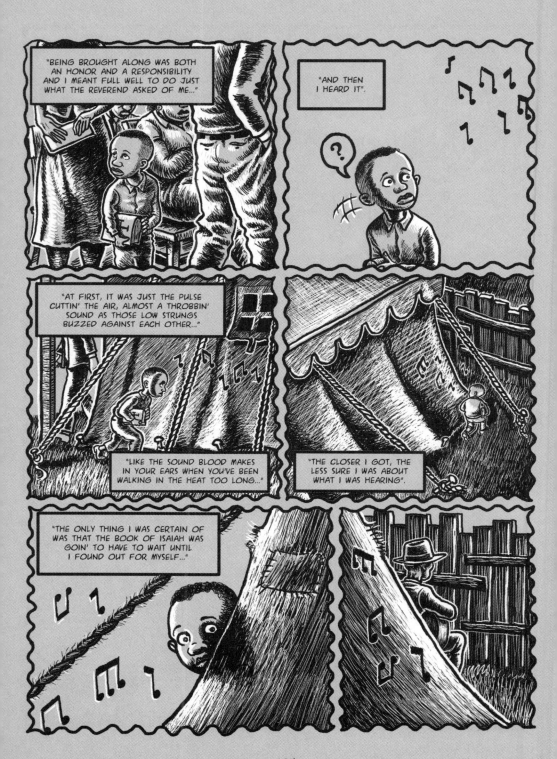

124

125

126

127

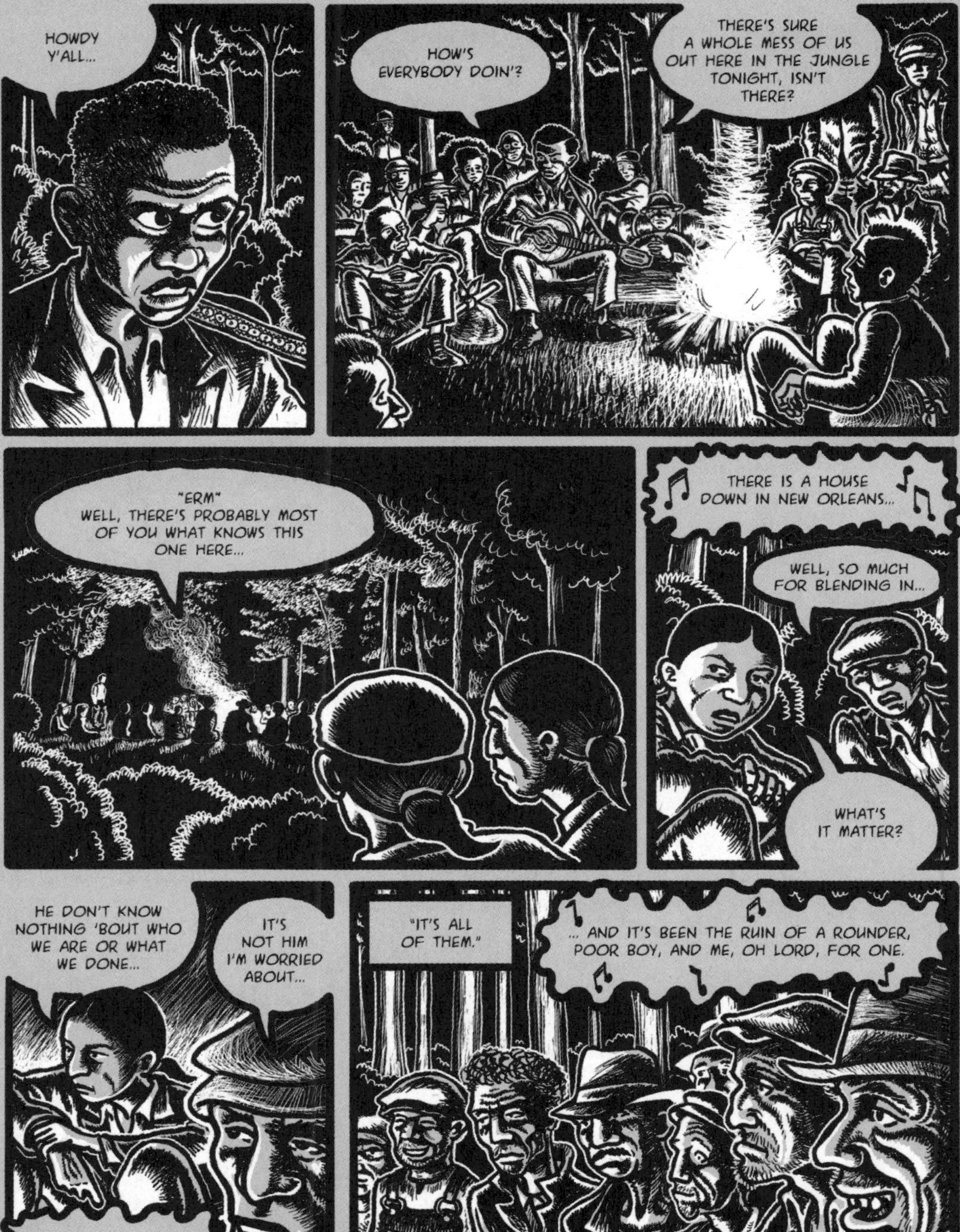
HOWDY Y'ALL...
HOW'S EVERYBODY DOIN'?
THERE'S SURE A WHOLE MESS OF US OUT HERE IN THE JUNGLE TONIGHT, ISN'T THERE?
"ERM" WELL, THERE'S PROBABLY MOST OF YOU WHAT KNOWS THIS ONE HERE...
THERE IS A HOUSE DOWN IN NEW ORLEANS...
WELL, SO MUCH FOR BLENDING IN...
WHAT'S IT MATTER?
HE DON'T KNOW NOTHING 'BOUT WHO WE ARE OR WHAT WE DONE...
IT'S NOT HIM I'M WORRIED ABOUT...
... THEY CALL THE RISING SUN...
"IT'S ALL OF THEM."
... AND IT'S BEEN THE RUIN OF A ROUNDER, POOR BOY, AND ME, OH LORD, FOR ONE.

129

130

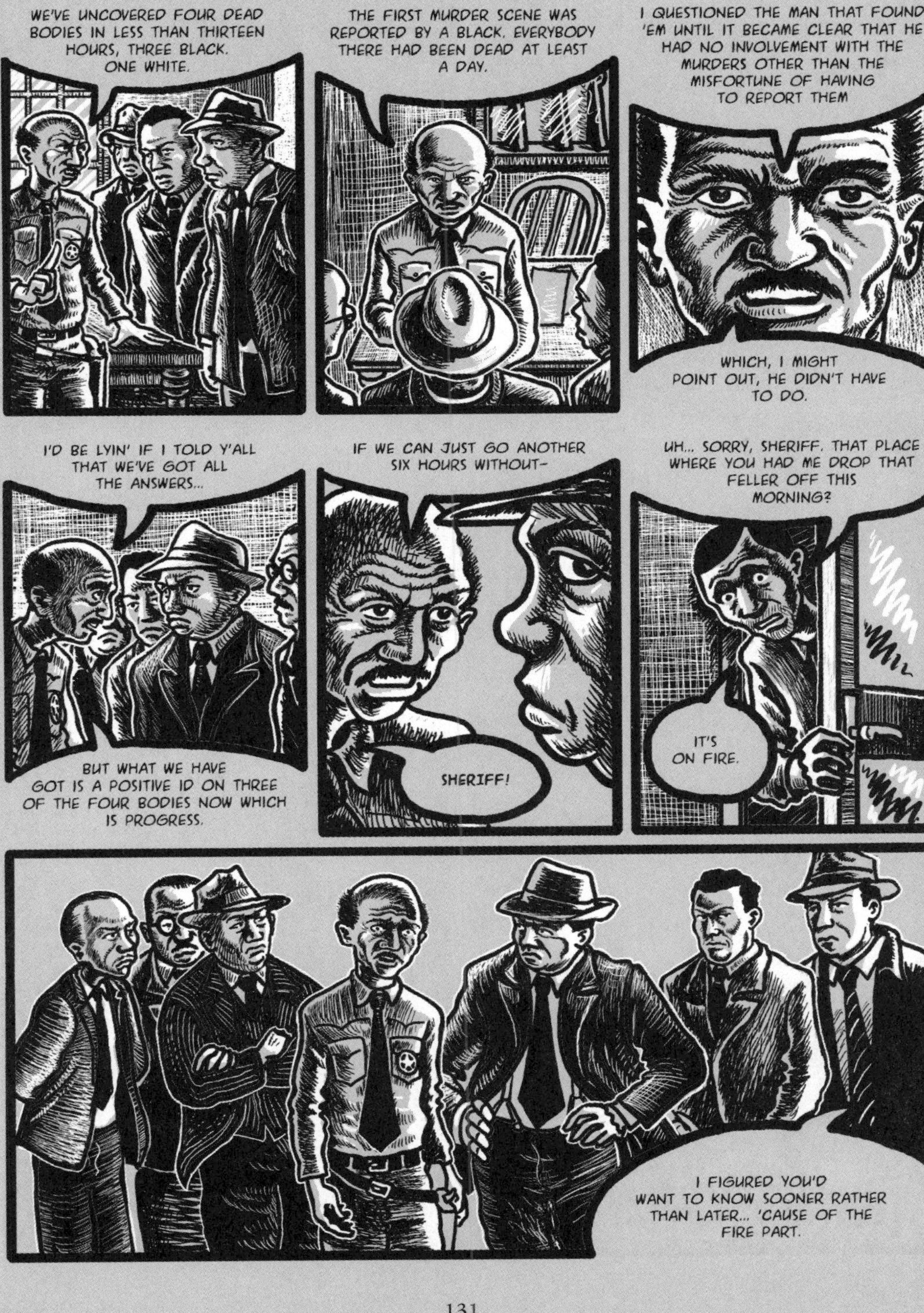

WE'VE UNCOVERED FOUR DEAD BODIES IN LESS THAN THIRTEEN HOURS, THREE BLACK. ONE WHITE.
THE FIRST MURDER SCENE WAS REPORTED BY A BLACK. EVERYBODY THERE HAD BEEN DEAD AT LEAST A DAY.
I QUESTIONED THE MAN THAT FOUND 'EM UNTIL IT BECAME CLEAR THAT HE HAD NO INVOLVEMENT WITH THE MURDERS OTHER THAN THE MISFORTUNE OF HAVING TO REPORT THEM
WHICH, I MIGHT POINT OUT, HE DIDN'T HAVE TO DO.
I'D BE LYIN' IF I TOLD Y'ALL THAT WE'VE GOT ALL THE ANSWERS...
BUT WHAT WE HAVE GOT IS A POSITIVE ID ON THREE OF THE FOUR BODIES NOW WHICH IS PROGRESS.
IF WE CAN JUST GO ANOTHER SIX HOURS WITHOUT-
SHERIFF!
UH... SORRY, SHERIFF. THAT PLACE WHERE YOU HAD ME DROP THAT FELLER OFF THIS MORNING?
IT'S ON FIRE.
I FIGURED YOU'D WANT TO KNOW SOONER RATHER THAN LATER... 'CAUSE OF THE FIRE PART.

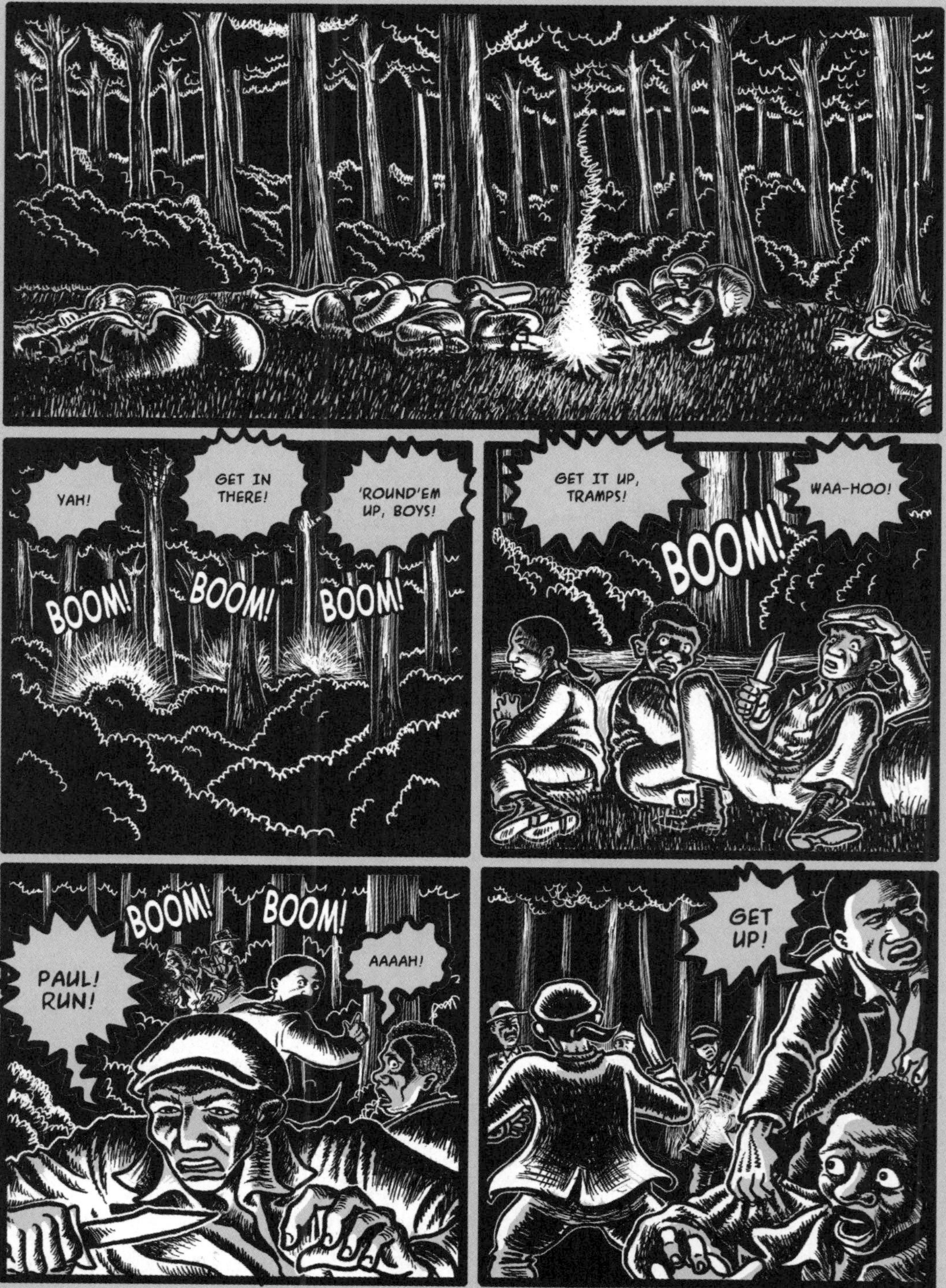
YAH!
GET IN THERE!
'ROUND'EM UP, BOYS!
BOOM!
BOOM!
BOOM!
GET IT UP, TRAMPS!
WAA-HOO!
BOOM!
BOOM!
BOOM!
PAUL! RUN!
AAAAH!
GET UP!

134

135

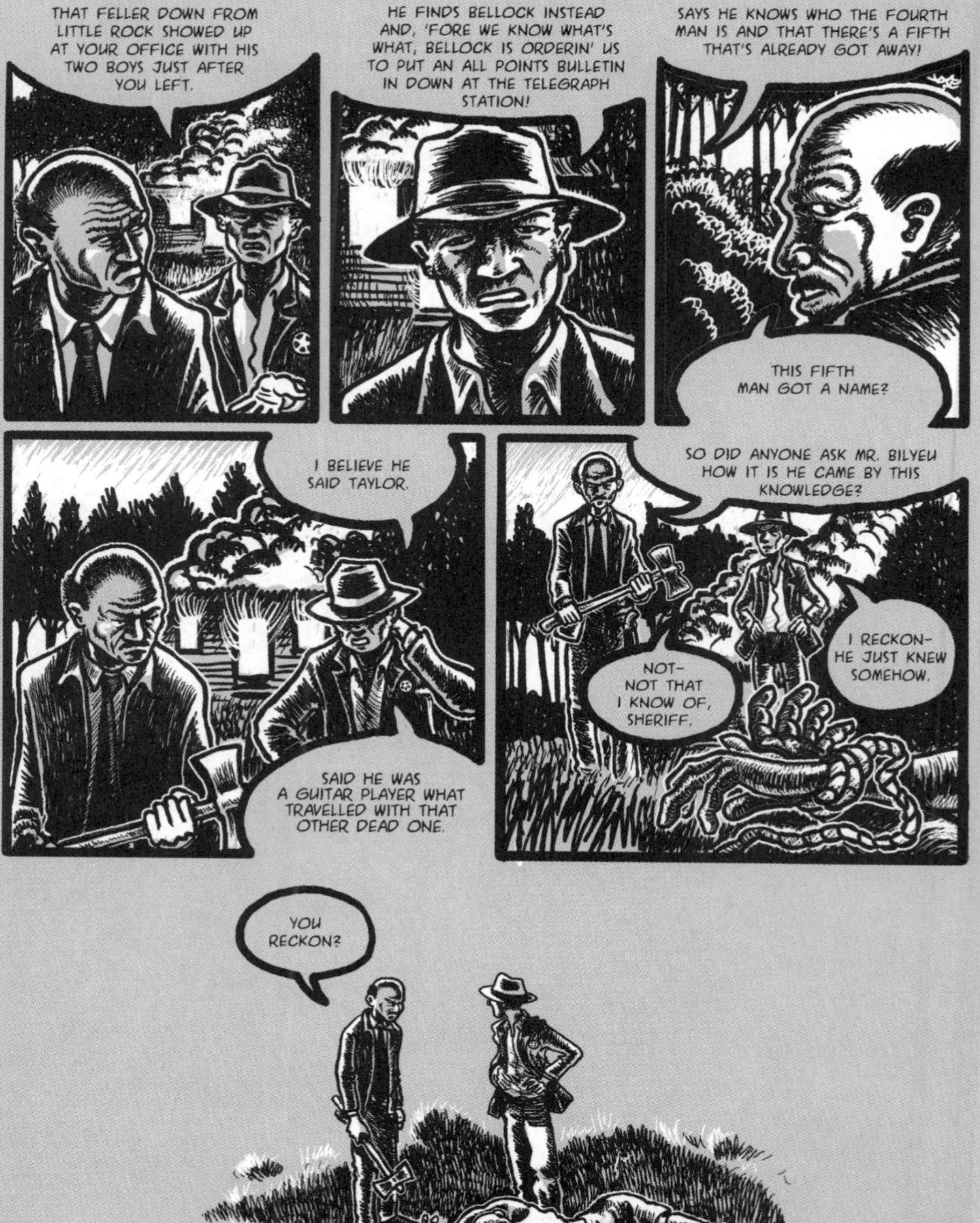
THAT FELLER DOWN FROM LITTLE ROCK SHOWED UP AT YOUR OFFICE WITH HIS TWO BOYS JUST AFTER YOU LEFT.
HE FINDS BELLOCK INSTEAD AND, 'FORE WE KNOW WHAT'S WHAT, BELLOCK IS ORDERIN' US TO PUT AN ALL POINTS BULLETIN IN DOWN AT THE TELEGRAPH STATION!
SAYS HE KNOWS WHO THE FOURTH MAN IS AND THAT THERE'S A FIFTH THAT'S ALREADY GOT AWAY!
THIS FIFTH MAN GOT A NAME?
I BELIEVE HE SAID TAYLOR.
SAID HE WAS A GUITAR PLAYER WHAT TRAVELLED WITH THAT OTHER DEAD ONE.
SO DID ANYONE ASK MR. BILYEU HOW IT IS HE CAME BY THIS KNOWLEDGE?
NOT— NOT THAT I KNOW OF, SHERIFF.
I RECKON— HE JUST KNEW SOMEHOW.
YOU RECKON?

143

144

145

147

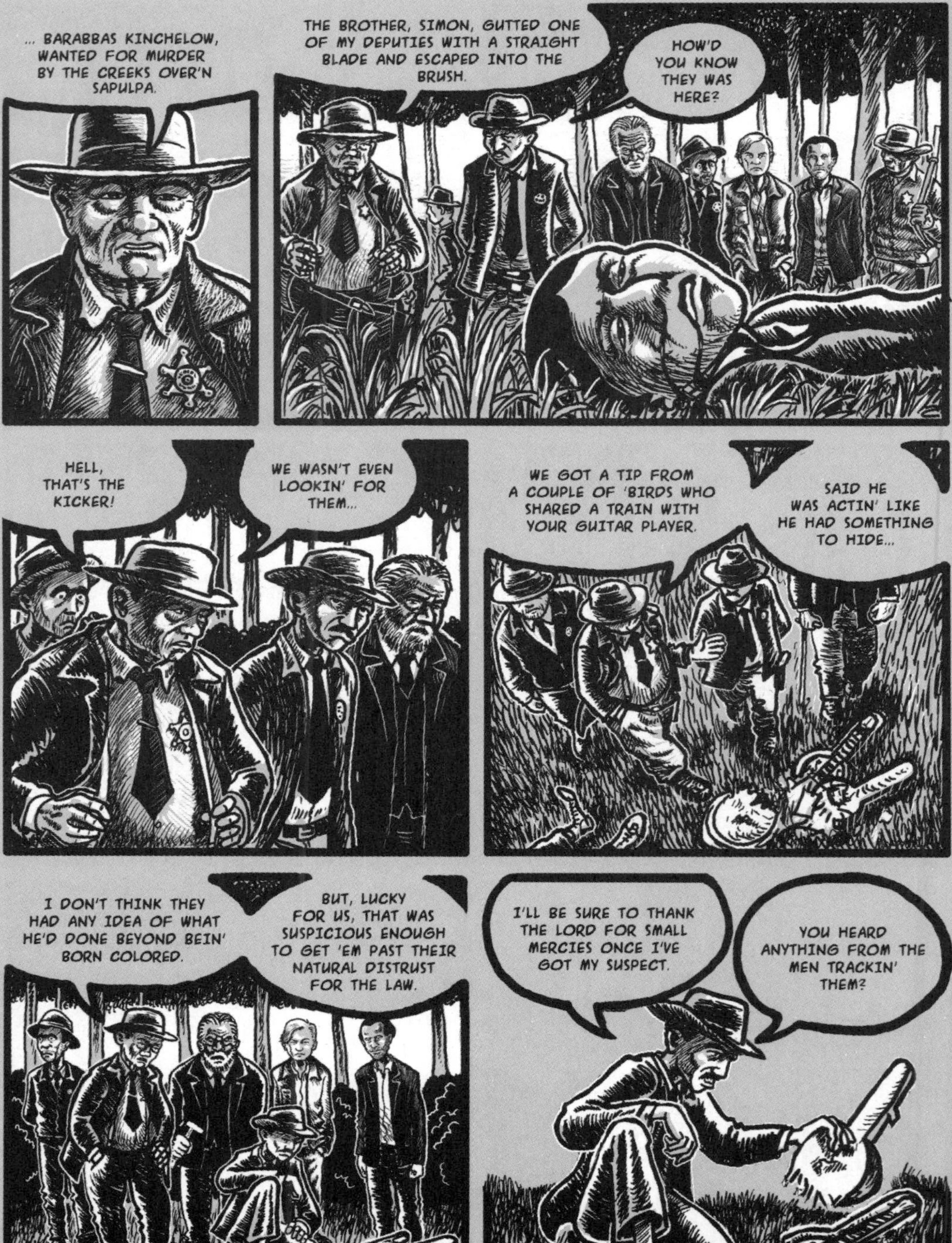
... BARABBAS KINCHELOW, WANTED FOR MURDER BY THE CREEKS OVER'N SAPULPA.
THE BROTHER, SIMON, GUTTED ONE OF MY DEPUTIES WITH A STRAIGHT BLADE AND ESCAPED INTO THE BRUSH.
HOW'D YOU KNOW THEY WAS HERE?
HELL, THAT'S THE KICKER!
WE WASN'T EVEN LOOKIN' FOR THEM...
WE GOT A TIP FROM A COUPLE OF 'BIRDS WHO SHARED A TRAIN WITH YOUR GUITAR PLAYER.
SAID HE WAS ACTIN' LIKE HE HAD SOMETHING TO HIDE...
I DON'T THINK THEY HAD ANY IDEA OF WHAT HE'D DONE BEYOND BEIN' BORN COLORED.
BUT, LUCKY FOR US, THAT WAS SUSPICIOUS ENOUGH TO GET 'EM PAST THEIR NATURAL DISTRUST FOR THE LAW.
I'LL BE SURE TO THANK THE LORD FOR SMALL MERCIES ONCE I'VE GOT MY SUSPECT.
YOU HEARD ANYTHING FROM THE MEN TRACKIN' THEM?

149

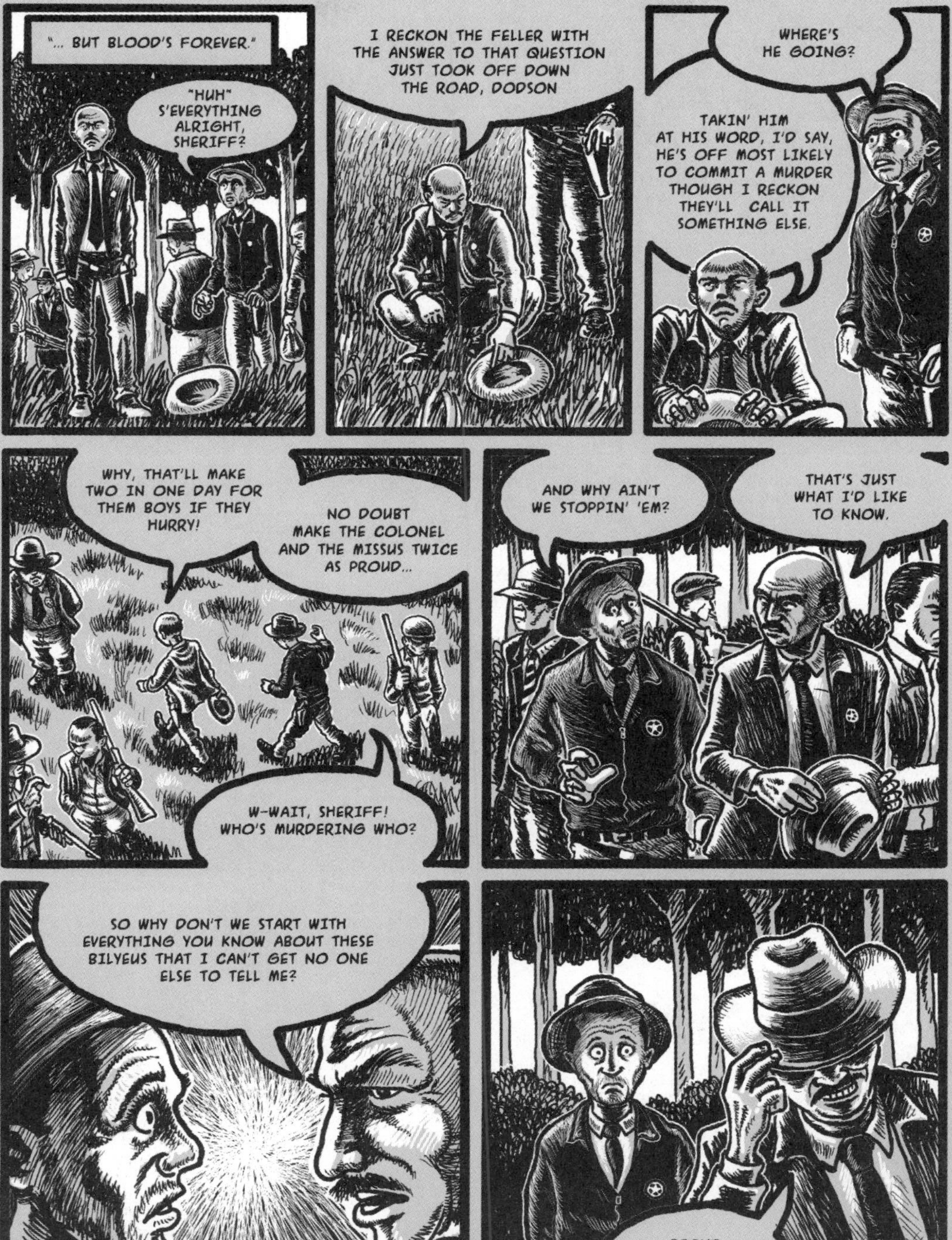

"... BUT BLOOD'S FOREVER."
"HUH" S'EVERYTHING ALRIGHT, SHERIFF?
I RECKON THE FELLER WITH THE ANSWER TO THAT QUESTION JUST TOOK OFF DOWN THE ROAD, DODSON
WHERE'S HE GOING?
TAKIN' HIM AT HIS WORD, I'D SAY, HE'S OFF MOST LIKELY TO COMMIT A MURDER THOUGH I RECKON THEY'LL CALL IT SOMETHING ELSE.
WHY, THAT'LL MAKE TWO IN ONE DAY FOR THEM BOYS IF THEY HURRY!
NO DOUBT MAKE THE COLONEL AND THE MISSUS TWICE AS PROUD...
W-WAIT, SHERIFF! WHO'S MURDERING WHO?
AND WHY AIN'T WE STOPPIN' 'EM?
THAT'S JUST WHAT I'D LIKE TO KNOW.
SO WHY DON'T WE START WITH EVERYTHING YOU KNOW ABOUT THESE BILYEUS THAT I CAN'T GET NO ONE ELSE TO TELL ME?
RIGHT AFTER YOU GO GET THE TRUCK...

153

154

10

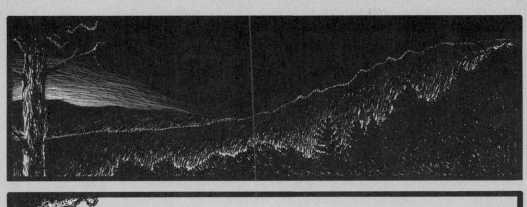

IS THAT A DAY FOR YOU THEN, MISTER DOUGHERTY?

THE DAY HAS BUT BEGUN AS NIGHT FALLS.

IF ANYONE OF MERIT COMES TO CALLING FOR ME, LET HIM KNOW I'LL BE DOWN THE LINE*

WHAT HAVE YOU GOT COOKIN' DOWN AT THE DREAMLAND TONIGHT?

COMBO OUT OF SHREVEPORT WITH A GIRL SINGER AS I RECALL IT.

SEEMS LIKE IT GETS A LITTLE HARDER EVERY SHOW TO FILL THE ROOM ENOUGH TO MAKE A BIG BAND PAY FOR ITSELF UNLESS YOU GOT ROYALTY UP THERE LEADING IT.

ARE YOU ABOUT DONE HERE FOR TONIGHT?

I SUPPOSE I'VE GOT ANOTHER TWENTY MINUTES OR SO OF TYPING LEFT TO DO AND THEN IT'LL BE A DAY.

WELL, DON'T LEAVE CECIL WAITING TOO LONG ON HIS DINNER OR I'M SURE TO HEAR ABOUT IT ON SUNDAY.

NOW IF THIS RAIN'D ONLY LET UP FOR A SPELL...

* "DOWN THE LINE" WAS A COLLOQUIAL EXPRESSION SPECIFIC TO LITTLE ROCK IN THIS PERIOD. "THE LINE" WAS THE MUSIC DISTRICT ON NINTH STREET.

KRAAAAAASSH!

OH!

NOW I'M GOIN' TO BE WET AND LATE FIXIN' DINNER, GLORIOUS...

OOH... WHY DIDN'T I BRING AN UMBRELLA TODAY?

LORD!

EEEEEEE—

NO! DON'T TOUCH M-MMF!

HUSH, NOW! AIN'T NO ONE GETTIN' HURT HERE!

JUS' TELL US WHERE WE CAN FIND J.L. DOUGHERTY...

160

I'M IN!

RIGHT WHERE HE SAID IT WAS.

DAMMIT! WAIT UNTIL THE DOOR IS SHUT!

CLIC!

TRY AND RELAX. WE GOT NOTHING TO WORRY ABOUT NOW.

SAYS YOU. I DON'T LIKE THIS...

HE GAVE US THE KEY TO HIS SHOP. WHAT MORE DO YOU WANT?

HE DIDN'T EVEN ASK US WHY WE DIDN'T COME IN OURSELVES.

LOOK AT US! I WOULDN'T WANT ME IN THERE EITHER!

WHERE'S HE AT, NOW, THEN? WE WERE THE ONES WALKING.

HE SAID HE HAD TO RUN THE WOMAN WE NEARLY SCARED TO DEATH HOME SO I DIDN'T SEE HOW I WAS IN A POSITION TO ARGUE WITH HIM.

DO YOU?

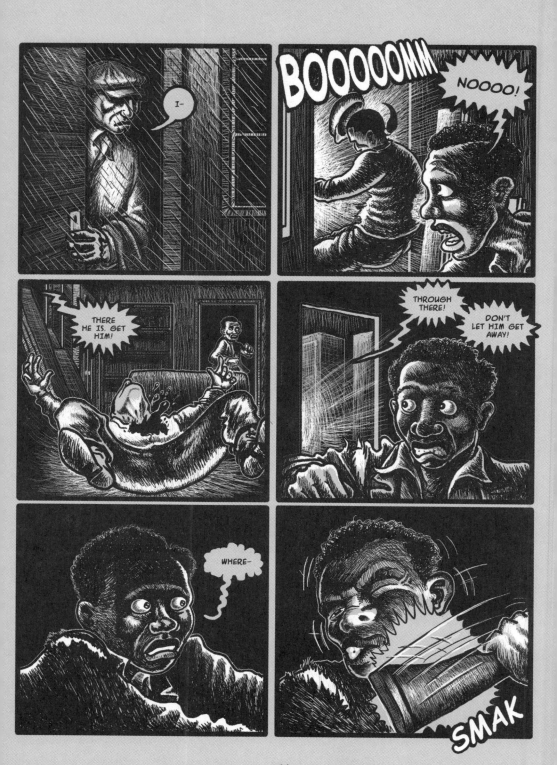

164

165

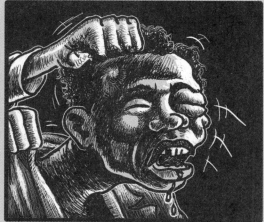

166

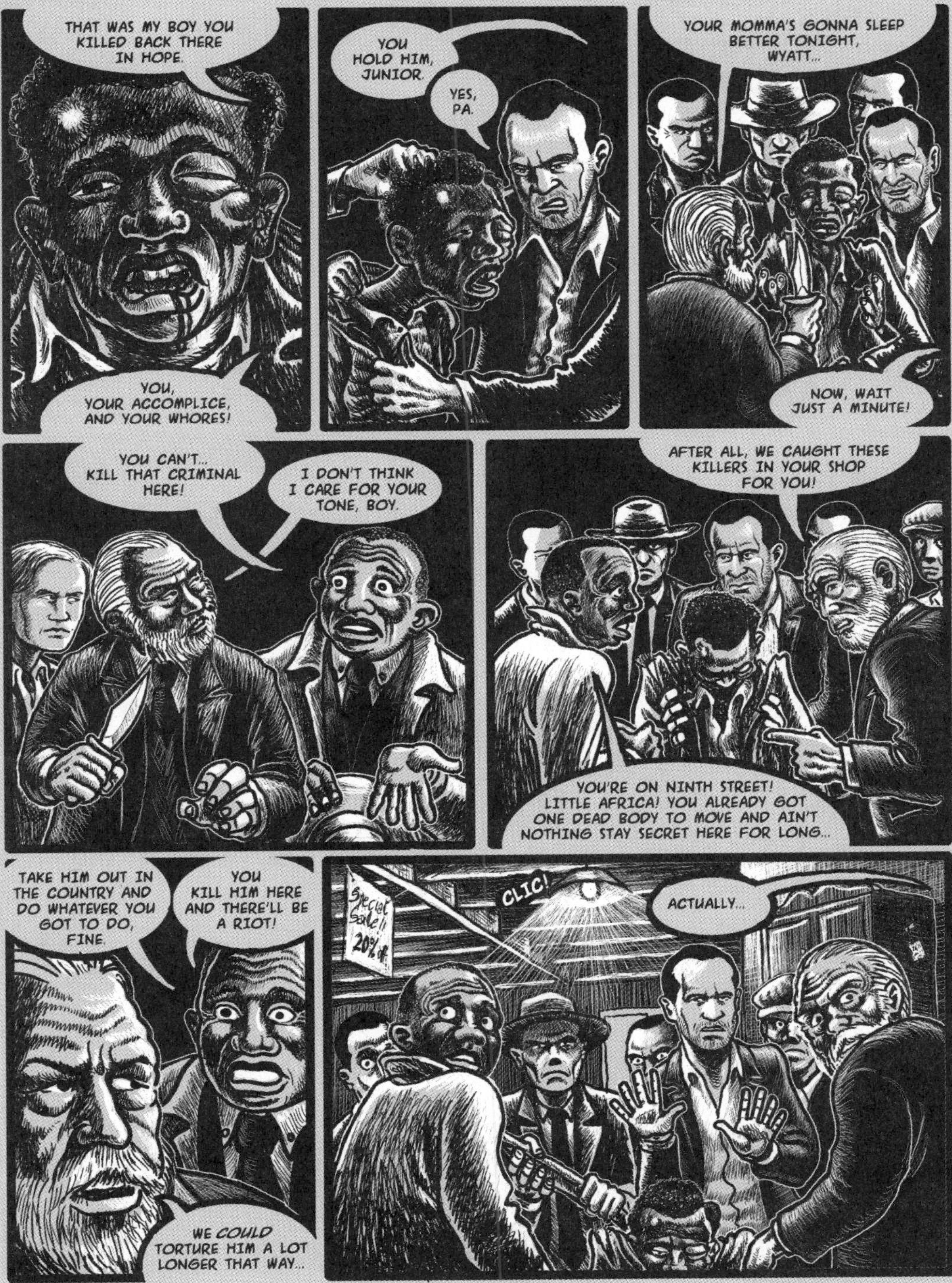
THAT WAS MY BOY YOU KILLED BACK THERE IN HOPE.
YOU, YOUR ACCOMPLICE, AND YOUR WHORES!
YOU HOLD HIM, JUNIOR.
YES, PA.
YOUR MOMMA'S GONNA SLEEP BETTER TONIGHT, WYATT...
NOW, WAIT JUST A MINUTE!
YOU CAN'T... KILL THAT CRIMINAL HERE!
I DON'T THINK I CARE FOR YOUR TONE, BOY.
AFTER ALL, WE CAUGHT THESE KILLERS IN YOUR SHOP FOR YOU!
YOU'RE ON NINTH STREET! LITTLE AFRICA! YOU ALREADY GOT ONE DEAD BODY TO MOVE AND AIN'T NOTHING STAY SECRET HERE FOR LONG...
TAKE HIM OUT IN THE COUNTRY AND DO WHATEVER YOU GOT TO DO, FINE.
YOU KILL HIM HERE AND THERE'LL BE A RIOT!
WE COULD TORTURE HIM A LOT LONGER THAT WAY...
Special Sale!! 20% off
CLIC!
ACTUALLY...

168

11

171

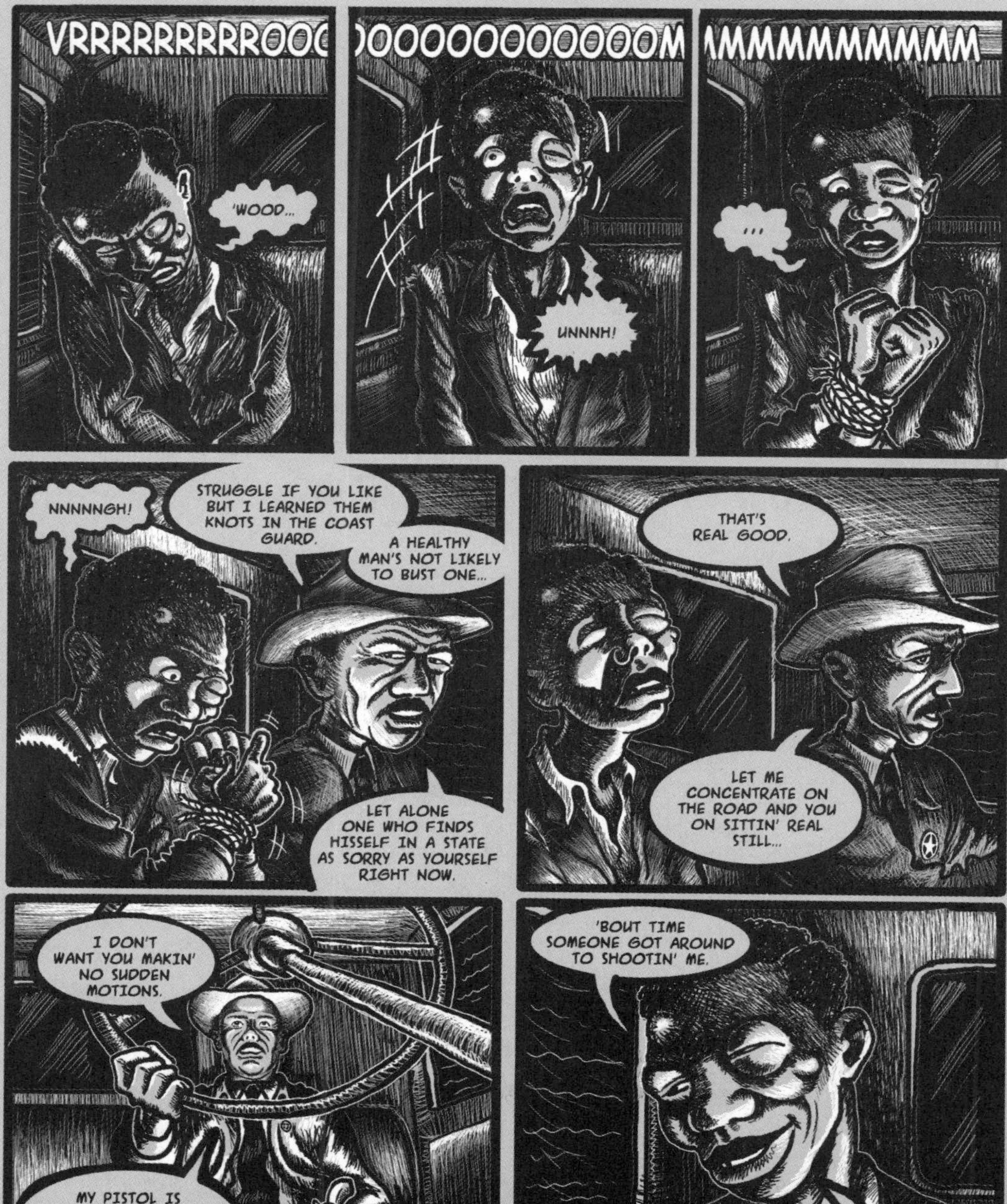
VRRRRRRRRROOOOOOOOOOOOOOOMMMMMMMMMMMM
'WOOD...
UNNNH!
...
NNNNNGH!
STRUGGLE IF YOU LIKE BUT I LEARNED THEM KNOTS IN THE COAST GUARD.
A HEALTHY MAN'S NOT LIKELY TO BUST ONE...
LET ALONE ONE WHO FINDS HISSELF IN A STATE AS SORRY AS YOURSELF RIGHT NOW.
THAT'S REAL GOOD.
LET ME CONCENTRATE ON THE ROAD AND YOU ON SITTIN' REAL STILL...
I DON'T WANT YOU MAKIN' NO SUDDEN MOTIONS.
MY PISTOL IS RIGHT HERE ON MY HIP AND I AIN'T OPPOSED TO SHOOTIN' YOU WHERE YOU SIT.
'BOUT TIME SOMEONE GOT AROUND TO SHOOTIN' ME.
I WAS STARTIN' TO WONDER IF THE LORD HADN'T DONE FORGOT 'BOUT OL' LEM.

173

174

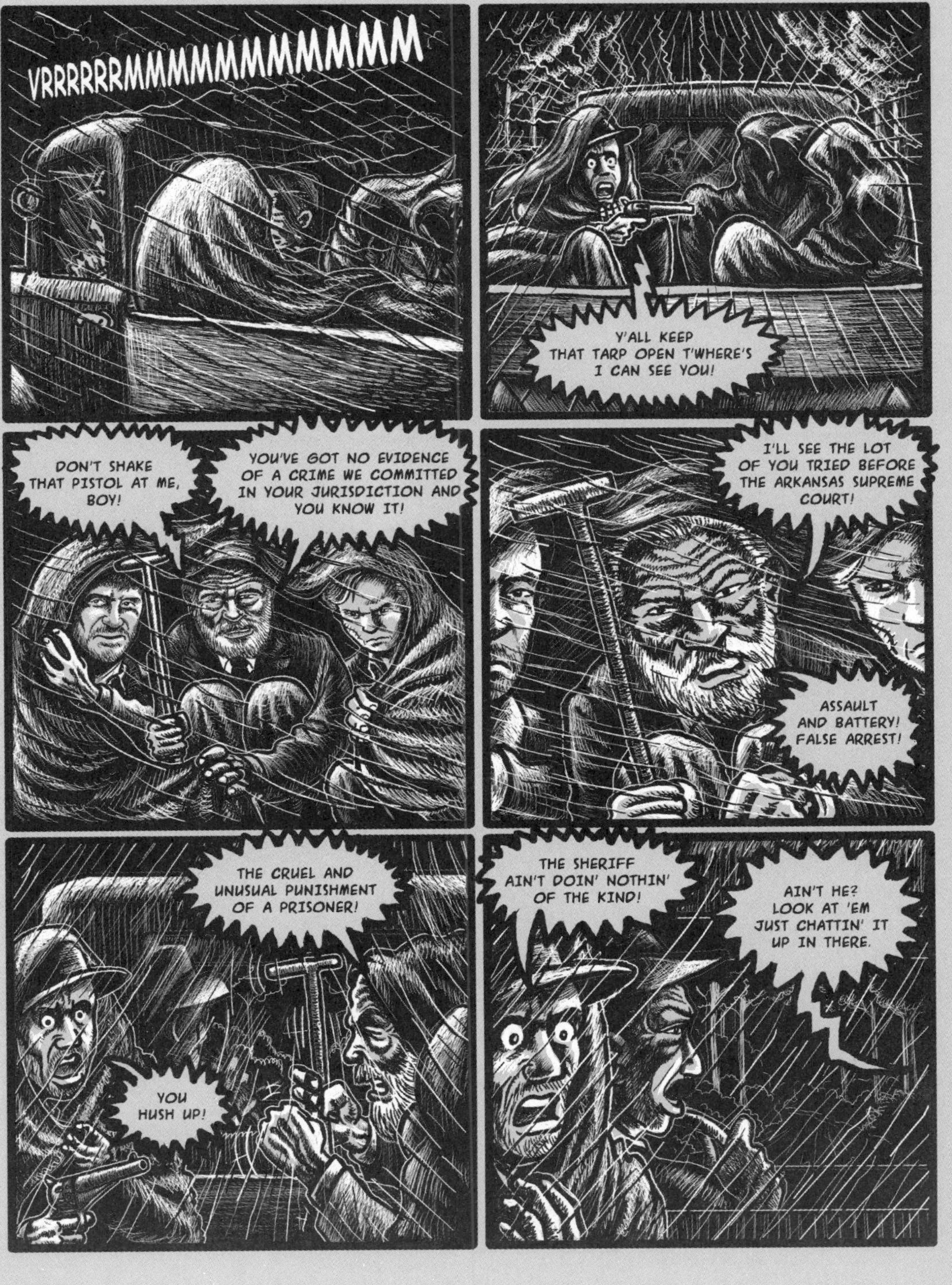
VRRRRRRMMMMMMMMMMMM
Y'ALL KEEP THAT TARP OPEN T'WHERE'S I CAN SEE YOU!
DON'T SHAKE THAT PISTOL AT ME, BOY!
YOU'VE GOT NO EVIDENCE OF A CRIME WE COMMITTED IN YOUR JURISDICTION AND YOU KNOW IT!
I'LL SEE THE LOT OF YOU TRIED BEFORE THE ARKANSAS SUPREME COURT!
ASSAULT AND BATTERY! FALSE ARREST!
THE CRUEL AND UNUSUAL PUNISHMENT OF A PRISONER!
YOU HUSH UP!
THE SHERIFF AIN'T DOIN' NOTHIN' OF THE KIND!
AIN'T HE? LOOK AT 'EM JUST CHATTIN' IT UP IN THERE.

176

177

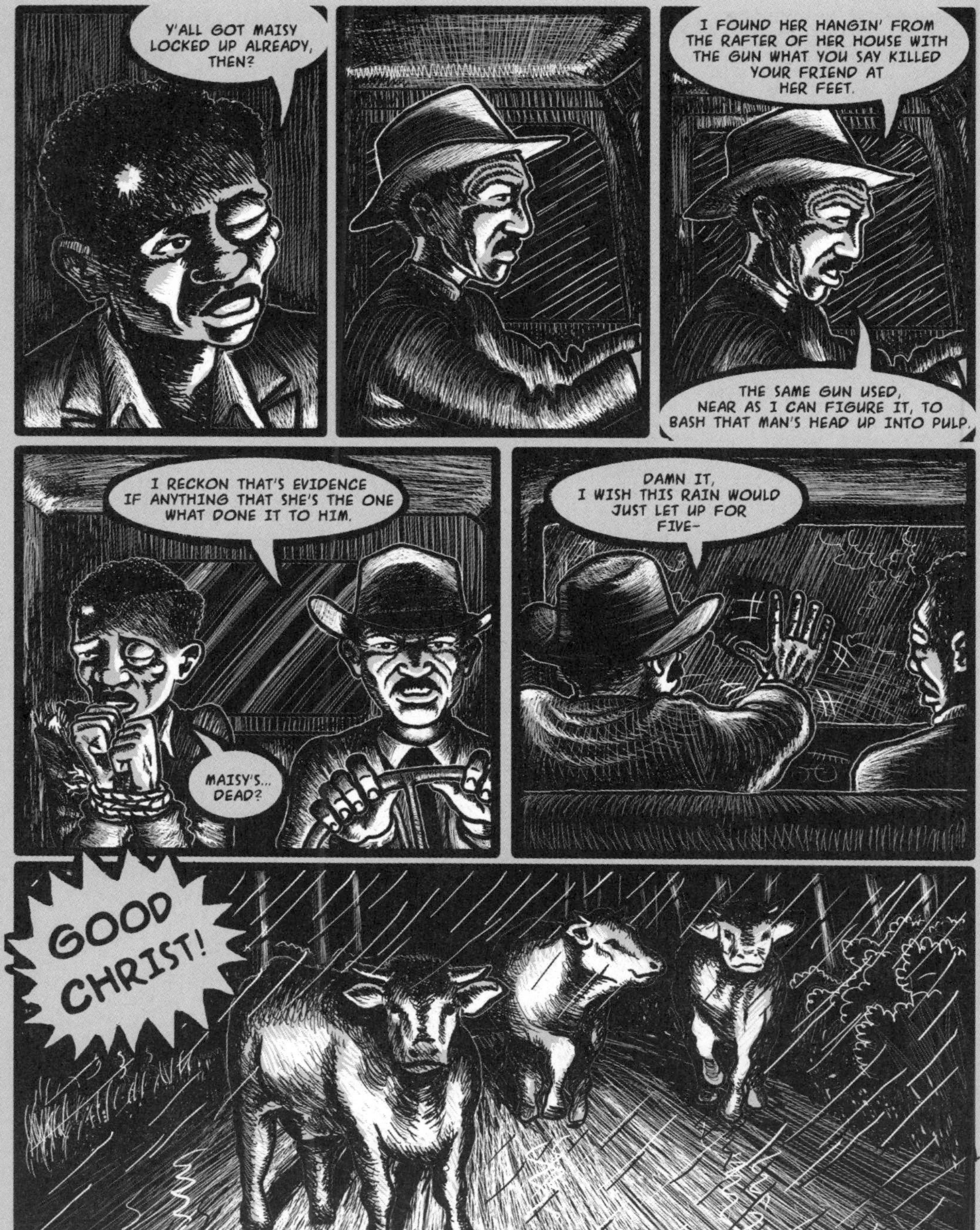
Y'ALL GOT MAISY LOCKED UP ALREADY, THEN?
I FOUND HER HANGIN' FROM THE RAFTER OF HER HOUSE WITH THE GUN WHAT YOU SAY KILLED YOUR FRIEND AT HER FEET.
THE SAME GUN USED, NEAR AS I CAN FIGURE IT, TO BASH THAT MAN'S HEAD UP INTO PULP.
I RECKON THAT'S EVIDENCE IF ANYTHING THAT SHE'S THE ONE WHAT DONE IT TO HIM.
MAISY'S... DEAD?
DAMN IT, I WISH THIS RAIN WOULD JUST LET UP FOR FIVE-
GOOD CHRIST!

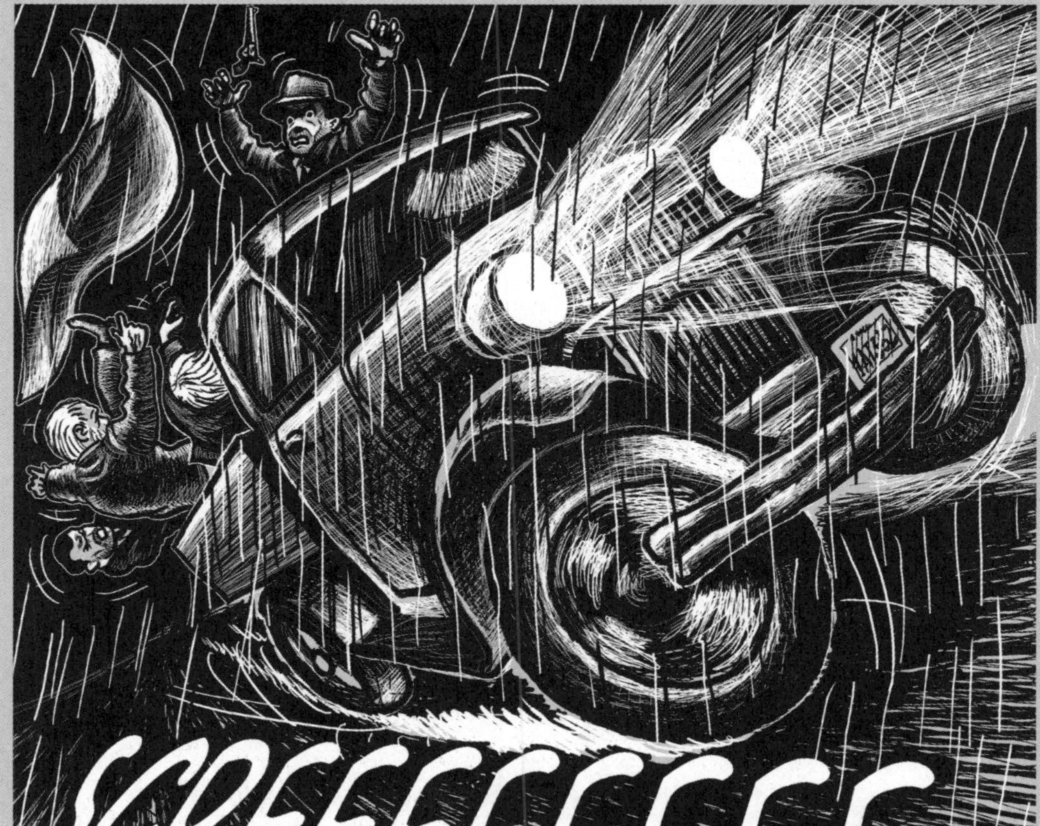
SCREEEEEEEEEE
EEEEEEEEE
SPLASH!

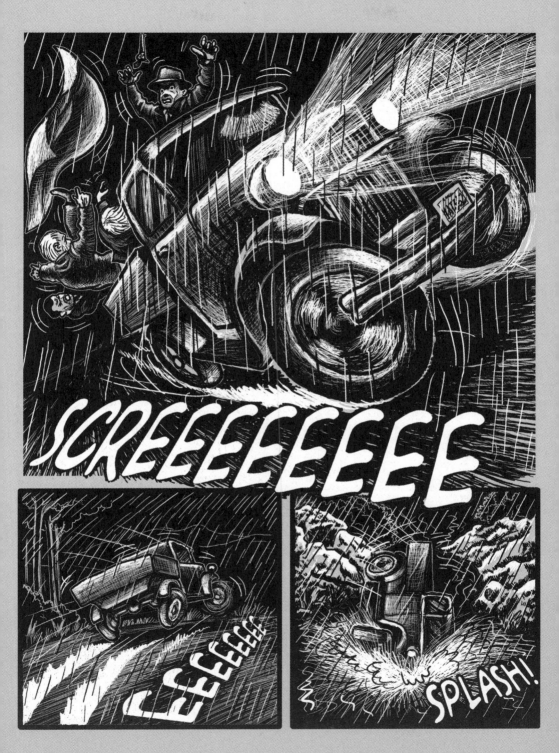

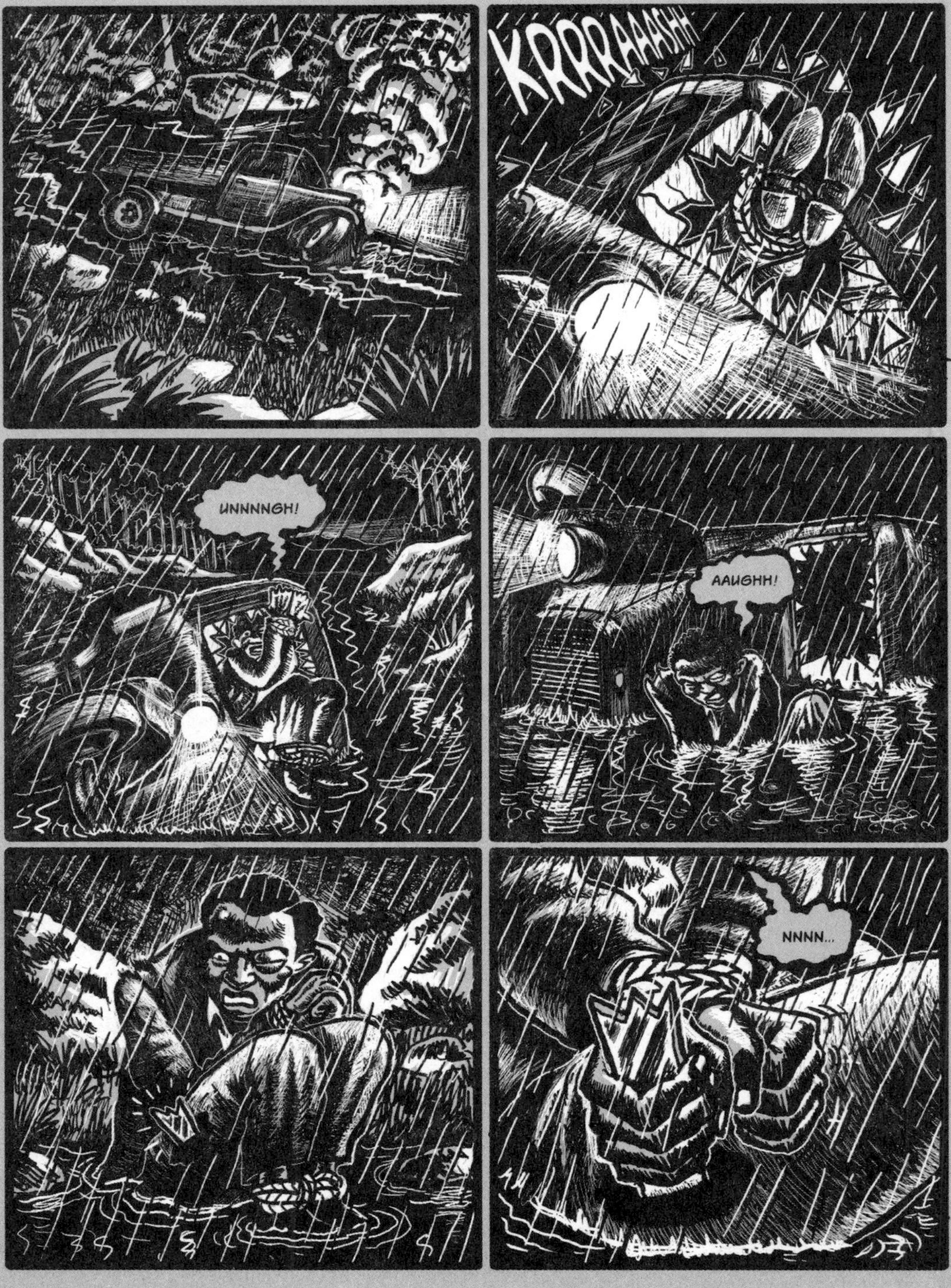
KRRRAAASHH
UNNNNGH!
AAUGHH!
NNNN...

182

12

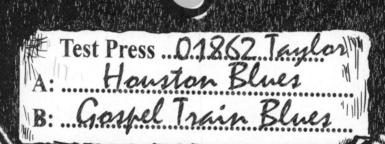

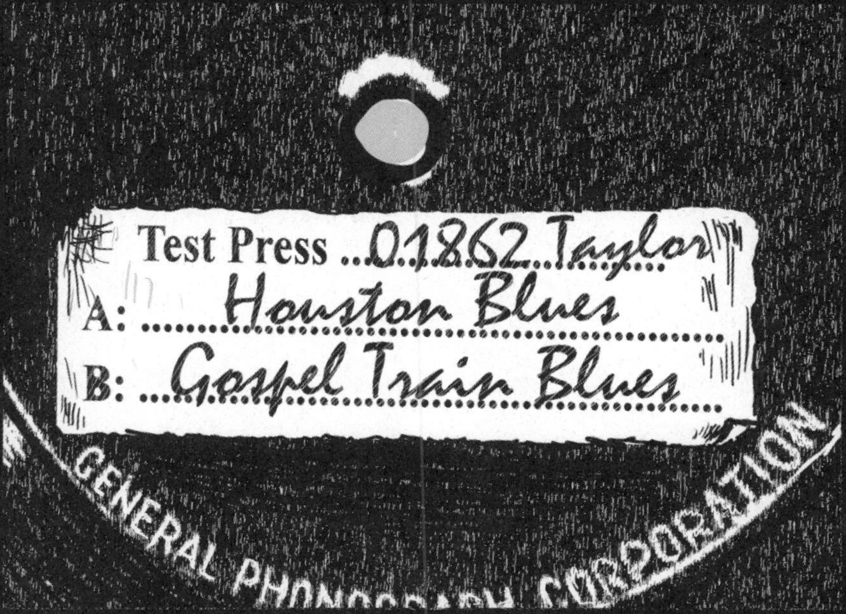

Test Press ...0.1862 Taylor
A: ....Houston Blues
B: ....Gospel Train Blues

GENERAL PHONOGRAPH CORPORATION

185

190

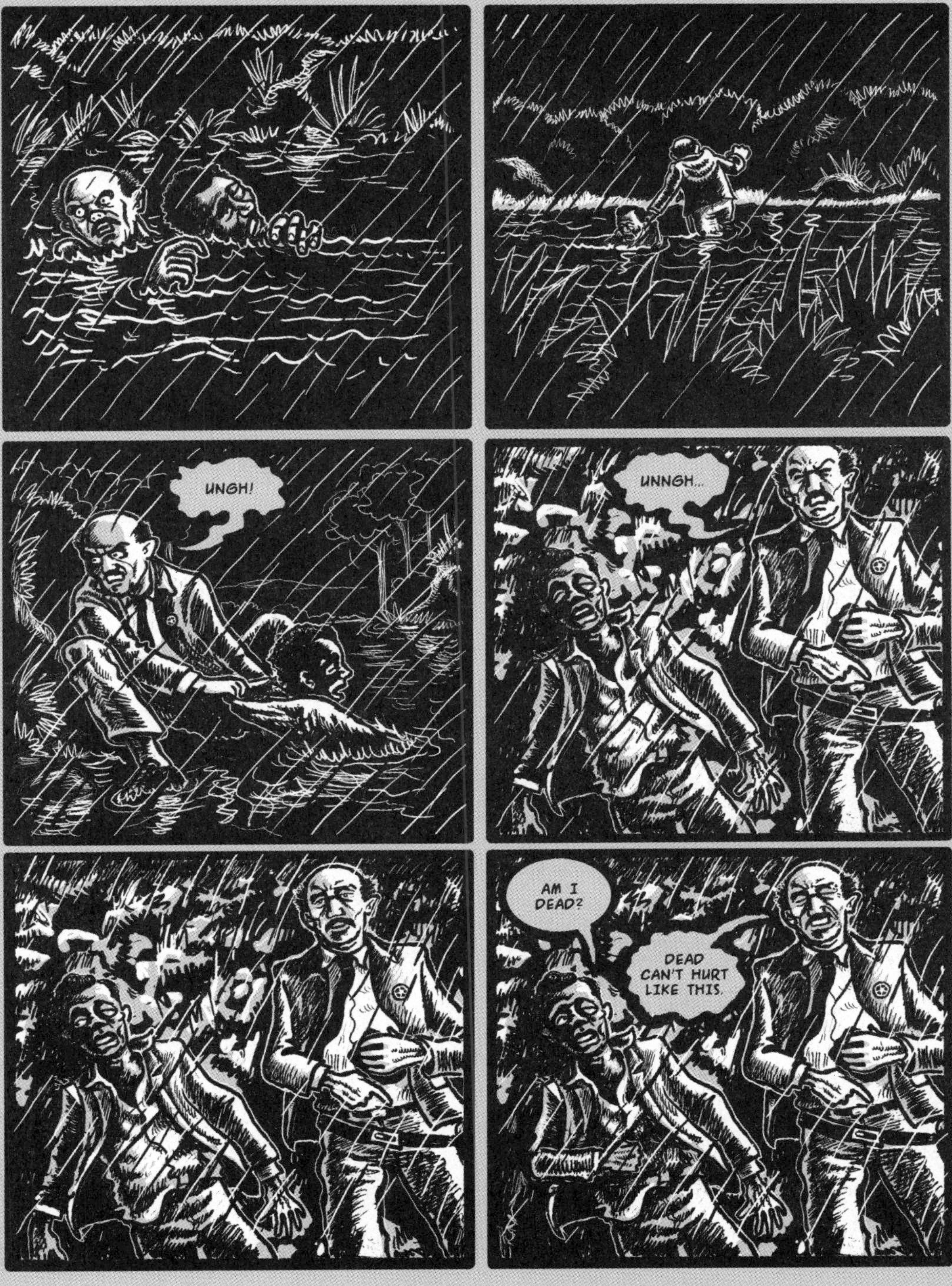
UNGH!
UNNGH...
AM I DEAD?
DEAD CAN'T HURT LIKE THIS.

193

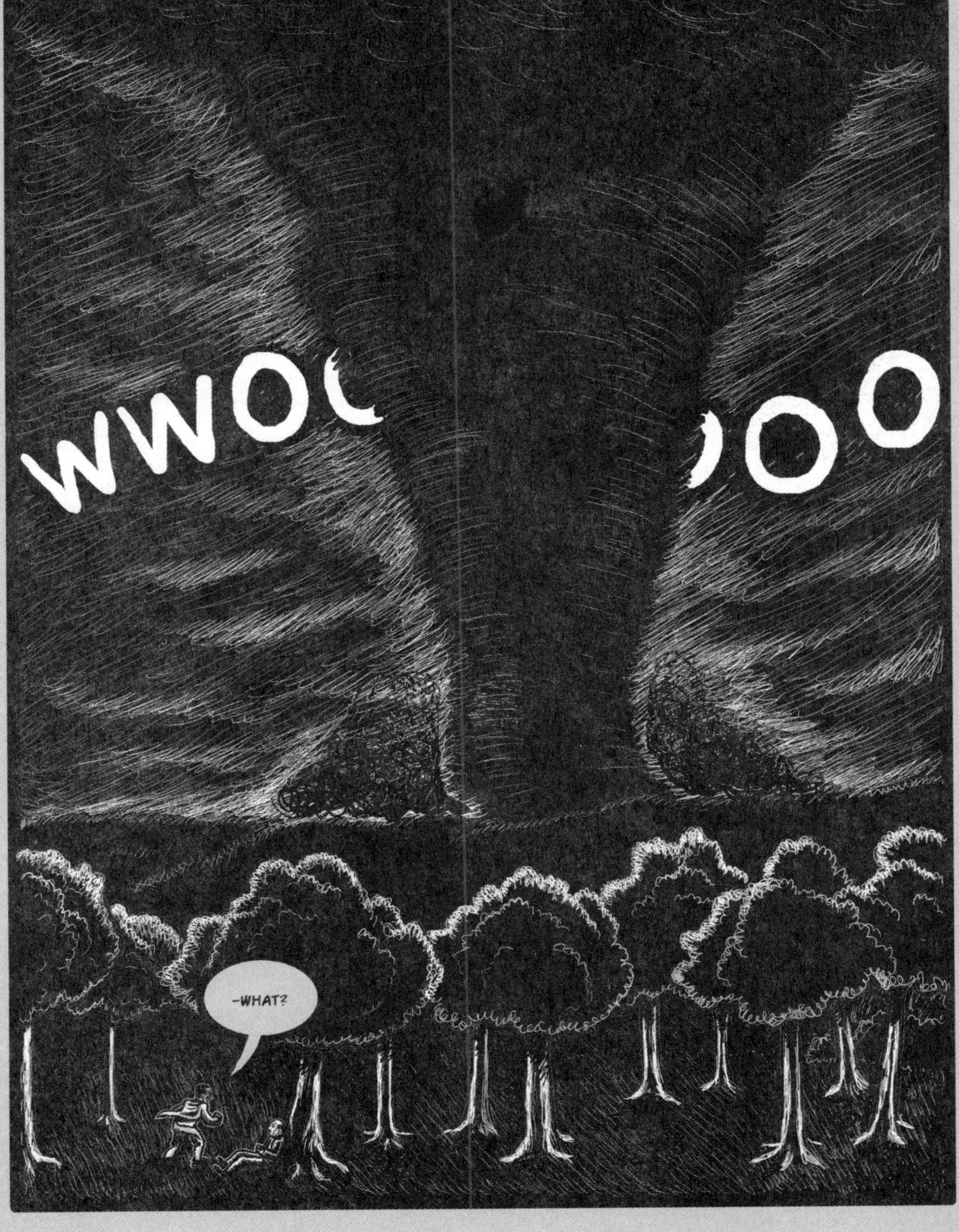
WWOO
OOO
-WHAT?

199

200

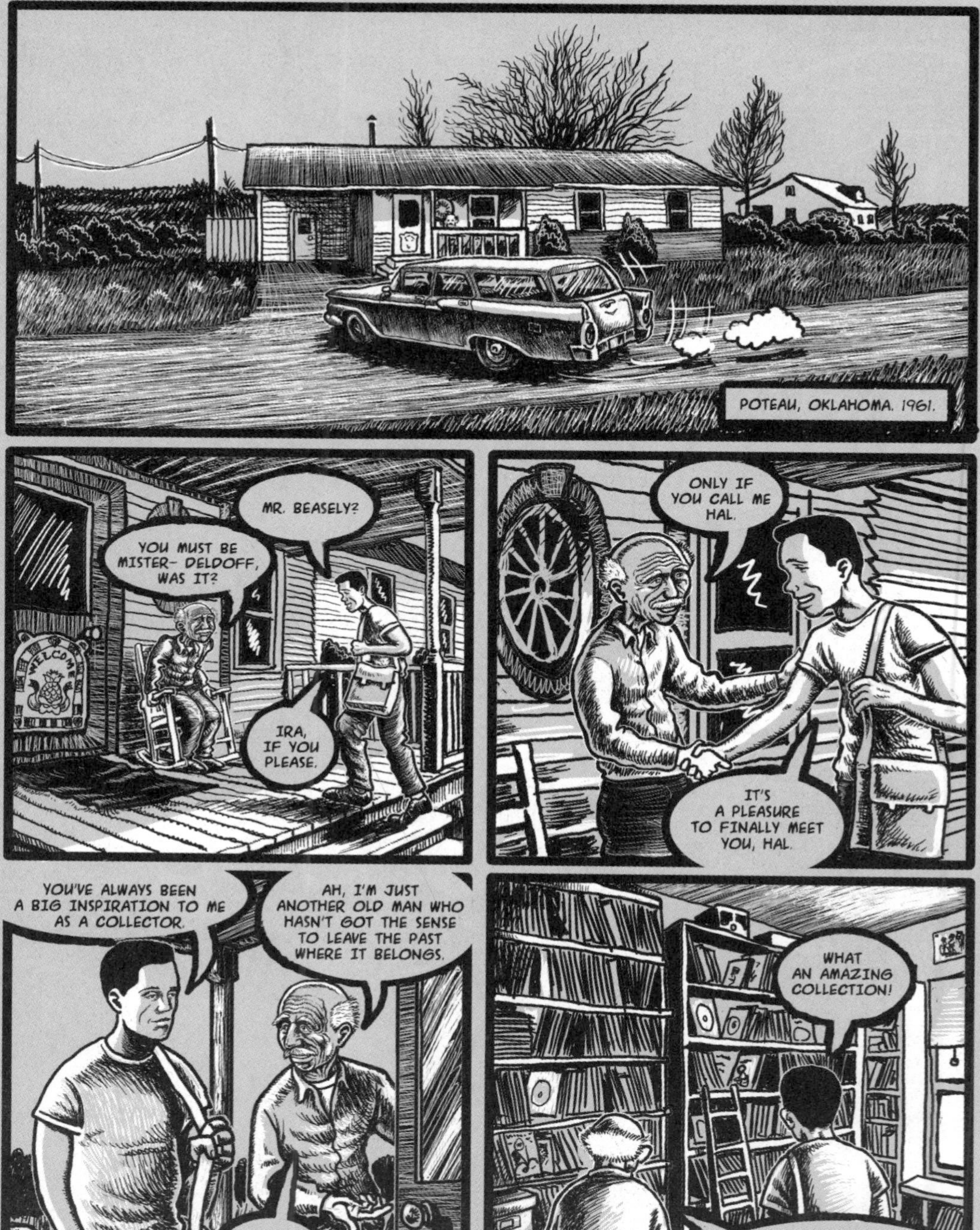
POTEAU, OKLAHOMA. 1961.
MR. BEASELY?
YOU MUST BE MISTER- DELDOFF, WAS IT?
IRA, IF YOU PLEASE.
ONLY IF YOU CALL ME HAL.
IT'S A PLEASURE TO FINALLY MEET YOU, HAL.
YOU'VE ALWAYS BEEN A BIG INSPIRATION TO ME AS A COLLECTOR.
AH, I'M JUST ANOTHER OLD MAN WHO HASN'T GOT THE SENSE TO LEAVE THE PAST WHERE IT BELONGS.
LET'S GO ON INSIDE.
WHAT AN AMAZING COLLECTION!
I GOT INTO THE RECORD HUNTING GAME EARLIER THAN MOST SO THERE WAS JUST A LOT MORE TO BE HAD AND MOSTLY FOR NOTHING.

203

205

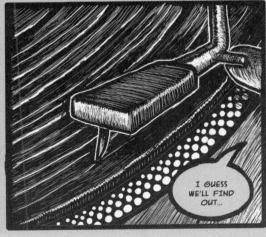

207

208